Development Agenda and Donor Influence in South Asia

Policy ownership of development agenda emerged as an important aspect in international development cooperation during the 1990s in the wake of evident failures of reform initiatives in developing countries steered by donor agencies, particularly the international financial institutions (IFIs), the World Bank (WB) and the International Monetary Fund (IMF).

The principal focus of this book is to examine Bangladesh's policy ownership in its PRSP by broadly analyzing the dynamics in the formulation process and examining the principal actors' contribution to the formulation process. This book also deals with several other dimensions of foreign aid and its changing features including the shifts in WB-IMF's approach to development cooperation. This book argues that the WB-IMF strongly influence Bangladesh's development strategies and agendas and in general the WB-IMF have not changed much in their aid relationship despite clear limitations of their previous reform models. Building on Bangladesh's current level of development the book advocates that Bangladesh needs to adopt a new model for development agenda setting.

Illustrating the influences of donor communities on the creation of development strategies in developing countries, this book presents a macro dynamics of the political economy of international development cooperation. It will be of interest to academics and professionals working on political economy, governance, public policy and development cooperation as well as South Asian Studies.

Mohammad Mizanur Rahman graduated from the University of Dhaka in Political Science and received his PhD from the Institute of Bangladesh Studies (IBS), University of Rajshahi, Bangladesh. He is a career civil servant in Bangladesh. He also worked as a Policy Specialist for over four years in the Aid Effectiveness Project of UNDP, Bangladesh. He published research articles in national and international journals and also contributed several book chapters.

Development Agenda and Donor Influence in South Asia

Bangladesh's Experiences in the PRSP Regime

Mohammad Mizanur Rahman

Routledge
Taylor & Francis Group
LONDON AND NEW YORK

First published 2018 by Routledge

2 Park Square, Milton Park, Abingdon, Oxfordshire OX14 4RN
52 Vanderbilt Avenue, New York, NY 10017

Routledge is an imprint of the Taylor & Francis Group, an informa business

First issued in paperback 2020

British Library Cataloguing in Publication Data
A catalogue record for this book is available from the British Library

Library of Congress Cataloging in Publication Data
Names: Rahman, Mohammad Mizanur, author.
Title: Development agenda and donor influence in South Asia: Bangladesh's experiences in the PRSP regime / Mohammad Mizanur Rahman.
Description: New York : Routledge, 2018. |
Series: Routledge studies in the growth economies of asia ; 141 | Includes bibliographical references and index.
Identifiers: LCCN 2018003739| ISBN 9781138489967 (hardback) | ISBN 9781351036382 (ebook)
Subjects: LCSH: Structural adjustment (Economic policy)–Bangladesh. | Economic assistance, Domestic–Bangladesh. | Economic development–Bangladesh. | Investments, Foreign–Bangladesh. | World Bank–Bangladesh. | International Monetary Fund–Bangladesh.
Classification: LCC HC440.8.Z9 P6345 2018 | DDC 338.91095492–dc23
LC record available at https://lccn.loc.gov/2018003739

ISBN: 978-1-138-48996-7 (hbk)
ISBN: 978-0-367-58941-7 (pbk)

Typeset in Times New Roman
by Taylor & Francis Books

My father, mother and mother-in-law and my wife, Marium, for their love and care

My sons, Labib, Afif and Zarif, in the hope that they may find some meaning from the work when they are grown-up

Bangladesh government's permanent secretary Ms. AFROZA Khan for giving me the opportunity to work autonomously beyond typical civil service norms while I worked under her guidance, and also for her exceptional care to my family

Dr. Stanley Bruce Thomson, MacEwan University, Canada for his unflinching academic support for over a decade though we have not met yet

Contents

Illustrations

Figure

Table

Boxes

Foreword

The collective demand for making the process of development both effective and beneficial for countries and communities in the Global South incited a precipitous yet deep desire to anchor the discussion of development in a new narrative that fosters a culture of participation and ownership. At the heart of this policy-relevant discussion is a realization that much of the success of development depends on the ability of official aid providers to meaningfully engage developing country partners – including public servants, civil society actors, and community groups – in the decision-making process. Apart from creating a space for different stakeholders to work together to promote an enabling setting for people's self-development, such an understanding of development planning is expected to help design better policies and programs that contribute to improving the poverty conditions which characterize much of the Global South. What it does, on one hand, is elucidate the widely-held myth of the incapacity of the Southern actors to make decisions based on their own priorities and conditions; on the other hand, it allows them to reduce their historical dependence on external actors. Greater emphasis on ownership and participation are also likely to steer global development efforts toward achieving greater efficiency, accountability, and transparency in the entire process of development.

Renewed interest in advancing a new bottom-up framework for development planning has created the need for scholars to offer an incisive assessment of the changing narrative of development. How is ownership understood? What opportunities do the concept of ownership and participation create for national and local actors to meaningfully influence the development agenda? Are civil servants, politicians, community organizations, and civil society actors able to develop a shared agenda for national development without external prompting? Dr. Mohammad Mizanur Rahman's monograph entitled *Development Agenda and Donor Influence in South Asia: Bangladesh's Experiences in the PRSP Regime* digs deep to answer some of these supremely important questions in the evolving context of Bangladesh. His exploration of Poverty Reduction Strategy Papers (PRSP) is inspiring in many ways. Despite the absence of a vibrant academic culture of research in Bangladesh's seemingly dysfunctional political landscape, he worked diligently to produce an analytically sophisticated study filled with fascinating insights that questions the effectiveness of the mainstream global development agenda sponsored by both International Financial Institutions and official aid agencies. Instead of being ideological and/or rhetorical, his research explores the various complex issues and formidable challenges that confront both donor agencies and governments in the Global South.

Dr. Rahman traces the evolution of development planning in Bangladesh, which has undergone a process of transformation in the last three decades, from its path to state-led development to a neo-liberal project of development. The country abandoned its initial socialist roots to embark on a journey to capitalist modernity that required continued support and engagement from external actors in reorienting its statist economy toward the market. Although Bangladesh's apparent success in advancing a private-sector led development agenda in recent years significantly lessened its overwhelming dependence on official aid, it has yet to set, as Rahman's study vividly displays, a structure in motion that questions outside experts' continued dominance in development planning. External agencies and consultants still assume a major responsibility for setting the country's national development agenda.

As an extraordinarily accomplished young development scholar and policymaker, Dr. Rahman produces an analysis that identifies the missing link between the official development narrative and the real practice of development planning. He has worked closely with a large number of public service institutions and development agencies in Bangladesh which provided new insights into the challenges and opportunities of democratic development, local development, and sustainable livelihoods in the Global South. His rich professional and academic experiences enabled him to explore both the discursive and normative processes of development intervention programs from a thought provoking perspective. Instead of delving into the abstract world of development theory, Dr. Rahman makes the conscious decision of guiding us in understanding the practical ways in which development is planned, delivered, and managed. By raising critical questions about the present global aid architecture, Dr. Rahman's study makes an effort to identify the inherent weaknesses of the current system constructed by major powers after the Second World War. It carefully re-examines the critical assumptions about official development cooperation that often fail to support people's self-help capacities.

While Dr. Rahman's research explores a country case study, his monograph contains much that will interest students and scholars of Comparative Politics, International Relations, Development Studies, Geography, Sociology and other interdisciplinary fields. I strongly believe that his monograph will stimulate debate and facilitate new research on ownership and participation in future.

Fahimul Quadir, PhD, Professor of Development Studies, Dean and Associate Vice-President, Graduate, Faculty of Graduate Studies, York University, Toronto, Canada

Preface

Policy ownership of development agenda emerged as an important aspect in international development cooperation during the 1990s. The issue came to the forefront in the face of failures of donor led development strategies in developing countries. The failure of Structural Adjustment Programs (SAP), introduced as a loan condition by the World Bank (WB) and International Monetary Fund (IMF) in early 1980s, contributed to the rise of interest in policy ownership. Against this backdrop, the WB and the IMF introduced the poverty reduction strategy paper (PRSP) as a new approach to poverty reduction and development of its loan recipient countries. Bangladesh adopted the PRSP replacing its traditional Five-Year development plan to ensure its access to WB-IMF loans. On the face of it, the PRSP was a loan condition; Bangladesh claimed that its PRSP had sufficient national ownership. The contested ownership in the PRSP process provided a unique opportunity to examine the state of national ownership in the development agenda in Bangladesh.

This book analyzes policy independence and national ownership in Bangladesh's PRSP by examining the dynamics in the formulation process and assessing the principal actors' contribution. The book also presents the shifts in WB-IMF policy of development cooperation and subsequent influence over development strategies of the developing countries including Bangladesh; analyzes political and civil society responses in relation to the PRSP process and content in Bangladesh; and examines line-Ministries involvement in the PRSP. Though the book examines Bangladesh's own dynamics of formulating a development agenda, it adds value by aptly narrating glimpses of global resistance to WB-IMF policy conditionality.

The book presents a country specific example highlighting donors' influence over public policy choice, but also provides a macro dynamic view of the political economy of international development cooperation. This case study ably flags that international development cooperation still favors a patron–client approach while apparently advocating country ownership and leadership. The inherent limitation of the donors in public policy choice of the recipient countries has been candidly exposed in this book.

The lessons of Bangladesh's experiences would be helpful to both practitioners and academics including the university student of development studies and public policies/administration to understand that the current approach of development providers does not work to strengthen country ownership. Loan recipient countries must be allowed to think and try to formulate their own terms of developing and managing the development agenda for the country.

The case is also important for other reasons. Bangladesh has been maintaining a momentum of economic growth with more reliance on its own resources but in terms of policy formulation it still heavily depends on international donors. This presents a contradictory situation which may encourage researchers and students of governance and political economy and policy makers to be more interested in understanding the root causes of such dependence. In fact, the research insights have significant potential to add value to the current body of literature.

The broader understanding of the current research is that national ownership of development policy or strategy demands a strong will and the commitment of national leaders to build a self-reliant economy. Development strategies and policies should assume eventual "graduation" (or an "exit plan") from aid and be supported by a concrete vision and realistic measures for growth promotion and domestic resource mobilization. Policies should move beyond mere slogan and be truly imbued with equitability and growth sustainability.

Bangladesh's steady economic progress calls for a new pathway to establish ownership in national development strategy. The changing scenario of the country's development financing also indicates that Bangladesh can no longer be fully dependent on aid and donor policy prescriptions. Bangladesh's development trajectory should be built around its own needs, priorities, and opportunities. Against this understanding and building on findings of the PRSP regime, this book argues that the country should take some proactive measures to strengthen its institutional ability, political culture, and people's true engagement for better policy making being independent of any external influence. This book finally advocates for a triangular model for development agenda underlying strong collaboration between government, private sector, and research.

Acknowledgement

This book is an outcome of my PhD dissertation. In the process of my PhD research and later on in developing this book, I received assistance from many individuals and institutions. While the list would be long if I mention all of them; however, it would be remiss of me if I do not mention at least some of them who played an important role in different forms and at different levels to help me finish either the dissertation, or the manuscript of this book. The first name should be Professor Jakir Hossain, PhD; I have no words to acknowledge his contribution to this research. He was the first supervisor of my PhD but due to his own academic pursuits he could not continue his supervisory role. Dr. Hossain set the research agenda and throughout the research tenure he guided me and enlightened me even while he was then at the Cornell University, and several thousand kilometers away from Bangladesh. I am highly grateful to Professor Shah M. Habibur Rahman, Professor M. Shamsur Rahman PhD for their excellent supervisory role. Both of them were extraordinarily helpful during my research journey. It is my responsibility to mention the name of Professor M. Shariful Islam, a former Syndicate member of the University of Rajshahi for his high level administrative cooperation which was crucial during the research period.

Professor Fahim Quadir, PhD of the York University, Canada played an important role in advising me to situate the research issues in the right perspective. Professor Fahim has been truly a regular source of academic guidance and support to me. It is my pleasure to mention that Dr. Fahim has kindly written the Foreword for this book which has enhanced acceptance of the book. I am highly grateful to him. The external examiner of my dissertation Professor M. Alauddin, PhD of the Queensland University, Australia provided some critical suggestions during his review; his suggestions eventually helped improve the scholastic contribution of the work. Professor Salahuddin M. Aminuzzaman, PhD of the Dhaka University was one of the members of the examiner panel of my dissertation. His guidance was also important in developing the book. I am very sincerely indebted to both of them.

I owe a great deal to Dr. Akbar Ali Khan, Bangladesh's former alternate executive director in the World Bank and Cabinet Secretary of Bangladesh, Professor Atiur Rahman of Dhaka University and former Governor of Bangladesh Bank, the central bank, Dr. Hossain Zillur Rahman, an eminent political economist of the country and the lead consultant of Bangladesh's PRSP, Dr. M. M. Akash of Dhaka University, Professor Anu Muhammad of Jahangirnagar University, Dr. Abul Barkat, President of Bangladesh Economic Association (BEA), Dr. Quazi Mesbahuddin Ahmed, former Member, General Economics Division (GED), Bangladesh Planning Commission, Lt. Col. (Retd) Farruk Khan MP, a former Minister, Dr. Osman Farruk, former Minister for education, and Dr. M. Mahbubur Rahman (late), Mr. Md. Momtazul Islam and Mr. Kamaluddin Ahmed, former permanent secretaries to the Government of Bangladesh for their valuable time for discussion on several aspects of Bangladesh's PRSP in relation to national ownership of development agenda. I am grateful to my friend Mr. Monowar Mostofa Jolly for he managed interview opportunity for me with some of the key informants mentioned above.

It is always difficult for me to express the contribution of Dr. Stanley Bruce Thomson of MacEwan University, Canada to my academic life; it is so great that words are hardly enough to express his contribution. He has been a great example of devoted academic mentoring; he has not seen me until now and he resides thousands of kilometers away, yet he is always committed to help me to excel in my academic and research career.

It is a pleasure for me to mention some of the names of my civil service colleagues for their encouragement, support, and cooperation at different stages of my professional and academic life. Many of them are my senior colleagues, some of them are my peers and some are junior colleagues. They are Mr. Delwar Hossain, Mr. Monowar Ahmed, Mr. Aftab Ahmad, Mr. Nurul Alam Miah, Dr. M. Shariful Alam, Dr. Fazle Rabbi Sadeque Ahmed, Dr. K.M. Kabirul Islam, Mr. Aktaruzzaman Talukdar, Mr. Mohammad Salahuddin, Mr. Md. Fahimul Islam, Mr. Abu Tahir Muhammed Zaber, Dr. Md. Rezaul Bashar Siddique, Mr. Shirajun Noor Chowdhury, Mr. Md. Anwar Hossain, Mr. Zahid Hossain Munshi, Mr. Md. Nazmul Huda Siddiqui, Dr. Abu Shahin M. Asaduzzaman, Mr. Abu Saleh Mohammad Ferdous Khan, Mr. Shah Alam, Mr. Mohammad Hasan Arif, Mr. Md. Hasan Maruf, Ms. Surayya Akhtar Jahan, Mr. Mahbubur Rahman Bhuiyan, Ms. Najia Islam, Mr. Mohammad Jashim Uddin, Mr. Mohammad Kamrul Hasan, Mr. Samiul Masud, Mr. Nawsher Ahmed Sikder. I remember my junior colleague Dr. Syed Abul Hasan, who worked in the GED, Planning Commission during the PRSP preparation phase, for his exceptional help in enabling me to access many official documents.

I had a wonderful stay at the Institute of Bangladesh Studies (IBS), University of Rajshahi mostly because of the congenial academic environment. IBS faculties and administrative staff are always highly supportive to its research fellows. As I write the acknowledgement, I express my deep regards and gratitude to my teachers at the IBS for their contribution to my academic pursuit and they include Professor P.K. Mitra, PhD (late), Professor M. Zainul Abedin, PhD, Professor Swarochish Sarker, PhD, Professor M Mostafa Kamal, PhD. I also acknowledge the cooperation of IBS the then Assistant Registrar Mr. Abdus Salam Akond and Secretary (Deputy Registrar) Mr. Zaidur Rahman.

It is a matter of extreme happiness for me to mention the support and contribution of Bangladesh government's permanent secretary Ms. AFROZA Khan and her husband Mr. Masud Ahmed Khan to my professional life and my family. They have been a trusted source of cooperation and support to my family.

I should put on record the support of the Government of Bangladesh as it gave me permission to carry out the PhD study and also the Social Science Research Council (SSRC), Ministry of Planning, Bangladesh and Institute of Bangladesh Studies (IBS) for the scholarships they provided me. However, I should mention that the opinions expressed in this monograph are of solely mine and do not represent the views and position of the government.

Dr. M. Kamrul Hasan from the UK, and Mr. S. M. Rasheduzzaman helped to ease my research efforts by providing different academic and logistic support. I remain grateful to them. I feel happy to mention Mr. Ali Ahmed for he has been inspiring me for many years to write an academic book based on my research. Though he lives in USA he makes calls to me every now and then, like a genuine elder brother, so that I should not sidetrack my attention from publishing a book. I remember Professor Tajul Islam PhD and Mr. Shah Ahsan Habib for their support to me in various ways. I also recognize Mr. Asad H. Chowdhury from the UK, Mr. Khondoker Zakaria Ahmed, Dr. Kazi Sohag and Kazi Obaidul Hoque for their love and encouragement as genuine well-wishers.

I wish to offer my sincere thanks to my wife Marium Begum, my sons Aamir Hamza Labib and Abdullah Omar Naseef Afif for they sustained many difficulties during my research tenure. My youngest son, Abdullah Yusuf Ali Zarif did not see me endure the pain of research but would see the joy of the publication of the book. I am sure they would be happy while they grow to understand the worth of this academic work.

I am sure my parents, uncle, siblings, and in-laws, particularly Mr. Khairul Anam will be very happy to see the publication of the book. They have helped me in many ways. It is my time to formally express my indebtedness to them.

I am happy to mention the sincere cooperation I received during the publishing process of this book from Dorothea Schaefter, Senior Editor, Lily Brown, Editorial Assistant, Asian Studies, Routledge, Daniela Amodeo, eProduction Editor, and copyeditor Elizabeth Nichols. I am greatly moved by their professional support. I express my sincere gratitude to them. As I conclude this acknowledgment, I take the opportunity to mention Professor Rehman Sobhan, Professor Nurul Islam, and Professor Anisur Rahman, who were the part of the independence of the country and always wanted to see Bangladesh follow its own path of development. My personal indebtedness to them is that their academic work influenced me very much and led me to revisit the political economy of development cooperation in Bangladesh's current context of development. I love to mention Dr. Just Faaland (late), the first country director of the World Bank to Bangladesh for his sincere love and feeling for Bangladesh and its people till his death and also for his high appreciation of my PhD thesis. Dr. Faaland, died recently having lived a life close to a century, unlike most of the World Bank staffs, tried to support the country beyond his official role in the struggling beginning years of this country after bloody war of Independence. I pay my deep respect to this great economist and human being.

Finally, I would like to take the opportunity to appreciate all the unnamed people who helped me in different ways in doing the research and inspired me all through my life. They remain in my heart. I hope the people of Bangladesh will one day defeat poverty and draw their own dreams of development independently. And on that day, no one would be happier than me. I look forward to those days.

Abbreviations

ADP	Annual Development Plan
ASRC	Administrative and Services Reorganization Committee
BDF	Bangladesh Development Forum
BEA	Bangladesh Economic Association
BIDS	Bangladesh Institute of Development Studies
BIPS	Bangladesh Institute of Parliamentary Studies
BWI	Bretton-Woods Institution
CAS	Country Assessment Strategy
CBOs	Community Based Organizations
CDF	Comprehensive Development Framework
CDP	Committee for Development Policy
CPIA	Country Policy and Institutional Assessment
CPT	Career Planning and Training
CSO	Civil Society Organization
CSP	Civil Service of Pakistan
DCN	Debt Crisis Network
DfID	Department for International Development
DSC	Development Support Credit
ECNEC	Executive Committee on National Economic Council
EFF	Extended Finance Facility
EHIPC	Enhanced Highly Indebted Poor Country
EPZs	Export Processing Zones
ERD	Economic Relations Division
ESAF	Enhanced Structural Adjustment Facility
FDI	Foreign Direct Investment
FFYP	First Five-Year Plan
FGD	Focused Group Discussion
FONDAD	Forum on Debt and Development
FYP	Five-Year Plan
GAP	Group for Alternative Policies
GED	General Economics Division
GoB	Government of Bangladesh
GPEDC	Global Partnership for Effective Development Cooperation

GPP	Good Practice Principles
HIES	Household Income and Expenditure Survey
HIPC	Highly Indebted Poor Country
ICCO	Inter Church Coordinating Committee on Development Projects
IDA	International Development Association
IFI	International Financial Institution
IMF	International Monetary Fund
IPC	Import Credit Program
I-PRSP	Interim Poverty Reduction Strategy Paper
ISI	Import Substitution Industrialization
JSA	Joint Staff Assessment
JSAN	Joint Staff Advisory Note
LCG	Local Consultative Group
LDC	Least Developed Country
LFS	Labor Force Survey
LICs	Low Income Countries
MDGs	Millennium Development Goals
MFA	Multi Fiber Agreement
MOE	Ministry of Establishment
MTBF	Medium-Term Budgetary Framework
MWCA	Ministry of Women and Children Affairs
NAFTA	North American Free Trade Agreement
NCB	Nationalized Commercial Banks
NGO	Non-government Organization
NIP	New Industrial Policy
NOVIB	The Netherlands Organization for International Development
NPDC	National Policy for Development Cooperation
NPFP	National Poverty Focal Point
NPRC	National Poverty Reduction Council
NSAPR	National Strategy for Accelerated Poverty Reduction
NSC	National Steering Committee
ODA	Overseas Development Agency
OED	Operations Evaluation Department
PARC	Public Administration Reforms Commission
PET	People's Empowerment Trust
PFP	Policy Framework Paper
PIP	Priority Investment Program
PPA	Participatory Poverty Assessment
PRGF	Poverty Reduction and Growth Facility
PRS	Poverty Reduction Strategy
PRSC	Poverty Reduction Support Credit
PRSP	Poverty Reduction Strategy Paper
RMG	Ready-made Garments
SAF	Structural Adjustment Facility

SAP	Structural Adjustment Program
SILICS	Severely Indebted Low Income Countries
SOEs	State-owned Enterprises
SUPRO	Sushashoner Jonno Procharavijan
SWAP	Sector-wide Approach Program
TA	Technical Assistance
TGs	Thematic Groups
TRIMs	Trade Related Investment Measures
TRIPs	Trade Related Intellectual Property Rights
WB	World Bank
WC	Washington Consensus
WDM	World Development Movement
WDR	World Development Report
WTO	World Trade Organization

Introduction: The context of policy ownership in development agenda and the PRSP regime[1]

Policy ownership of development agenda emerged as an important aspect in international development cooperation or foreign aid during the 1990s in the backdrop of past failures of reforms initiatives in developing countries steered by different donor agencies, particularly the international financial institutions (IFIs), the World Bank (WB) and the International Monetary Fund (IMF). The disappointing results of the Structural Adjustment Programs (SAP), introduced as a loan condition by, the WB-IMF, also known as the Bretton Woods twins, in the early 1980s, contributed to the rise of interest in policy ownership. Though SAP was thought to become an agenda for overall restructuring of an economy for faster poverty reduction and creation of employment opportunities, however, it appeared as "nothing else but neo-classical economics espousing a firm belief in the market's 'invisible hand,' the rationality of economic actors' choice, and a minimalistic vision of the states' regulation of economies" (Lopes: 2012, 70).

Poor countries were forced to accept SAP as a policy conditionality of the WB and IMF; the influence of the WB and IMF became much stronger in the SAP regime, particularly in the aftermath of the debt crisis of 1982 (Chang: 2007). Yet, in practice, much of the policy measures under the package did not work; practically, the failures of SAP could be attributed to its inbuilt structural deficiencies. It influenced developing economies to open up their markets without adequate social protection and it essentially weakened the capacity of the state thus creating market failures. The resultant shock of market failures caused severe hardship on the lives and livelihoods of the poor of the developing economies. It is argued that these failures make SAPs questionable and irrelevant (McCutchan: 2010).

Another critical inadequacy of SAP is that they considered reforms as part of neo-liberal trajectory giving the market the ultimate authority, but from an apolitical stance. Thus taking for granted that the market would be able to govern the economy without considering the socio-political context of the economy. Due to its overly economic thrust, it put much importance on policy conditionality to ensure effectiveness of reforms packages from a technocratic point of view (Heidhues and Obare: 2011). IMF staff also admitted, despite some successes, the neoliberal agenda that was pursued under the

Washington Consensus or structural adjustment program (SAP) hurt many of the developing economies by creating more inequalities that have significant implications both in terms of social and economic cost (Ostry, Loungani, and Furceri: 2016).

Chang (2007, 18) further argued

> … the World Bank and the IMF have imposed on developing countries standard policy packages that are considered to be universally valid by the rich countries, rather than policies that are carefully designed for each particular developing country – predictably producing poor results as a consequence. Another result is that, even when their policies may be appropriate, they have often failed because they are resisted by the locals as impositions from outside.

The essence of Chang's arguments is that a development agenda could not be successful if it is anchored within a technocratic and apolitical perspective. Moreover, social buy-in or in other words national ability to demonstrate a country's ownership over the agenda is crucially important. The disappointing results of the SAP regime forced the international development community to undertake soul-searching to pinpoint the reasons behind the failures. It was then identified that for reforms to be successful the aid recipient country must have the freedom to choose the reform strategies (Stiglitz: 2002). It was a clear movement towards ownership in development policy.

Stiglitz (2008) underlined, while sharing his thoughts on the post-Washington Consensus (PWC) as a response to address the gaps of SAP and/or WC, that development policies should not be within the confines of Washington, i.e. the WB-IMF and the US establishment. It means it should not be an issue of of donors' and international financial institutions' influence only because they provide financial assistance to developing economies. The main reason for such argument is that there is no 'one-size fits all' approach as the situation varies from country to country. It was argued that rampant liberalization of the economy, while understanding that it worked well in some developed countries, is not prudent and that engagement of the developing countries in development policies is important (Stiglitz: 2008). Thus, it emerged from Stiglitz's discussion that one of the major features of the PWC is the engagement of stakeholders.

Despite criticism surrounding PWC that it is also an extension of the previous neoliberal WC, some argue that PWC is a major departure from the WC. The argument was that the former moves away from policy conditionality and resorts to country ownership and recognizes the importance of effective state institutions (Ruckert: 2006). The theoretical premise of the PWC underlined that it was an outcome of the change in thinking of the World Bank about development strategy that was spelled out by the Bank's Comprehensive Development Framework (CDF), which was espoused by its President in 1999. Among the key features of CDF, country ownership and country-led partnership were prominent as there was evidence that past failures were because of the lack of country ownership (Wolfensohn: 1999; Stiglitz: 1998).

At the same time, on the theoretical front, change was also taking place as to the definition of development and poverty in the context of the new argument for human development and well-being spearheaded by the UNDP building on the lessons of past reforms that sought to see development from a more technocratic point of view. The World Bank's World Development Report 2000/01 recognized the multidimensional aspect of poverty. This signaled a departure from the previous growth-centric and market-led development model of the WB and IMF. It recognized that poverty has many faces and poverty is an outcome of multiple factors.

The Report's theoretical underpinning is rooted in the WB's flagship study, *Voices of the Poor* (WB: 2000). The study was generated by interviews and/or discussions with over 50,000 poor people from forty-seven countries in different regions of the world. The Report concluded with suggesting the need for reform in development cooperation to attack poverty more effectively. One of its key arguments in doing so was that local conditions have to be considered if the country has to be strengthened (WB: 2001). It is evident that in the backdrop of past failures and new realization of development, the ownership agenda has gained currency in development dialogues and discourses over time.

The Millennium Development Goals (MDGs) became another watershed event that brought the aid effectiveness agenda to the forefront of global discussion. Following the MDGs, several dedicated international forums and meetings took place underscoring the need for country ownership in making aid deliver results. The most prominent such high-level meeting was the Paris Declaration that provided five key principles[2] for effective aid as a global agreement and formalized country ownership in development cooperation as being one of the five principles. However, these principles were further sharpened by Accra Agenda for Action[3] followed by Busan Partnership Document.[4] Following the Busan High Level Meeting on Aid Effectiveness, the Global Partnership for Effective Development Cooperation (GPEDC)[5] emerged to advocate for effectiveness of development cooperation within the key principles of Paris declaration.

Thus, in the wake-up call of the Comprehensive Development Framework (CDF), the World Bank and the IMF opted for introducing a new strategy replacing previous Structural Adjustment Programs (SAP). This new strategy is anchored in the principles of the CDF. The new strategy became popularized as the *Poverty Reduction Strategy Paper* (PRSP) as it aimed to explicitly deal with poverty reduction in the aid receiving countries. The core CDF principles are (a) long term and holistic, (b) country ownership and stakeholders' participation, (c) result oriented, and (d) country led partnership. Therefore, all PRSPs were expected to translate the principles of the CDF while developing a development framework at country level.

An overview of PRSP

Arguably, a PRSP emphasized that ownership can be achieved through the participation of major stakeholders ranging from the public to private sector and civil society organizations (CSOs). Any developing country of either of the WB's Highly Indebted Poor Country (HIPC)[6] category or within the IMF's Poverty Reduction and Growth Facility (PRGF)[7] category willing to receive concessional loans had to develop a PRSP and have it approved by the Bank-Fund. Bangladesh, as a loan recipient under the PRGF category of the IMF, committed to preparing a PRSP as the major development strategy for poverty reduction replacing the traditional Five-Year Plan (FYP).

A PRSP document was supposed to be grounded within core elements of the CDF and the explicit aim of a PRSP was poverty reduction (Christiansen and Hovland: 2003). The principles underpinning the PRSP approach suggested that these strategies should be:

- Country-driven and owned, predicated on a broad-based participatory process for formulation, implementation, and outcome-based progress monitoring;
- Results-oriented, focusing on outcomes that would benefit poor;
- Comprehensive in scope, recognizing the multidimensional nature of the causes of poverty and measures to attack poverty;
- Partnership-oriented, providing a basis for active and coordinated participation of development partners (bilateral, multilateral, nongovernmental) in supporting country strategies; and
- Based on a medium and long-term perspective for poverty reduction, recognizing that sustained poverty reduction cannot be achieved overnight (WB: 2002).

There are four major assumptions built into a PRSP.

- Macroeconomic and structural policies to support sustainable growth in which the poor participate.
- Improvement in governance, including public sector financial management.
- Appropriate sectoral policies and programs.
- Realistic costing and appropriate level of funding for the major programs (WB: 2002).

Full PRSPs are expected to summarize the priority public actions over a three-year horizon by inclusion of tables (a) presenting the country's macroeconomic framework; (b) summarizing the overall public expenditure program (capital and recurrent) and its allocation among key areas; and (c) setting out key policy actions and institutional reforms and target dates for their implementation (a policy matrix) (WB: 2002).

Ownership agenda in PRSP and the polemics: Overview of global evidence and the need for further research

While PRSP was claimed to have been a major paradigm shift within the WB-IMF development milieu, it also has engendered many criticisms globally. Critics have challenged the core principles of a PRSP in terms of content, intention and procedure. Some critics have argued that governments are being forced to implement Bank-Fund strategies to obtain loans from either the Bank-Fund or other bilateral donors. As deeply indebted and cash strapped governments do not usually have access to alternative sources of development finance, therefore, the Bank-Fund policies are becoming more powerful than national laws and policies. Crucial national policies related to trade, investment, assets ownership, natural resources, fiscal management, banking, public administration, social development, and even judicial systems are determined more by Bank-Fund and donor pressures than by domestic priorities and aspirations (Malaluan and Guttal: 2003).

Ownership seemed to have been the buzzword in the PRSP process but, in reality, experience suggests the 'ownership' issue has been more of a rhetoric than reality (Malaluan and Guttal: 2003; Oxfam: 2004). Non-Government Organizations (NGOs), consumers' rights groups, research institutes, peasants, political parties, etc. in many countries have rejected the structure, content, and process of PRSPs on the count that the ultimate ownership is with International Financial Institutions (IFIs). While every PRSP is followed by a joint staff assessment (JSA) by the Bank-Fund, the assessment note decides the fate of the document as to whether or not the strategies, presented in the PRSP, constitute a sound basis for concessional assistance from IMF and World Bank (WB: 2002). In terms of the structure of approval, it clearly points out that a PRSP is very much WB-IMF signal dependent. Guttal (2000) has argued that recipient countries have been practically forced to do a PRSP in line with the Bank-Fund model. Having critically analyzed the PRSP process, Guttal (2000) pointed out that a PRSP was not the outcome of people's felt need, for people were not properly invited to participate and characterized the participation as 'manipulated consent'.

Sobhan (2002) argues that ownership does not only mean that the policies are developed and shaped by the stakeholders and indigenous in nature, but also the benefits coming from the public policy must be shared by the stakeholders. Thus, participation is to determine the felt need of the poor and then to meet those needs. The consensus over policy proposal by ruling and opposition political parties is also essential for developing ownership.

Although the stakeholders' participation is one of the major underpinning principles of a PRSP to ensure national ownership of development agenda by loan receiving countries, the time limit given to prepare PRSPs has made real participation impossible and thus the formulation process has been questionable (Guttal, Bendaña and Wanguza: 2001; McGee, Levene and Hughes: 2002). Moreover, participation was by and large limited to inviting prominent and well-resourced NGOs to offer their perspectives on pre-prepared documents. Real stakeholders such as peasants, workers, professional groups, community leaders, local government institutions, women groups, etc. have not been fairly included in the process. Local people have also not been involved in the process to design strategies for nationally meaningful development plans. Parliamentary involvement has also been undermined and thus resulted in creating a narrow prospect for policy consensus and national ownership. Many have argued that a PRSP is, in terms of economic development strategy, not a new one rather an extension of previous policies of a structural adjustment regime. There was no major change in the PRSP and it ignored many important issues, like bottom-up land and agrarian reform, protection of common pool or common property resources, redistributive and equity enhancing financial and economic policies, progressive taxation, strengthening domestic markets and economic capacities, food and production sovereignty, the rights of communities to their natural resources, the protection of workers and the environment in relation to foreign investors, and assurances of social rights and entitlements to domestic populations (Malaluan and Guttal: 2003; Guttal, Bendaña and Wanguza: 2001). The central roles that the Bank-Fund has in global policymaking and governance would have a leveraging role on PRSPs beyond debt relief and concessional loans. PRSPs have been key policy instruments through which the world's major donors relate with low-income countries, and countries undergoing economic crises. The low-income countries are on the verge of being virtually cut off from international aid, trade and finance without a Bank-Fund approved PRSP. The US, EU and other OECD members have fully endorsed the PRSP framework and agreed to base their respective official aid programs to low income and crisis-ridden countries on the PRSP. Many bilateral donors have agreed to co-finance poverty-reduction credits, grants and technical assistance in line with the PRGF and Country Assessment Strategy (CAS) loan packages. The Netherlands and Japan have contributed 20 million USD to establish a special multi-donor trust fund to build the capacity of countries to prepare PRSPs in accordance with WB principles. The WB administers the trust fund and final approval for country proposals rest in the hands of the Bank, UN and external donors (WB 2002; Malaluan and Guttal 2003). Instead of mere participation, Stewart and Wang (2003) examined PRSP ownership from a national empowerment perspective. Empowerment means that national actors have greater say and contributions to policy design. While participation does not necessarily ensure true and effective engagement of key actors, it has varied forms and connotations such as information sharing, consultation, etc. Moreover, participation is contingent upon some factors such as who participates, whether it does truly influence the design or merely endorse the externally designed program. While Stewart and Wang (2003) viewed that a generalized interpretation of the nature and quality of engagement varied, they mentioned there had been extensive participation in many countries; particularly in Vietnam and Rwanda where government played a substantial role. However, donors' involvement including IFI representatives was evident at various levels. Strong engagement was noted in Tanzania and in Malawi, where engagement with the IFIs was less transparent. The major actors who were more or less excluded from the process were the parliamentarians, trade unions, and women and marginalized people. What is more important is that in many cases, participation was excessively selective and groups out of favor with the government were often not invited. In other cases, NGO participation was limited to international NGOs, or NGOs in the capital area. In most cases, smaller and rural NGOs, generally those who have most contact with the poor, were excluded from the process.

World Development Movement (WDM) (2005) made an exhaustive analysis of 50 completed PRSPs. The report held the view that conditionality was a basic component in IFI aid infrastructure. Since the 1970s poor countries were exposed to various forms of conditions although there were changes in the names of loans, such as during the structural adjustment regime the WB loan was called structural adjustment credits (SAC) while the IMF loan was a structural adjustment facility (SAF). In the face of global resistance, loans were later renamed by the WB as a poverty reduction support credit (PRSC) and by the IMF as a poverty reduction and growth facility (PRGF). However, it was evident that the same conditionality continued. It labeled the PRSP as an outcome of policy conditionality. The major findings the report mentioned are as follows:

- There were further trade liberalization measures in 72 per cent of the PRSPs. Despite compelling evidence such as rising poverty, rising unemployment, increased wage inequality and reductions in average wages as the outcomes of economic liberalization in poor countries, in only two cases was an 'alternative trade policy' included. Laos recognized a need for protection of certain sectors, while Ghana mentioned holding a review of trade liberalization policy. Being faithful to the policy outlined in the PRSP, the Ghanaian parliament in 2003 passed a budget to increase the import duty on poultry products to protect Ghanaian farmers who were being priced out of the domestic market by subsidized European poultry. However, after a phone call from the IMF, the legislated increase was removed by the Ghanaian Government after two weeks. Thus Ghana was pressured by the IMF to revert to trade liberalization.
- 90 per cent of the PRSPs included privatization, and 62 per cent specifically include water privatization/greater private sector involvement in water supply services. Despite recorded failure of the private sector none of the PRSPs included a review of any privatization policies or a specific goal to keep water and sanitation under public management.
- 64 per cent of PRSPs included investment deregulation and none mentioned the possible need to regulate investors to ensure reinvestment of profits in the country, joint ventures with local companies, technology

transfer or employment of local people; policies recognized by development policy analysts as potentially useful in creating spill-over benefits for domestic economies from Foreign Direct Investment (FDI).
- 96 per cent of PRSPs included fiscal stringency; normally that the government should not resort to borrowing from the domestic economy. But the history suggests that Continental Europe, the US, and Japan during their rapid economic growth maintained large programs of public expenditure, and even large budget deficits. Denying governments the ability to borrow domestically seriously hinders their ability to manage the economy.

It was argued "if countries really were free to promote their own choice of poverty reduction strategy in PRSPs, there would have been significant variation between countries and adaptation of policies to suit local circumstances (rather than a high degree of similarity) and have been range of 'alternative' approaches (rather than an adherence to the narrow confines of the Washington Consensus). However, this is not the case" (WDM: 2005, 11). It concluded saying "The homogeneity of PRSPs across such a range of widely differing countries, and the dearth of alternative policy approaches on these key economic issues, suggests that ownership of the economic policies in such countries is still a pipedream" (WDM: 2005: 12).

The WDM (2005) report attempted to see the PRSPs in a broader context of the mechanisms – both overt and subtle – that donor institutions and donor governments used to influence the policies of poor countries. Despite IFIs and some donor countries' claims that PRSP were country owned, the WDM report (2005) argued that in practice it was extremely difficult, if not impossible, for the poorest countries to truly determine their own development strategies for three key reasons. First, the preexisting WB/IMF policies influenced the content of the PRSPs and as such instead of starting afresh these IFI determined policies were generally 'cut-and-paste' into the PRSP with no further analysis or scrutiny. For example, in Gambia, Ghana, Guinea, Malawi, Mali, Mozambique, Nicaragua, Sierra Leone and Yemen, water privatization was already a condition of a WB and/or IMF program before being included in the PRSP. These countries had little choice but to include water privatization within the document. In theory, IMF and WB policy conditions were supposed to be determined by the content of PRSPs, but in practice, in many cases the PRSP content was determined by already existing IMF and WB conditions. Second, the influence of WB/IMF officials was evident in many countries where in the final PRSPs many points either were incorporated or omitted at the request of the officials. The third reason is very crucial in that the ultimate approval of the PRSPs lies with the board of directors of the WB/IMF. Thus, the loan receiving countries would try to incorporate strategies that would please the WB/IMF and not take any risk of being rejected by the board. As one Finance Minister has revealed, "We don't wish to second guess the Fund. We prefer to give them what they want before they start lecturing us about this and that. By doing so, we send a clear message that we know what we are doing – i.e., we believe in structural adjustment" (WDM: 2005, 8).

The WDM report (2005) mentioned that the WB's Operations Evaluation Department (OED) itself concluded, "The Bank management's process for presenting a PRSP to the Board undermines ownership. Stakeholders perceive this practice as 'Washington signing off' on a supposedly country owned strategy" (p. 8). It further pointed out that this problem was compounded by the structure and functioning of the IMF and WB boards where rich countries held 62 per cent of the votes, despite only possessing 21 per cent of the world's population and providing 23 per cent of the WB and IMF's income. Developing countries, which provide 77 per cent of the institutions' income and hold 79 per cent of the world's population, have just 38 per cent of the votes on the IFI boards.

Jones and Hardstaff (2005, 6) held a similar argument:

> So poor countries are now faced with an international financial landscape where loans, debt relief and aid are all subject to meeting economic policy conditions determined by the IMF and World Bank and their political masters in the developed world. To obtain concessional loans from the Bank and Fund, a country has to agree a programme with economic conditions attached. To receive debt relief through the HIPC initiative, countries must have an IMF programme in place, implement further conditions contained in their 'decision point document' (agreed with the Bank and Fund) and create and implement a PRSP.

McKinley (2004) questioning the quality of participation in a PRSP observed that while participation was important for building effective strategies, participation by itself could not guarantee pro-poor outcomes. In many cases the participation was nominal in the sense that it was government sponsored one-off consultation with civil society and community groups. He observed that the purpose was to elicit a rubber stamp for strategies already formulated. Participation was more focused on the process and less on content. Civil society contribution in terms of giving input and influencing strategies was marginal. McKinley (2004, 4) observed,

> The call by the international donor community for national 'ownership' of PRSPs usually implies that national stakeholders are encouraged to agree with a pre-determined set of external policy recommendations. They have had little opportunity to choose among various policy options, much less formulate their own. At best, the scenario is one of 'choice-less' participation, with negligible scope for real policy choice. The most severe problems are in the realm of economic policymaking. In this area, there is still little latitude for choice or debate. External conditionalities remain tightly binding, despite the recent muted rituals of

> critical self-examination generated by the research departments and independent evaluation offices of international financial institutions.

He argued that if there were true participation then there would have been different perspectives, thus abandoning the present one-size-fits-all approach and creating country specific strategies. Invariably all countries undergoing the PRSP experience shared more or less the same approach. Moreover, broad-based debate and dialogue was required before a strategy was finally adopted.

Rowden and Irama (2004) underscored the asymmetrical power relationship between the dependent loan receivers and the powerful international financial institutions in the analysis of independence of the borrowers. By their analysis the IFIs are also the gatekeepers to the bilateral lending sources. The IFIs, due to dependency of the poor countries on access to low-interest loans, exerts greater leverage and political power on the borrowing economies. The PRSPs according to the IFI guidelines must undergo first a Joint Staff Assessment (JSA) and then to the Board of Directors of the WB/IMF.

> in the eyes of many of these lower-income borrowing governments, the principle (principal) purpose of the PRSP is to cave-in to enough standardized neoliberal policies to secure their access to desperately needed external financing. If the purpose of PRSPs was to actually formulate 'country owned' homegrown policy prescriptions, then the executive boards of the IFIs would not undercut the sovereignty of their borrowers by requiring that they first approve PRSPs as a condition for extending credits, grants and debt relief.
>
> (Rowden and Irama: 2004, 10)

A summary reveals an overall scenario as well as cross-country experiences concerning the real perspective of participation in a PRSP (Rowden and Irama: 2004). It argued that governments wanted the CSOs to play the traditional role of implementers and voicing basic needs of the downtrodden people and not of a supplier of alternatives policies and paradigms. In other words, governments did not want CSOs to challenge the development strategies of the IFIs. The Angolan experience showed that CSOs' participation was limited to discussing social issues but not the macroeconomic issues. The same experience existed in Bolivia where the NGO network CEDLA noted, "The participation of Bolivian civil society in the definition of macroeconomic programs is virtually nil, above all with reference to the PRGF" (Rowden and Irama: 2004, 28).

In 2002 the civil societies in Ghana, Malawi, Mozambique, Tanzania, Zambia and Bolivia came up with the consensus that they were totally unable to influence macroeconomic policy or even engage governments in dialogue about it. Honduran NGOs complained of being excluded from workshops on the macroeconomic chapter of their PRSP. That chapter was included in the final document without ever having been circulated to CSOs or parliamentarians for discussion and input. Another study of six African PRSPs and interim-PRSPs policy discussions noted that the workshops rarely discussed sequencing of policy reforms or alternative policies and possible trade-offs, and only in only one (Uganda) was there discussion on the impact of structural adjustment. Vietnamese NGOs said their national policies on poverty "may well be country-owned", but "there will be little that is country-owned in terms of the macroeconomic framework in which such policies will be carried out, if Vietnam wants the loans" (Rowden and Irama: 2004, 29).

The Operations Evaluation Department (OED) of the WB ran an independent evaluation on the PRSP initiative in 2003. The evaluation report admitted the inbuilt tension between the BWI conditionality attached to the PRSP initiative and the thrust for a country-owned development strategy for the borrowing countries which resulted in bringing a shift in the agenda. The countries, instead of looking at making a PRSP in their own context, focused on completing the document and prepared standardized strategies to ensure access to concessional loans. It also reported the frustrations of the CSOs as to the impact of participation,

> that this openness has had only limited impact on the design of PRSPs or on domestic policy, with the exception of greater attention to governance concerns in some countries. Moreover, participatory activities have sometimes waned once the PRSP was formulated, suggesting that governments were concerned more about fulfilling donor requirements than about achieving systemic change. Along these dimensions, participation has not achieved all its aims.
>
> (WB: 2004, 46)

EURODAD's (2007) groundbreaking research on Good Practice Principles[8] (GPP) provides a substantial picture of continuation of policy conditionality which was earlier heavily criticized. Those criticisms led the WB-IMF to endorse the notion of policy ownership to give the borrowing countries a chance to come up with policy alternatives to deal with local problems and better economic impact.[9] EURODAD analysis suggests that two years on from the implementation of the GPPs, more than two thirds of loans and grants (71%) from the WB's IDA still have sensitive policy reforms attached to them as conditions.

The majority of these are privatization related conditions. This report also finds that as a share of overall conditions, economic policy conditions have at best remained unchanged and at worst gone up slightly, now constituting a quarter of WB conditions in poor countries. In short, this report highlights serious concerns with the WB's implementation of GPPs. However, the continued use of conditionality in sensitive areas such as privatization and liberalization is of significant concern.

According to the WB data, there has been a reduction in the overall number of conditions attached to WB finance packages. They report that the average number of conditions has fallen from 46 per loan prior to the GPPs, to 37 per loan today. The report interpreted that this reduction is largely due to a fall in the number of non-legally binding conditions, from 33 per loan before the GPPs to 24 today. Legally binding conditions,[10] however, have remained unchanged at 13 per loan.

However, the apparent reduction in number may misleadingly give an overly optimistic picture and thus the report suggests treating the numbers with a degree of caution. The reason it argues that the WB is "bundling" numerous policy actions into one overall condition. For example, according to WB data, Uganda has only eleven conditions in its PRSC V. However, when EURODAD counted the policy actions contained within each of these conditions, they found that Uganda had thirty-eight separate policy conditions. In a sample of 1,341 WB conditions, EURODAD found that almost 7 per cent of WB conditions contained multiple policy actions. If these are counted as separate condition, the number of overall conditions increases by 12 per cent. The report commented that economic policy conditions[11] remained virtually unchanged, if taken as a percentage of overall WB conditions. According to WB data, pre-GPPs economic policy conditions stood on average at 8 per loan and around 17 per cent of overall conditions. Over the two-year period of the GPPs being implemented, this reduced to an average of 6 per loan, which represents 16 per cent of all conditions.

To sum up the global experience, it appears that there is much room to contest the quality of participation and the level of ownership in PRSPs. It is explicitly evident that many of the policy strategies of SAP either continued or were further strengthened in PRSPs. Despite claims by the WB-IMF that the aid recipient countries would be able to set their own development agenda through participatory approaches, this did not happen. And it creates a premise for research of Bangladesh's ownership in its PRSP.

PRSP and Bangladesh

Bangladesh emerged through a bloody war of independence in 1971 and the war ravaged the economy of the country resulting in high dependence on foreign aid regime both in terms of financial assistance for managing its development, and policy dependence in development strategy. Despite attempts soon after independence to take an independent posture, the country had to embrace foreign aid because of multiple vulnerabilities on different fronts of the economy. It is evident from aid inflow data in Bangladesh that the country was greatly dependent on food aid and commodity aid for the first two decades after independence (GoB: 2016). Dependence on food and commodity aid depicted Bangladesh's critical dependence on foreign aid in the beginning years. Gradually, partnership with donors was transformed into development partnership with more engagement in development project financing. In a sense Bangladesh's PRSP was an outcome of the country's historical partnership with donors and a continuation of its past engagement with donors through different policy and structural interventions and financial assistance. The evolution of Bangladesh's partnership with donors is explained in detail in Chapter 3 of this book.

In regard to Bangladesh's decision to prepare a PRSP, it could be said that the decision was taken within the milieu of the country's past legacy of partnership with donors to obtain credit under PRGF program of the IMF in Bangladesh Development Forum (BDF)[12] Meeting 2000. Economic Relations Division (ERD) of the Finance Ministry played a lead role in developing the I-PRSP[13] and submitted it to the IMF in 2003. In October 2005 Bangladesh officially released the full PRSP prepared under the management of the National Steering Committee (NSC).[14] General Economics Division (GED) of the Planning Commission coordinated the task. Bangladesh PRSP titled as *Unlocking the Potential: National Strategy for Accelerated Poverty Reduction* (NSAPR) (GoB: 2005) claims to have outlined a comprehensive medium-term strategy in a sound macroeconomic environment for implementing pro-poor growth, effective safety-net programs and human development. The strategy asserts to have been made broad-based and operational by emphasizing social inclusion and empowerment, promoting good governance, highlighting better service delivery practices and bringing care for environment and sustainable development to the center stage. The implementation of PRSP strategies has been anchored on a 'medium-term macroeconomic framework' supporting sustained growth and poverty reduction, which are steps towards attainment of MDGs (GoB: 2005). There have been four strategic blocks enunciated in the document: (a) macroeconomic environment for pro-poor economic growth; (b) critical sectors for pro-poor economic growth; (c) effective social safety nets and targeted programs; (d) human development.

With Bangladesh's decision to prepare a PRSP replacing the previous five-year planning approach, there had been substantial criticism with regard to the PRSP content and process as in other countries undertaking PRSPs. Many academics challenged Bangladesh's PRSP process and the efficacies of the strategies (Ahmad: 2005; Hossain: 2004; Titumir: 2002; Rahman: 2003; Sobhan: 2002, 2002a, 2002b, 2003; Akash: 2002). Rehman Sobhan consistently argued for policy independence and ownership for harnessing local demand driven policy interventions for poverty reduction. Sobhan aptly made the issue of policy ownership, in its own right, a major agenda for research. The major criticisms attributed to PRSP are: (a) lack of political will to eradicate poverty; (b) imbalanced distribution of wealth; and (c) lack of ownership in national poverty reduction strategy. But the government, on the other hand, has claimed that the PRSP has been prepared through proper consultations with stakeholders at different levels, ranging from Upazilla[15] to divisional/national levels (GoB: 2005).

As the debate continues, it has provided a rationale to undertake research on the state of Bangladesh's ownership in the PRSP, the major government development agenda aimed at poverty reduction. The principal focus of this book is to examine Bangladesh's policy independence or dependence in its

PRSP by broadly analyzing the dynamics in the formulation process and examining the principal actors' contribution to the formulation process. Nevertheless, the study also sheds light on the following issues as part of dealing with several other dimensions of aid and policy shifts:

- Understanding the shifts in WB-IMF policy of development cooperation and subsequent influence over development strategies of the developing countries including Bangladesh;
- Analyzing political and civil society responses in relation to the PRSP process and content in Bangladesh;
- Examining line-Ministries' involvement in the making of PRSP;
- Providing some policy implications in order to make a pro-people, home-grown, and country felt-independent development agenda for Bangladesh.

Like many other countries, the PRSP in Bangladesh seemed not to have evolved as a demand of local need and in effect, the issue of ownership in Bangladesh's PRSP has highly been questionable and contested. While a good body of literature in relation to unfolding the influences of the WB-IMF in Bangladesh's development agenda is available, an attempt to undertake research on PRSP policy ownership with the primary aim of exploring policy leverage of the Bank-Fund in PRSP as a case study and the level of engagement of local actors demands justification from a national perspective. Sobhan (1982), Islam (1991, 2003), Rahman (1991), Syeduzzaman (1991, 2004), Akash (2004), Barkat (2002), Bhattacharya and Titumir (2001), Faaland (1981), Muhammad (1998), and Rahman (1993) have provided insights into the policy influences on the Bank-Fund over Bangladesh's development agenda over the years. Many of these writers had the privilege to closely observe the dynamics of donor influences from within. Many of these individuals were key figures in the government, particularly on the Planning Commission. They have very poignantly narrated the dynamics of an uneven engagement of a newly independent poor country with powerful organizations such as the WB-IMF.

While past works discussed donors' influence from a general point of view, this book presents a detailed case study of donors' influence over Bangladesh's national strategy process. It also tries to understand the role of different key actors in the formulation process of a development agenda. By capturing broadly the dynamics of the engagement of key actors in the development planning this book provides new insights into development agenda setting. This book argues that it is true that the WB-IMF strongly influence Bangladesh's development policies and agendas, but it is equally important to understand that Bangladesh is committed to ensuring ownership of our national development agenda. It further argues that policy ownership does not automatically come about, but it is the outcome of the relentless and committed persuasion of major actors in the State. Moreover, as poverty continues to be a daunting challenge for Bangladesh, a strong commitment to poverty reduction through policy consensus is strongly needed.

While participation of key actors is recognized as a fundamental element to ensure local ownership, a PRSP strongly demands participation of major players of the society apart from government functionaries. In other words, to qualify for national ownership a PRSP has to prove that the actors have been given ample opportunity to interact with the entire process from beginning to end. But in the case of Bangladesh, all major actors have decried that they have not been given due opportunity. The book is geared to unfolding that debate also.

One of the major contributions of this book is that it analyzes, with particular reference to Bangladesh, whether the Bank-Fund (departing from SAP approach) truly did want to give space to the loan receiving countries to draw their own agenda of development. What is captured is the elaborate dynamics of development agenda setting in Bangladesh. As mentioned earlier while understanding the influences of the Bank-Fund are important, it is more important to understand the local scenarios (i.e. the readiness of the State and other actors to pursue independent strategies). It can safely be said that there has not been much light shed on that area in Bangladesh.

Why Bangladesh's policy ownership still merits discussion when PRSP does not exit

Domestic dimension

Bangladesh, once identified as the test case for development (Faaland and Parkinson: 1976), fared well over the last couple of decades on different fronts of development. It has beaten the level of abject poverty. Bangladesh's achievements on several targets during the MDG regime were remarkable and globally applauded. Significant progress was made in areas of poverty reduction, ensuring food security, primary school enrolment, and gender parity in primary and secondary level education, lowering the infant and under-five mortality rate and maternal mortality ratio, improving immunization coverage; and reducing the incidence of communicable diseases (GoB: 2015). Bangladesh is now the second largest apparel exporter in the world. Over 4 million workers are engaged in garment industries and 90 per cent of them are women resulting in phenomenal change in women's empowerment and employability (Adnan et al.: 2015).

Bangladesh has been successful in steadily maintaining a growth rate of over 6 per cent for a decade through an export-led growth trajectory which has resulted in transitioning the economy from agriculture to manufacturing (IMF: 2017). The recent World Bank Update on Bangladesh's economy (WB: 2017) also held an optimistic scenario for the economy; however, the WB pointed out certain areas of weakness that require attention to sustain current progress. The growth rate surpassed the 6 per cent rate in fiscal year 2015–16 registering at 7.11 per cent. The GNI per capita in 1970s was below 200 USD and that now rose to 1465 USD in the same fiscal year.[16] Rapid growth already elevated the position of the country from low-income to lower to middle-income category in 2014 (WB: 2016). Despite many severe challenges, such as natural calamities, confrontational domestic politics, poor governance and weak institutional ability, Bangladesh's development success is considered a 'surprise' by many (Asadullah, Savoia and Mahmud: 2014).

On the development financing front, the change is also highly significant. While in the beginning Bangladesh's development budget used to almost fully depend on external financing, particularly foreign aid but currently foreign assistance accounts for only 2 per cent of the country's GDP (GoB and AP-DEF: 2016). On the other hand, ODA represents 5 per cent of capital formation (GPEDC: 2016). Private sector, domestic revenue and remittances are playing an important role in development financing. The seventh five-year plan (2016–20) projected that around 70 per cent of resources for public investment will come from the domestic private sector and only 2.7 per cent from ODA (GoB: 2015). Remittances have been maintaining steady inflow of over 12 billion USD annually for last couple of years with record high over 15 billion USD in the 2014–15 fiscal year. Clearly, the contribution of ODA or international development aid is declining significantly in the changing development financing landscape of Bangladesh.

In such a changing scenario it is important to look more critically at why the influences of the international financial institutions and development aid continue to stay as formidable as it used to be in the early years of the country when aid was a major source of development financing. For example, Bangladesh has been struggling to manage its development partners (DPs) to finalize the national policy for development cooperation (NPDC) or foreign aid policy. Started in 2011, the country still has not been able to make the policy formally operational until October 2017.[17] Moreover, it is also important to point out that many officials working in the Economic Relations Division (ERD), Ministry of Finance[18] commented that donors continue to influence the decision-making process of the projects and the influence is much greater than that of their financial contribution. Thus, it is important to ask why Bangladesh is failing to exert its ownership over its development agenda. And against this backdrop, a study of national ownership of development agenda makes sense. While Bangladesh's case may offer lessons to other developing countries, Bangladesh also may look at the practices of other countries to strengthen its national ability to choose its own development agenda by offsetting external influences.

GPEDC's 2016 Monitoring Survey Report (GPEDC: 2016) reveals Bangladesh's aid dependence in a practical manner. While Bangladesh's ODA per capita is slightly over 15 USD and ODA's contribution to GDP is 2 per cent, Bangladesh scored 3 out of 6 in country policy and institutional assessment (CPIA); on the contrary, as an example, Rwanda's[19] ODA per capita is over 91 USD and ODA's contribution to GDP is over 13 per cent, but it scored 4 in CPIA. Rwanda is progressing in all indicators of use of a country system, whereas; Bangladesh has seen negative performance. Donors' use of a national procurement system is 88 per cent in Rwanda but it is only 21 per cent in Bangladesh presenting a dismal situation. Bangladesh's dependence does not match its scale of economic development. Clearly, there are some issues in aid management in Bangladesh which calls for further investigation.

On the other hand, it is essentially important to note that given Bangladesh's current development momentum, the country needs a different type of development trajectory which should not be as technocratic as usually suggested by donor agencies. Bangladesh needs an engaged discussion among key national actors to recalibrate its own means and pathways for development. And for this, Bangladesh has to undertake strategic interventions in different areas of development going beyond generic prescriptions offered by different technocratic models. Bangladesh already has been identified as a lower-middle income country by the World Bank; it has also initiated formal steps to be graduated from the Least Developed Country (LDC) list.[20] Moreover, the country's leadership often argues that the country aspires to be a member of the developed countries by 2041. These essentially indicate the country's deep commitment to development. Countries that experienced momentum in development followed such policy strategies that matched their own development expectations. The example of Korea, China, India and Vietnam could be relevant to Bangladesh in this regard. While Bangladesh's development success is encouraging, it is a fact that it is one of the most densely populated countries and also one of the most climate vulnerable countries in the world. Therefore, Bangladesh needs a development trajectory that not only exploits the opportunities but at the same time addresses the vulnerabilities. And, this kind of strategy requires practical and prudent understanding of the context, both domestic and global, and also an ambitious leadership. Within such milieu, Bangladesh needs to move forward to manage its development goals.

International dimension

In terms of time frame the book seems a late arrival as the formal PRSP agenda lapsed a few years back. But if we critically look at the current architecture of global aid and development agenda, it is found that the architecture is still dominated by rich countries and international financial institutions. It is evident that despite positive changes and better spaces for the poor countries to influence the global decision-making process and institutions due to high level dialogue and discussions on aid effectiveness, the scope for influencing the poor countries by the rich countries rather has been more legitimate and formal with the emergence of the global institutions. After the Busan meeting in 2011 on aid effectiveness, Global Partnership for Effective Development Cooperation (GPEDC) emerged as the global platform guiding and steering the development cooperation agenda. GPEDC, though apparently an inclusive platform having representation of both donor and recipient countries and CSOs in the steering committee, is likely to be influenced by the OECD countries because of their inherent power and role and secretariat functions. On the other hand, the development regime is heavily dominated by the 'Trinity' of the World Bank, IMF and WTO. With that in mind, it is very unlikely for the poor and developing countries to completely ignore the influence of the Trinity that seem to serve the purpose of the rich countries (Chang: 2007; Peet: 2009). Nevertheless, country ownership emerged as a strong principle of aid effectiveness, but, in reality, it is still far below the horizon (UKAN and BOND: 2013). So, the relevance of researching ownership agenda merits continuance. Given the hard reality at the global level, the smart approach would be that the poor or developing countries should gradually look forward to more autonomy in policy articulation which builds on previous experiences. Therefore, although, as such, PRSP is not in place, the approaches and strategies that the Trinity aspires to are very much in practice and preaching. Lessons learned in the PRSP regime shall continue to maintain its relevance to all developing countries aiming to avert past failures and aspire to be more independent in terms of policy making. Country level analysis always has the potential to inform other peer countries to build effective and strategic approach to smartly manage donor induced development policies and strategies. The PRSP agenda was a major package of the WB and IMF; and thus, its comprehensive analysis is likely to provide critical insights to policy makers of today. The World Bank and IMF continue to financially aid underdeveloped and developing countries. It is therefore critical that the errors of the past be brought to light and scrutinized so that these errors are not repeated. Further we cannot ignore the global influence that these policies have had and the book provides an opportunity to revisit, rethink and evaluate the value of such institutions.

Assessing Bangladesh's country ownership in PRSP: methodological consideration

The principal focus of this study is to understand policy (in)dependence in Bangladesh's PRSP by broadly analyzing the dynamics in the formulation process and examining principal actors' contribution to the formulation of the document as a principal development strategy. The study thus captures (a) the shifts in WB-IMF policy of development cooperation and subsequent influence over development strategies of poor countries including Bangladesh; (b) political and civil society responses in relation to PRSP process and contents in Bangladesh; (c) line-ministries' involvement in the making of PRSP. While the current research makes efforts to understand the role of various key actors in the formulation process of a development agenda such as PRSP, the research argues that alongside researching WB-IMF's policy influence over Bangladesh's development policies and agendas, it is equally important to understand that the country is committed to ensuring ownership of the national development agenda. The present study further argues that policy ownership does not automatically come in but it is the outcome of the relentless and committed persuasion of major actors in the State. Moreover, as poverty continues to be a daunting challenge for Bangladesh, a strong commitment to poverty reduction through policy consensus is strongly needed.

While participation of key actors is recognized as a fundamental element to ensure local ownership, PRSP strongly demands the participation of major players of the society apart from government functionaries. In other words, to qualify for national ownership a PRSP has to prove that the actors have been given adequate opportunity to interact with the entire process from beginning to end. The study elaborately captured the dynamics of development agenda setting in Bangladesh. As said earlier, while understanding the influences of the WB-IMF is important, it is more important to understand the local scenario or in other words, the readiness of the state and other actors to pursue independent strategies. And it could safely be said that to date there has not been much light shaded on that area in Bangladesh.

The current research, in pursuing aforesaid objectives, has identified some key issues to deal with and those issues have constituted the focus of the research. In capturing those issues, it has shed light on Bangladesh's engagement with the WB-IMF from a historical point of view. Searching the context of PRSP in Bangladesh is a major point of discussion in this work. In understanding broadly the question of national ownership in Bangladesh's PRSP the answers to the following research questions were sought out:

a Who were the actors in the making of the PRSP in Bangladesh?
b What was the scope of participation?
c How did the principal actors, such as the parliament, political parties, civil society and bureaucracy interact with the process?
d What was the influence of the donors in the process?

The research, being explorative in nature, has largely been dependent on qualitative data. It employed hosts of research tools for data collection (e.g. secondary data – books, reports, newspaper articles etc.; primary data – interviews). The major objective of the study was to search for ownership, which could be ascertained through analysis of participation of stakeholders in the PRSP.

Myriad criticisms as to the process and contents emanating from different CSOs, and academics, have required thorough checking to gauge the level of participation and the quality of preparatory process. Major views expressed about participation by different scholars, especially synthesized in the analytical framework chapter, have been categorically examined to comment on participation process of PRSP in Bangladesh.

Desk research captured the shifts in development cooperation at national and international levels. The case study method was used to gain broader understanding about CSO and political activism and to comprehend the government run participation process. Key interviews of different actors, such as political elite, government officials, and principal activists of the

CSOs intensively helped to provide insight on the total process of creating a PRSP. The individuals interviewed for the study included: government officials including permanent secretaries – 27, top political leaders – 3, academic and CSO leaders – 12, 2 senior level private sector functionaries, and the lead consultant recruited for preparing PRSP. Among the prominent interviewees were: Bangladesh's alternate director in the World Bank and former cabinet secretary, former minister for education and World Bank official, secretaries to the government, the lead consultant for preparing PRSP, the member-secretary of the National Steering Committee (NSC), the President of the Professional Economists' Association – Bangladesh Economic Association (BEA), the chief of the largest civil society network closely involved in the entire process and some senior and mid-level public officials in different ministries, close aides in the General Economics Division (GED), Planning Commission, Chairman of the largest private sector commercial bank; and managing director of the SME Foundation.

The interviews seemed to have been able to represent a cross section of stakeholders. Various published documents relating to PRSP and the research reports were consulted. Besides, a FGD was conducted in Chakoria Upazilla, Cox's Bazar district to grasp the understanding of local actors. Public officials, community leaders and NGO leaders attended the FGD. There were a number of conversations on different occasions with various key actors to capture the ownership process comprehensively. There were three seminars to share the progress and findings of the research: two in the Institute of Bangladesh Studies (IBS) and one in Dhaka. The Dhaka seminar was attended by a good number of career public servants and NGO activists. Observations and comments made in the seminars/discussions were incorporated into the study.

The research benefited immensely from my professional engagement as a career civil servant; I worked in several ministries and was able to see critically the internal dynamics of policy formulation and national ownership not only in PRSP but also in other development strategies and reforms initiatives. Direct involvement in government ministries enabled me to carefully read the mind of both public officials and political leadership.

I also worked with the UNDP Bangladesh for close to five years and supported the government as a policy specialist to ensure effectiveness of foreign aid. My role in UNDP enabled me to look at policy making process and influences of donors from a different angle. In fact, my professional role was much helpful to understand the complexity of policy ownership in Bangladesh. Looking back, it seems that the challenges persisted during PRSP regimes still continue and it provides the premise of a study on PRSP even after some years of its departure.

Organization of the book

The book is divided into five chapters including the introductory chapter. The **Introduction** presents the context for the study in terms of the shift in the development strategy leading to a PRSP. It discusses the importance of policy ownership for Bangladesh. It analyzed the changes taking place within the development financing landscape for the country in which the contribution of domestic revenue, private sector and remittances is increasing, while the proportionate contribution of foreign aid is declining. Moreover, at the global level, there are changes that underscore national ownership over the development agenda. Under this context, this chapter argues that Bangladesh's policy ownership agenda still has relevance and importance for further discussion and analysis.

Chapter One presents the historical perspectives concerning the different dimensions of WB-IMF's development agenda. This chapter focuses on the structural adjustment program (SAP), the predecessor of PRSP, and its associated issues. It also discusses the impact of SAP on the developing economies. SAP, due to its extremely negative impact on the economy of the poor countries, encountered popular resistances across the world and it resulted in bringing new understanding about development strategy within WB-IMF. The PRSP was an outcome of strategy and policy changes. Thus, this chapter explores the background of the PRSP. While discussing the evolution of WB-IMF strategies, the chapter covers the structural inadequacies of the policies. This chapter makes a contribution to global knowledge as this summarizes the historical dimension of WB-IMF sponsored development agenda from a global point of view providing a quick and easy reference to the readers.

Chapter Two provides the analytical framework of ownership in a development strategy. It discusses different dimensions of stakeholder engagement in a development agenda formulation. This chapter also analyzes the potential role and contribution of some key stakeholders in the context of development strategy in general and in particular, a PRSP. It aims to pinpoint why stakeholder roles are important to ensure true ownership in development agenda. Finally, it showcases Korea's example to demonstrate country ownership in a development agenda.

Drawing on secondary materials, **Chapter Three** provides an overview of Bangladesh's engagement with WB-IMF. This chapter is essentially a quick guide for the readers to understand the ups and downs in the relationship. It particularly focuses on Bangladesh's initial years when the country was in the middle of deep challenges; while it opted to maintain autonomy in development thinking, yet it had to accept the conditional lending of the Bank-Fund. This represents the vulnerability of a developing country which still bears relevance to understand the political economy of development cooperation. This chapter unfolds that since Bangladesh's independence, donors play important roles in the development strategy.

Chapter Four is the key chapter of this book as it discusses multiple dimensions of stakeholder engagement in the formulation process of Bangladesh's PRSP. The chapter is split into two major parts. The first part of this chapter attempts to present an overview of Bangladesh's PRSP: targets, goals, key issues in building strategies, monitoring and evaluation features, Joint

Staff Advisory Note, etc. The first part presents the government versions, while the second part highlights on the ground realties. Essentially, there were gaps between the official version and the practical situation. The second part analyzes the real scenario of ownership by examining the level and quality of engagement of major stakeholders. This chapter identifies that 'an accidental' coalition of three individuals contributed to developing the PRSP in Bangladesh. Broadly, the findings of this chapter make it clear that Bangladesh's dismal experience in PRSP formulation corroborates experiences of other developing countries that adopted the PRSP development model.

Finally, building on Bangladesh's experience in regard to policy dependence in PRSP, **Chapter Five** argues for a new model for Bangladesh. Bangladesh's economy is changing, so is its development financing. Thus, this book identifies that Bangladesh needs to build strong partnership with its private sector and research bodies for effective and strategic guidance to ensure ownership in development strategy and highlights the experiences of Korea and India.

Notes

1 Elaborately discussed in Chapter 4.
2 The Five Principles are: Ownership; Alignment; Harmonization; Managing for Results; and Mutual Accountability. Available at: http://www.oecd.org/dac/effectiveness/45827300.pdf.
3 For details: https://www.oecd.org/dac/effectiveness/45827311.pdf.
4 For details: http://www.oecd.org/development/effectiveness/49650173.pdf.
5 For details http://effectivecooperation.org/.
6 The HIPC Initiative entails coordinated action by the international financial community, including multilateral institutions, to reduce to sustainable levels the external debt burden of heavily indebted poor countries that pursue IMF and World Bank-supported adjustment and reform programs, but for whom traditional debt relief mechanisms are insufficient (http://www.imf.org/external/np/sec/pr/1999/pr9957.htm).
7 On November 22, 1999, the Enhanced Structural Adjustment Facility (ESAF) was renamed the Poverty Reduction and Growth Facility (PRGF), and its objectives were changed to support programs to strengthen substantially and in a sustainable manner balance of payments positions, and to foster durable growth, leading to higher living standards and a reduction in poverty. The PRGF is a concessional IMF facility for assisting eligible members that are undertaking economic reform programs to strengthen their balance of payments, and improve their growth prospects. PRGF loans carry an interest rate of 0.5% and are repayable over 10 years with a 5½-year grace on principal payments. (Please see http://www.imf.org/external/np/sec/pr/1999/pr9957.htm).
8 GPP is a WB sponsored review of its conditionality policy launched in 2005 in response to growing international criticism, from developed and developing countries alike, that the WB was still attaching too many intrusive and, at times, harmful economic policy conditions to its development finance to poor countries. The review resulted in the WB defining five "Good Practice Principles" that were intended to govern the way WB staff apply conditionality. These principles aimed to reduce the overall number of conditions attached to WB lending and ensure that those attached respected and were drawn from nationally developed poverty plans

in recognition that developing country ownership is the bedrock of successful development (EURODAD: 2007, 3).

9 The specialty of the report is that EURODAD was able to use WB's own conditionality database, made available to EURODAD for the first time in a welcome gesture in WB transparency (p. 6).

10 According to WB definitions only "legally binding conditions" are conditions, as they have the legal power to suspend finance. However, EURODAD along with many other NGOs have argued that non-legally binding conditions should also be counted as conditions, given that they influence recipient countries decisions and are used as a guide to assess performance of a loan throughout the year (EURODAD: 2007, 6).

11 EURODAD has counted as economic policy all conditions which related to financial and private sector development, economic management, privatization and privatization related activities, public enterprise reform, liberalization, trade and other issues related to trade like the removal of non-trade barriers, regulatory reform, exchange rate changes, customs, debt management and fiscal policy (ibid, 7).

12 BDF is a high level meeting that is held periodically between policy makers of the government and development partners. Ministers and Headquarter based policy makers of donor agencies and countries join this meeting to discuss on government's development trajectory and priorities.

13 Bangladesh, given the time constraint, initially developed an interim PRSP (I-PRSP) and later developed a full-blown PRSP. The WB-IMF had given loan receiving countries opportunity to prepare an I-PRSP if they failed to manage to develop a full PRSP within a given time.

14 Bangladesh government formed the National Steering Committee (NSC) under the leadership of the Principal Secretary to the Prime Minister to lead the PRSP formulation tasks.

15 An upazilla is a sub-district and a basic administrative unit in Bangladesh.

16 http://www.bbs.gov.bd/site/page/dc2bc6ce-7080-48b3-9a04-73cec782d0df/GDP.

17 An insider, in a recent interview, explained that the main reason for not finalizing the aid policy is that the development partners do not simply come under a policy framework. Their issues are not very substantive and moreover, those have been clarified several times, yet they do not show their willingness to support the government in finalizing the draft. This represents a dilemma of past legacy for both the donors and public officials. Donors on the ground are failing to understand that within the current level of development, they cannot influence the government as they used to do in the past. Yet, public servants and policy makers are also equally failing to exert their autonomous position. Considering the fact the country is no more critically dependent on the donors, public servants and policy makers should steer the process of policy making. The subservient situation of national actors could be explained as Sobhan (1996) argued perhaps is the state of mind when they prefer to leave their role on the donors or a 'cosy accommodation with dependency' as Mule (1997: 7) pointed out.

18 Lead ministry for the government to manage foreign aid/ODA.

19 Rwanda is now often cited as a good case study of demonstrating country leadership in development cooperation.

20 Economic Relations Division (ERD), Ministry of Finance is coordinating with Committee for Development Policy (CDP) of the UN. Bangladesh's several high-level missions met CDP officials and also CDP officials visited Bangladesh in October 2017 for discussion on a formal roadmap for graduation.

Bangladesh is expected to be recommended for graduation from the LDC list at the triennial meeting of the CDP (12–16 March 2018) and is expected to be graduated formally from the LDC list in 2024 upon complying with satisfactory performance during the transitioning period. The government has already undertaken several programs and events to celebrate the beginning of its graduation (http://www.thedailystar.net/business/govt-getting-ready-celebrateldcgraduation-1545127).

References

Abugre, Charles. "Still Sapping the Poor: A Critique of IMF Poverty Reduction Strategies", World Development Movement, London: 2001.

Adnan, A.T.M.*et al.* "Export Trend of Bangladesh: The Dominance of Ready-Made Garments Industry" in *Research Journal of Business, Economics and ICT*, Vol. 10, Issue 1, pp. 25–31, 2015.

Ahmad, Qazi Kholiquzzaman. "Poverty Reduction Strategy Paper: Repackaging Old Medicine" in *Journal of Bangladesh Economic Association*. Bangladesh Economic Association: Dhaka: pp. 111–118, 2005.

Akash, M.M. "Aid and Poverty" in *Revisiting Foreign Aid: A Review of Bangladesh's Development 2003*, CPD and UPL: Dhaka: 2004.

Akash, M.M. "Poverty Reduction Strategy Paper: What, Why & for Whom", Action Aid Bangladesh: Dhaka: 2002.

Asadullah, Niaz; Savoia, Antonio; and Mahmud, Wahiduddin. "Paths to Development: Is there a Bangladesh Surprise", *World Development* Vol. 62, pp. 138–154, 2014.

Barkat, Abul. Bangladeshe Baideshik Riin o Shahajjoyo Kotokhani Prpyojon: Goto Tin Dashakaer Aviyaggatar Political Economy [How Much Foreign Aid Does Bangladesh Really Need? The Political Economy of Last Three Decade's Experience] in *Bangladesh Economic Association Journal 2002* [in Bengali]: Dhaka: 2002.

Bhattacharya, Debapriya and Titumir, Rashed A.M. *Bangladesh Experience with Structural Adjustment: Learning from a Participatory Exercise*, CPD: Dhaka: 2001.

Chang, Ha-Joon. *Bad Samaritans: The Myth of Free Trade and the Secret History of Capitalism*, Bloomsbury Press, London: 2007.

Christiansen, Karin and Hovland, Ingie. *The PRSP Initiative: Multilateral Policy Change and the Role of Research*, Working Paper 216, Overseas Development Institute, London: 2003.

EURODAD. *Untying the knots: How the World Bank is failing to deliver real change on conditionality*: 2007, Available at: http://www.eurodad.org/uploadedfiles/whats_new/reports/untying%20the%20knots%20-%20how%20the%20wb%20is%20failing%20to%20deliver%20real%20change%20on%20conditionality.pdf; last accessed 12 December 2017.

Faaland, Just and Parkinson, J.R. *Bangladesh: The Test Case for Development*. C. Hurst & Company: London and UPL: Dhaka: 1976.

Faaland, Just. "The Debt Liability of Pakistan" in Faaland, Just (ed). *Aid and Influence: The Case of Bangladesh*. Chr. Michelsen Institute: Bergen: 1981.

GoB and AP-DEF. *Strengthening Finance for the 7th Five Year Plan and SDGs in Bangladesh: Findings from an Independent Development Finance Assessment*: 2016.

Government of Bangladesh (GoB). *Unlocking the Potential: National Strategy for Accelerated Poverty Reduction*, General Economics Division, Planning Commission, Dhaka: 2005.

Government of Bangladesh (GoB). *Millennium Development Goals: Bangladesh Progress Report, 2015*. General Economics Division, Planning Commission, Dhaka: 2015.

Government of Bangladesh (GoB). *Seventh Five-Year Plan FY2016-FY2020: Accelerating Growth, Empowering Citizens*, General Economics Division, Planning Commission, Dhaka: 2015.

Government of Bangladesh (GoB)/Economic Relations Division (ERD). *Flow of External Resources into Bangladesh*: 2016.

GPEDC. *Making Development Cooperation More Effective: 2016 Progress Report*; 2016.

Guttal, Shalmali. "The End of Imagination: The World Bank, IMF and Poverty Reduction": 2000. Available at: http://www.globalpolicy.org/socecon/develop/devthry/poverty/2000/guttal.htm.

Guttal, Shalmali, Bendaña, Alejandro and Wanguza, Helen. "The World Bank and the PRSP: Flawed Thinking and Failing Experiences". Available at: http://www.worldbank.org/poverty/strategies/review/jsouth1.pdf.

Heidhues, Franz and Obare, Gideon. "Lessons from Structural Adjustment Programmes and their Effects in Africa", *Quarterly Journal of International Agriculture*, vol. 50, no. 1: 55–64: 2011.

Hossain, Jakir. "Lost in the Queue: Equality, Rights and Livelihood". The Innovators: Dhaka: 2004.

IMF. "Bangladesh: 2017 Article IV Consultation – Press Release: Staff Report", *IMF Country Report* No. 17/247, Washington, DC: 2017.

Islam, Nurul. "Economic Policy Reforms and the IMF: Bangladesh Experience in the Early 1970s" in Sobhan, Rehman (ed.) *Structural Adjustment Policies in the Third World: Design and Experience*. UPL: Dhaka: 1991.

Islam, Nurul. *Making of a Nation Bangladesh: An Economist's Tale*. UPL: Dhaka: 2003.

Jones, Tim and Hardstaff, Peter. *Denying Democracy: How the IMF and World Bank Take Power from People*, World Development Movement (WDM), London: 2005.

Lopes, Carlos. "Economic Growth and Inequality: The New Post-Washington Consensus", *RCCS Annual Review* [Online], vol. 4, no. 7, 2012, Online since 01 October 2012, connection on 05 October 2016. http://rccsar.revues.org/426; doi:10.4000/rccsar.426.

Malaluan, Jenina Joy Chavez and Guttal, Shalmali. "Poverty Reduction Strategy Papers: A Poor Package for Poverty Reduction". Focus on the Global South: 2003. Available at: http://www.cadtm.org/IMG/pdf/prsp.pdf.

McCutchan, Andrew. 'Understanding the Inefficacy of Structural Adjustment Programs in Latin America', Master's Thesis, School of Economics and Management, Lund University: 2010.

McGee, R., Levene, J. and Hughes, A. "Assessing Participation in Poverty Reduction Strategy Papers: A Desk-based Synthesis of Experience in sub-Saharan Africa". IDS: London: 2002.

McKinley, Terry. "Economic Policies for Growth and Poverty Reduction: PRSPs, Neoliberal Conditionalities and 'Post-Consensus' Alternatives" presented in International Development Economics Associates (IDEAs) International Conference on THE ECONOMICS OF THE NEW IMPERIALISM, School of Social Sciences (SSS-I) Committee Room, Jawaharlal Nehru University (JNU), New Delhi, 22–24 January, 2004.

Muhammad, Anu. "Actors, Victims and Rhetoric: A Deconstruction of 'Development' Exercises" in Bayes, Abdul and Muhammad, Anu (eds). *Bangladesh at 25: An Analytical Discourse on Development*. UPL: Dhaka: 1998.

Mule, H., *"Partnership for Capacity Building in Africa. A Report of the Working Party on the Impact of Bank Policies, Instruments and Operational Practices on Capacity Building in Africa"*World Bank: Washington, DC: October, 1996.

Ostry, Jonathan D., Loungani, Prakash and Furceri, Davide. "Neoliberalism: Oversold?", *IMF Finance and Development*, vol. 53, no. 2: 2016.

OXFAM International. From 'Donorship' to Ownership? Moving Towards PRSP Round Two, *OXFAM Briefing Paper*, No. 51: 2004.

Peet, Richard. *Unholy Trinity: The IMF, World Bank and WTO*, 2nd Edition, Zed Books, London and New York: 2009.

Rahman, Anisur. *The Lost Moment: Dreams with a Nation Born through Fire.* UPL: Dhaka: 1993.

Rahman, Saifur. "Structural Adjustment Policies" in Sobhan, Rehman (ed.) *Structural Adjustment Policies in the Third World: Design and Experience.* UPL: Dhaka: 1991

Rahman, Habibur. "PRSP and Bangladesh": 2003www.prsp-atch.de/ laenderprofile/ bangladeshch_doku/iprsp.doc.

Rowden, Rick and Irama, Jano Ocaya. "Rethinking Participation: Questions for Civil Society about the Limits of Participation in PRSPs", Discussion Paper, ActionAid USA/ActionAid Uganda, Washington, DC: 2004.

Ruckert, Arne. "Towards an Inclusive-Neoliberal Regime of Development: From the Washington to the Post-Washington Consensus" in *Labour, Capital and Society*, Vol. 39, Issue 1, pp. 34–67: 2006.

Sobhan, R. "Aid Dependence and Donor Policy: The Case of Tanzania with Lessons from Bangladesh's Experience" in *Aid Dependency: Causes, Symptoms and Remedies; Project 2015*. Sida: Stockholm: 1996.

Sobhan, Rehman. *The Crisis of External Dependence: The Political Economy of Foreign Aid to Bangladesh.* UPL: Dhaka: 1982.

Sobhan, Rehman. "Policy Independence and Political Accountability", Centre for Policy Dialogue, Dhaka: 2002a.

Sobhan, Rehman. "The Incapacity of Structural Adjustment Reforms to Eradicate Poverty: An Agenda for Change", Centre for Policy Dialogue [CPD], Dhaka: 2002

Sobhan, Rehman. "The Political Economy of the State and Market in Bangladesh", Centre for Policy Dialogue, Dhaka: 2002b.

Sobhan, Rehman. "Aid, Governance and Policy Ownership in Bangladesh". CPD: Dhaka: 2003.

Stewart, Frances and Wang, Michael. "Do PRSPs empower poor countries and disempower the World Bank, or is it the other way round?", QEH Working Paper Series – Working Paper Number 108: 2003.

Stiglitz, Joseph E. "Towards a New Paradigm for Development: Strategies, Policies, and Processes" – the Prebisch Lecture 1998, October 19, 1998 at UNCTAD, Geneva: 1998.

Stiglitz, Joseph E. "Is there a Post-Washington Consensus Consensus?" in Serra, Narcís and Stiglitz, Joseph (eds) *The Washington Consensus Reconsidered: Towards a New Global Governance*, pp. 41–56. OUP and IPD Series: 2008.

Stiglitz, Joseph E. *Globalization and Its Discontents.* Penguin Books: 2002.

Syeduzzaman, M. "Aid and Policy Reforms in Bangladesh" in *Revisiting Foreign Aid: A Review of Bangladesh's Development 2003*, pp. 295–350. CPD and UPL: Dhaka: 2004.

Syeduzzaman, M. "Bangladesh's Experience with Adjustment Policies" in Sobhan, Rehman (ed.) *Structural Adjustment Policies in the Third World: Design and Experience.* UPL: Dhaka: 1991.

Titumir, R.A.M. "The Saga of PRSP: Penned in a Pegged Perspective", ActionAid Asia: Bangkok: 2002.

UNAN and BOND. "Country Ownership: The Only Way Forward for Development Cooperation": 2013.

Wolfensohn, James D. *A Proposal for a Comprehensive Development Framework* – A Discussion Draft to the Board, Management and Staff of the World Bank Group, June 21, 1999.

World Bank (WB). *Bangladesh Country Snapshot*, Washington, DC: 2016

World Bank (WB). *Bangladesh Development Update*, The World Bank Office, Dhaka: 2017.

World Bank (WB). Klugman, Jeni (ed.), *A Sourcebook for Poverty Reduction Strategies (Vol. I and II)*, Washington, DC: 2002.

World Bank (WB). *The Poverty Reduction Strategy Initiative: An Independent Evaluation of the World Bank's Support Through 2003*, Operations Evaluation Department (OED), Washington, DC: 2004.

World Bank (WB). *Voices of the Poor: Can Anyone Hear Us?*: 2000.

World Bank (WB). *World Development Report 2000/2001: Attacking Poverty*, Oxford University Press, London: 2001.

World Development Movement (WDM). *One size for all: A study of IMF and World Bank Poverty Reduction Strategies*, London: 2005.

1 The political economy of the WB-IMF's influences over development agenda

Contextualizing PRSP from a global point of view

Introduction

Since the Second World War the World Bank-IMF led development strategies underwent dramatic shifts. In order to understand the present policy discourses we need to know the policy context that contributed to the shifts in the strategies of the Bretton Woods Institutions (BWIs). Indeed, much of today's PRSPs are owed to the previous strategies. Until the 1970s development policy was dominated by an import substitution industrialization (ISI) strategy advocating for the promotion of large-scale modern industries by means of strong government interventions in the market, such as trade protection, directed credits, and subsidies. In the 1980s a new paradigm emerged with the market as a universally efficient mechanism for allocating scarce resources and promoting economic growth. It represented a major assault on national developmentalism in the context of which the state had played an active role in the developmental process. This new paradigm advocated a new development model based on the primacy of individualism, market liberalism, outward-orientation, and state contraction. The organizing principle of the paradigm was the notion of a minimal state whose principal role was confined to that of serving law and order, macroeconomic stability, and the provision of physical infrastructure (Öniş and Şenses: 2003). The new paradigm also had other names. Some called it neo-liberalism, some market fundamentalism, and some free-market economics or Washington Consensus (Broad: 2004). The emergence of the neo-liberal regime may also be attributed to the defeat of the US in the Vietnam War that caused the relative decline of American power and triggered the development of hegemonic stability and regime theories in American universities (Pramono: n.d.).

The new regime under the gloss of the Structural Adjustment Program (SAP), thought to have been a panacea, failed miserably in promoting economic stability and sustainable growth. Instead it substantially contributed to the debt crisis in the 1980s through to the 1990s. The crisis went to the extent that a global movement against the bilateral and multilateral donors emerged across the world. This was particularly true in the Northern hemisphere where strong policy advocacies in favor of easing international economic governance to benefit the poor nations were taking place. Indeed, the decade of 1990s was full of such activism. At one stage the UN and the G7 took interest in the multilateral economic strategies and they discussed it in their successive summits. Eventually, through an evolutionary process today's much talked about Poverty Reduction Strategy Paper (PRSP) concept appeared as a conditional mechanism to get concessional loans from the World Bank and the IMF. Alongside the WB-IMF, all major bilateral donors endorsed the PRSP as means of partnership.

This chapter captures the contributing factors to the policy evolution of BWIs, which eventually laid the foundation of policy context of a PRSP. In doing so it sheds light on SAPs and the political and economic underpinnings with particular reference to developing economies. It also explores the interface between the debt crisis and policy shifts in the BWIs. It further details the PRSP agenda and finally takes a brief stocktaking of BWIs' claims in the PRSP agenda vis-à-vis the realities on the ground through a look at the body of literature.

The chapter is split into two major parts. The first part deals with the dynamics of policy leverage imposed through the SAP on poor countries. The second part captures changes in BWIs' policies, which premise the policy context of PRSP, as outcomes of various factors such as BWIs' policy failures and the contemporary popular struggles and resistances. It also pinpoints the context of PRSP. The contribution of this chapter is that it presents an overview of the evolution of development strategies spearheaded by international donors and rich countries from a global point of view. This historical development is important to follow the dynamics of global policy changes and influences of powerful countries and financial institutions. Moreover, it makes a ready reference to the readers from a political-economic point of view for understanding the interface between politics and economic development.

Part 1: Structural adjustments and the political economy of policy leverage of IFIs on poor countries

Structural Adjustment Program: looking back

The shift in strategy in BWIs or IFIs (both are used as interchangeably to refer to the WB and IMF) can be accounted for in the backdrop that most of the rich countries in the West following the oil crisis underwent severe recession and inflation from 1973 onward (Easterly: 2002). The economic disturbance in the North also affected the developing economies. Thus, the 1970s were a time of impending economic crisis, forestalled in many cases by recourse to borrowing on a massive scale. It hurt the investment and saving scenario and eventually contributed to worsening problems of unemployment. The state-led development model of previous decades came under a huge challenge (UNRISD: 1994). Most developing countries took huge loans from the IFIs to adjust to the economic crisis, but in the end were caught by a debt crisis. The crisis prompted the IFIs to carry out a comprehensive transformation of third world economies in order to *adjust* them to the requirements of the world market. Caught in the trap of development on credit, they had no other choice but to submit to the conditions of the Bank and the Fund for taking new loans (Gélinas: 1995).

The new paradigm of BWIs, emerging in response to the crisis phrased as a structural adjustment, refers to a comprehensive program for economic reforms, including the management of macro-economy and various economic policies. The WB and IMF deemed the program necessary when they realized that short-term responses, including new loans and debt rescheduling, to the debt problem would not solve it on a long-term basis. They believed that the indebted developing countries had to improve their own economic structures and policies. While the focus of the paradigm was to structural adjustment, Stiglitz (1998) argued that like the previous models SAP also viewed development as a technical problem requiring technical solutions. It failed to capture development from a comprehensive point of view. However, the new regime was said to have been the agenda of the industrialized G7 countries. Since these countries had large shares in the WB and IMF boards they could influence decisions of both bodies (Juichi: n.d.). But, Stiglitz on the contrary argued, with overwhelming representation on the board of the IMF, the G7 countries should have been obliged to incorporate a broader range of views of developing countries and borrower nations as their decisions affected the poor countries in a very significant manner (Stiglitz: 2003).

Dynamics of aid conditionality

The dramatic shift occurred through the SAP not only narrowed down the role of the state in economic development but also dismantled control of the state in economic issues that was earlier carried out in the form of protectionism (Hayami: 2003). It resulted in serious erosion of developing countries' power in setting their development agenda and giving considerable authority to BWIs in influencing development policies through conditionality mechanisms. As an outcome of the leverage in the 1980s most poor countries had initiated programs of economic liberalization and adjustment under the sponsorship of the BWIs (Lapeyre: 2004; Girvan: 2005). The emergence of SAP, also known as neoliberal counterrevolution, was concomitant to the assumption of powers of new conservative leaders in both the UK and the US, respectively Margaret Thatcher and Ronald Reagan (Mavroudeas and Papadatos: 2005; Broad: 2004). These leaders were the staunch advocates of neoliberal premises that free markets and private enterprises were the main wheels of economic development and government intervention in the economy was the primary cause of disturbance and poor economic growth (Stiglitz: 2002). It was also argued that structural adjustment was the result of the convergence of the debt crisis with the rise to power of groups espousing radical free-market ideas, especially in Great Britain and the United States (UNRISD: 1994).

The essence as conceived in SAP as the new development paradigm was that the objectives of poverty reduction and growth were best served by reliance on market forces and private enterprise and the role of the state was to be restricted to a minimum of essential functions. While the policy advice was universalistic in nature, the policy relied largely on the 'trickle down' theory that liberalization would lead to integration to economic growth, and economic growth eventually to poverty reduction. Given the strong perception about the correlation between growth and poverty reduction, structural policy reforms were presumably designed to achieve efficiency and growth objectives, and promote poverty reduction. Lapeyre (2004, 4) observed that:

> In this context, the central objective of macroeconomic policy became the control of inflation through monetary policy, devaluation and the attainment of budgetary balances. Led by Thatcher and Reagan, the policy side of the 'counter-revolution' resulted in curbs on trade unions, reduction in taxes and welfare expenditure, the privatization of state enterprises, reduction or abolition of subsidies and price controls, deregulation of key sectors of the economy, and liberalization of exchange restrictions. The solution to the crisis, in the North as in the South, was to allow the market to determine how economic resources can more productively be allocated, and to rely on market forces as the principal determinant of economic decision.

The aid conditionality (Box 1.1) accompanied by SAPs compelled developing countries to open-up their economies to global competition and to substantially reduce the role of government. Developmentalist theories and policies were discredited, marginalized and dismissed. The governments of the South became convinced of the "magic of marketplace" (Lapeyre: 2004). By 1990s neoliberal globalization was a universally accepted phenomenon although China, India, and a few countries of Southeast Asia could maintain a degree of policy autonomy due to the successes of their own approaches to economic development and the level and size of their industrial development, particularly that of India and China. The IFI policy influence became pervasive and it was made to be permanent with the shift in the political and ideological spheres that marked the fall of socialism and proclaimed the "end of history" as espoused by Fukuyama (Girvan: 2005, 2–3).

Box 1.1 Premises of BWIs aid conditionality

- Drastic *reduction* of trade barriers protecting the local economy from foreign competition;
- Deep *reduction or elimination* of subsidies and price controls, which distorted internal prices for a number of goods and services;

- *Restructuring* of the financial system and weakening or removal of controls on the movement of capital;
- *Privatization* of state-owned firms;
- *Elimination* of control on private foreign investment;
- *Reduction* of the role of the state, not only in the economy but also in the provision of social services.

Source: UNRISD: 1994

SAP as Washington Consensus and the 'Realpolitik'

The remarkable shift in development policies and conditionality of the Northern rich countries and the BWIs in the 1980s in the end led to codifications of the terms to serve as the universalistic one-size-fits-all formulae approach to development irrespective of the variance in economic and social realities of countries, particularly in the South. John Williamson, a then World Bank manager, phrased the strategies in 1989 to tackle the Latin American economic crisis as the Washington Consensus (WC) – a tripartite solidarity of economic development policy between the World Bank, the IMF, and the US Treasury, all incidentally situated in Washington (Williamson: 2000). However, in the face of the growing stiff criticism of the WC, Williamson argued that his term was misused and equated with neoliberalism, which he did not intend. While Williamson claimed that his policy prescriptions for the Latin American economic reforms were misconstrued (Williamson: 2000), George (2007) interpreted that the political foundation of the consensus was clearly beyond Williamson's sense.

> What was this scenario about in political terms? The WC, in the broad, beyond-Williamson sense, was clearly intended to put a stop to any nationalistic leanings towards State-led development policies, particularly import substitution or the protection of national industries or local agriculture [the term 'food sovereignty' had not yet been invented]. It was also about opening one's economy to the largest private actors in world markets, that is, to transnational corporations, banks and other major financial actors like pension funds. It came down to forcing the government to leave the currency, jobs, local businesses, social system and *tutti quanti* to the decisions of outsiders, interested only in quick profits and possessed of far greater financial clout than most Central banks. It was, above all, a strategy invented by the North designed to ensure that Southern countries continued to service their debts, but could never hope to pay them off. This in turn would ensure that they continued to obey orders, those of the broad WC.
>
> (George: 2007, 6–7)

With the debt crisis in Mexico the US treasury motioned to the IMF to continue with the WC based on reform measures aiming at financial liberalization and this continued into the 1990s. Almost all developing countries, including the former socialist countries with the fall of the Berlin wall in 1990, were exposed to the US-backed WC. The policy premises of WC eventually constituted the foundation of the bilateral agreements negotiated by the US and other developed countries of the North and in effect influenced loan-receiving countries of the South. The formation of NAFTA involving the US, Canada, and Mexico (1993) and the World Trade Organization (WTO) (1994) by governments of the world clearly suggested for the down play of government's role in economic affairs and widespread proliferation of an open economy going clearly in line with the policy packages of the WC. The WTO expanded corporate protectionism (including strengthening so-called trade-related intellectual property rights or TRIPs) and reduced government ability to direct domestic economic policy (by making illegal various trade-related investment measures or TRIMs). The US Treasury Department, the IMF, and other key disciples of the WC in essence expanded Williamson's original 10 tenets[1] to include capital liberalization (in addition to trade liberalization). They proposed a 'multilateral investment agreement' to require countries to treat foreign investment exactly the same as domestic. Thus, the Washington Consensus became the only way. The desirability of its policies was presented as an objective economic truth. Anyone not with that program was, in the dismissive words of *New York Times* columnist Thomas Friedman on "a Noah's ark of flat-earth advocates, protectionist trade unions, and yuppies, looking for their 1960's fix" (Broad: 2004).

The WC imposition of conditionality over developing economies to continuously pursue capital market liberalization and massive privatization before their financial sectors were resilient enough was viewed as the outcome of a representation crisis of developing countries on the boards of the WB-IMF. The policies of the WB-IMF, accused of having harmed developing economies, could not have been so if they (the borrowing countries) had had proper representation in the leadership of the WB-IMF (Birdsall: 2003; Stiglitz: 2002). Thus, the assumption as to the *realpolitik* is that the WC was framed primarily to serve the economic interest of the developed nations. A related argument, widely held even by many who endorse the general direction of the institutions' policy advice, is that the imbalance of power makes them prone to prolonged reliance on universal (and in some cases, possibly wrong-headed) 'recipes'for economic reform. Thus also less open than they otherwise would be to home-grown approaches taking into account local institutional and political constraints (Birdsall: 2003).

Pramono (n.d.) characterizing liberalism as the embodiment of 1) democracy, (2) sustainable free trade, (3) democratic global governance through international organizations, and (4) effective collective security (multilateralism) argued that the very liberalism had come to an end (with the end of the Cold War) as multilateral decisions in the global political economy were increasingly taken over by the autocracy of the IMF and the WB. Both the IMF and the WB behaved like the medieval church that had a doctrine, a rigidly structured hierarchy preaching and imposing this doctrine, and a quasi-religious mode of self-justification. Their decisions, which affected more than 80 per cent of the population on the planet and the majority of which went largely unchallenged, must be implemented as a matter of faith. And their fundamentalist decisions that resulted in the dislocation of entire communities, displacement of peoples, destruction of the environment, and concentration of wealth in the hands of a few rich entrepreneurs, must be accepted by the poor majority as a necessary suffering for salvation of future lives. Consequently, the good global governance, which the liberals initially wanted to attain by promoting international organizations, was undermined by neoclassical fundamentalism. Thus, Pramono (n.d., 120) concluded "what then should one call liberalism in the absence of these four tools of liberal peace? Perhaps, one might call it 'genocidal neoliberalism'".

Washington Consensus – the failure of the formulae approach

The Washington Consensus visibly advocated a market led economy with very little role for the government. Privatization and liberalization were heavily given prominence in the discourse as if they were ends rather than means to more sustainable, equitable and democratic growth. Referring to the development of East Asian nations and even that of the US, Stiglitz (1998) criticized the minimalist state notion of the consensus. Even though many countries followed the dictums of the consensus, they did not grow. In the East Asian case, government played a very critical role in economic development and ran heavy industries such as steel mills. Greater successes in the US were credited to government and without such government interference or involvement in previous decades the capitalist economy was exposed to widespread social problems and economic instability.

> Governments intervened in trade, though more to promote exports than to inhibit particular imports. And governments regulated financial markets, engaging in mild financial restraint, lowering interest rates and increasing profitability of banks and firms (as opposed to financial repression, which results in negative real interest rates.) Many of the policies on which the governments focused were simply areas that had been ignored in the past; these included, for example, the heavy emphasis on education and technology, on closing the knowledge gap between them and the more advanced countries.
>
> (Stiglitz: 1998, 10–11)

Stiglitz (2002), referring to the development strategies of advanced industrial countries such as US and Japan, questioned the appropriateness of the application of built-in policies in the WC for countries in the early stages of development or transition. Both Japan and the US adopted protection measures to grow their industries strong enough to compete with foreign companies. The resultant impact of inappropriate policies had been so that the intentions of the WC were not materialized – anywhere. In Latin America – the most obedient pupil – growth was less than the expectation. The successes in Sub-Saharan Africa were also limited and they eventually proved the critics' concerns about the effectiveness of the WC reform agenda (Rodrik: 2006).

Economic Growth in the 1990s Learning from a Decade of Reform was an important publication from the WB (2005) that attempted to understand the reforms dynamics of the 1990s. The WB former Vice President and the coordinator of the work, Gobind Nankani, in the foreword to the book endorsed the inadequacy of the WC as formulae of development and suggested the consideration of some vital factors such as rigorous institutional, social analysis and country context during policy making. He unequivocally undermined a universalistic formulaic approach to development. To put it in his words:

> The central message of this volume is then that <u>there is no unique universal set of rules</u> (underline mine). Sustained growth depends on key functions that need to be fulfilled overtime: accumulation of physical and human capital, efficiency in the allocation of resources, adoption of technology, and the sharing of the benefits of growth. Which of these functions is the most critical at any given point in time, and hence which policies will need to (be) introduced, which institutions will need to be created for these functions to be fulfilled, and in which sequence, varies depending on initial conditions and the legacy of history. <u>Thus we need to get away from formulae and the search for elusive 'best practices'</u> (underline mine), and rely on deeper economic analysis to identify the binding constraints on growth. The choice of specific policy and institutional reforms should flow from these growth diagnostics. This much more targeted approach requires recognizing country specificities, and calls for more economic, institutional, and social analysis and rigor rather than a formulaic approach to policy-making.
>
> (WB: 2005: xiii)

Some leading economists[2] from both developing and developed countries through the Barcelona Development Agenda (Forum BARCELONA: 2004) analyzed the prospects of growth and development of nations and provided seven sets of lessons that were expected to serve the priorities of reforms. While all the lessons were important, their appraisals with regard to the WC seemed more important. Hinting at the WC they said that no single set of policies could guarantee to ignite sustained growth. Further, successful states experienced various difficulties and also adopted various policies regarding regulation, export and industrial promotion, and technological innovation and knowledge acquisition. They recommended that countries should be free to experiment with policies suited to their specific circumstances. While they suggested for a balance between the state and the market, they also cautioned that "encouraging developing nations to copy mechanically the institutions of rich countries as international financial institutions tend to do is not guaranteed to yield results, and can do more harm than good" (Forum BARCELONA: 2004, 2).

The results of SAPs were especially dismal in low-income countries and countries in Africa, Asia and Latin America experienced economic and social stagnation or decline. Essentially, they lost two decades of progress. To some extent, Africa was a 'forgotten continent'. Forcing the developing countries to be exposed to uneven and stiff competition in markets by opening up their economies virtually brought disastrous consequences both socially and economically. Poor farmers in developing countries simply could not compete with the highly subsidized goods from Europe and America. Jobs were systematically destroyed before the countries' industrial and agricultural sectors were able to grow strong and create new jobs. Even worse, the IMF's insistence on developing countries maintaining tight monetary policies led to interest rates that would make job creation impossible even in the best of circumstances. And because trade liberalization occurred before safety nets were put into place, those who lost their jobs were forced into poverty. Liberalization had thus, too often, not been followed by the promised growth, but by increased misery. And even those who did not lose their jobs were hit by a heightened sense of insecurity (Stiglitz: 2002). McCutchan (2010) made a deeper and cross-country study on the impact of SAP considering some countries of Latin America and he identified that the market liberalization agenda advocated under SAP did not accompany any social security measures to address the adverse effects of liberalization and eventually it resulted in weakening the state and compounding the plights of the poor people in the face of resultant economic shocks. It meant there was clear incoherence in the policy approach of SAP. The advocates of SAP considered that a universal approach would be effective for all countries irrespective of their level of development. This assumption seemed fallible. Oberdabernig (2010) conducted a major study on the impact of SAP taking all participating countries in the study and concluded that SAP had a negative impact on poverty reduction and income distribution. One of his arguments for such dismal results is that SAP advocated liberalization without providing any accompanying measures to offset the effects of liberalization.

The other allegation against SAP was that policies were undertaken in non-transparent and secretive ways as they were ignoring national interest. Thus, the chief economist of Inter-American Bank Ricardo Hausman had compared SAP to military tanks that rolled through a nation inflicting collateral damage (Abugre: 2001). Poverty reduction not only noticeably failed but in parts of the world such as the former USSR and Eastern Europe poverty was actually accentuated. Inequalities sharply increased; endemic poverty coexisted with extravagant accumulation of wealth and obscene level of conspicuous consumption. Levels of corruption were accentuated, and corruption was underwritten by abuse of the democratic process and violation of human rights (Sobhan: 2002). Stiglitz (2002) thus appropriately accused IMF for damaging the various aspects of economy it got involved in. Indonesia and Thailand encountered more damage after the crisis in 1997 as they followed IMF instructions and the same situation was prevalent in Latin America.

Part 2: Policy failure, popular struggle and PRSP policy context

The dynamics of debt crisis and debt relief

It was evident that SAP proved counterproductive to low-income countries. The immediate impact of SAP was that it plunged countries deep into debt crisis perpetuating their low economic growth and insolvency. While the impact was emerging, global voices against the BWIs and debt crisis were also taking ground across the world enjoying huge popular support. Celebrities, priests, faith institutions, activists and academics all joined hands to stand against all unjust policies and strategies. The internal evaluation in IFIs and popular movement helped both the IFIs and G7 leaders understand of the necessity of policy shift and it finally created a space for the PRSP agenda. This part of the chapter unfolds the debt crisis dynamics and the emergence of CDF leading to PRSP.

Dynamics of the crisis

The debt crisis had a huge impact on international economic governance and it was formally exposed when Mexico, in 1982, declared its inability to service its debt liability. The debt crisis was linked to economic crises of the 1970s. In order to overcome the crises in the 1980s SAP by the WB and IMF were adopted in many of the poor economies to reschedule the debt burdens and to ensure servicing debt liability. Civil society organizations viewed that the crisis was located in broader international and national contexts where the rich North wanted to dominate the poor South. The debt crisis contributed to both the perpetuation of Northern policy influence and the continuation of poverty. The policies imbued in SAPs failed to promote the improvement of economic conditions in the poor economies and instead established a permanent linkage with debt. Without considering local potentialities BWIs and other bilateral donors in a perpetuating way provided debts to the poor countries, which ultimately created debt-hung[3] situations for most of the countries. In addition, the discriminatory global trade regime promoted a system, instead of global balance in trade accounts, where surplus economies maintained their surpluses by keeping the deficit economies in deficit (Tagle and Patomäki: 2007). Jubilee Debt Campaign et al (2001) clearly held SAP responsible for perpetual indebtedness; the structural adjustment programs trapped the countries of the South into a perpetual cycle of debt dependence and underdevelopment. This policy constituted economic terrorism and genocide on the peoples of the South. The World Bank also attributed the crisis to the failure of SAPs (Gautam: 2003).

The United States and Western Europe were also held responsible for their reluctance to reform the BWIs as the crisis was deeply rooted into their policies. Particularly, the failure to de-link the system from the US dollar as the key currency indeed led to the explosion of international interest rates at the end of the 1970s and then, as a consequence of the extension of roll-over credits by the banks to debtor countries at very high rates (to repay the banks), to the outbreak of the debt crisis in 1982.

The crisis provided three lessons. First, the creditor countries were consciously delaying debt reduction measures to give the banks sufficient time to build up reserves for the eventual debt reduction that would have to come. Second, while the debtor countries failed to form a debtors' cartel to act together to deal with the problem favorably, the creditor countries had their own effective cartel, the Paris Club,[4] and almost full control over the IMF and the World Bank as instruments to guide the economic policies of debtor developing countries. Third, the creditor countries and the BWIs were successful in convincing the poor countries to liberalize and adjust economic structures to regain credit worthiness. However, this policy eventually proved to be inhibiting economic development in debtor countries (Teunissen and Akkerman: 2004).

While rescheduling measures through SAPs resulted in increased stocks of debt and debt burden ratios for the poorest debtors, the multilaterals initially totally overlooked the issue and opted to continue with adjustment policies. The bilateral donors appreciating the gravity of the problem thought to reschedule the liability and there had been progresses in rescheduling terms in the Paris Club. The 1988 G7 meeting held in Toronto, Canada decided rescheduling terms whereby one third of the poorest countries' debts could be cancelled by either forgiving part of the debt or granting concessional interest rates but it was later altered in London Summit of G7 in 1991. The new terms mentioned that up to fifty percent of the poorest countries' debts could be cancelled. In 1994 in the Naples Summit the portion of debt to be cancelled further increased amounting to 67 per cent of the total debt liability. However, a condition they imposed was that only countries with a good economic record would be awarded this concession (Blanco: 2005).

In the face of persistent economic troubles in the 1970s and the 1980s low-income countries (LICs) resorted to loans from various sources, bilateral, multilateral, and commercial to fill deficiencies in their economic systems. The Northern rich countries and the IFIs, without much consideration of the capacity of LICs to pay back the debt, opted for providing debt primarily to ensure their creditworthiness and enable them to service their previous liability. The Northern support under the SAP arrangement was heavily associated with stringent conditionality that further worsened the economic condition in the South particularly Sub-Saharan Africa.

Increasing poverty and a general perception of development failure of the SAP strategy and, more importantly, the inability of LICs to repay debt brought tensions in global economic governance. It is interesting to note that at the beginning of crisis the BWIs did not pay attention to the rescheduling of debt or cancellation of debt but in the 1980s the bilateral lenders started thinking in terms of rescheduling debt liability. The World Bank viewed the crisis as a short-term cash flow problem and thought it would be amenable to policy reforms such as SAPs. But by the early 1990s the WB had come to realize that reforms measures that lacked ownership were not working as expected (Gautam: 2003; Callaghy: 2004).

Debt crisis and the debt cancellation movement

Whatever successes in streamlining third world debt so far achieved owed largely to movements orchestrated by individuals, priests, and NGO networks against debt burdens. The debt issue, although emerging with the formal declaration of its inability to repay debt liability in 1982 by Mexico, was not readily recognized for a considerable time by creditors either bilateral belonging to Paris Club, commercial with London Club, or multilateral such as the World Bank and the IMF. SAPs, instead of proving effective, devastated the economies of Latin America and Sub-Saharan Africa causing economic deterioration and inflicting huge losses on the economies of reforming countries. The continued and persistent efforts of devoted individuals, networks, and groups brought the issue to the forefront of discussion of world economic players. Apart from research, demonstration, and public engagement these persistent individuals and groups lobbied G7 leaders to be sympathetic to the unjust debt burden of the Southern countries.

Before the watershed event with Mexico declining to pay back her debt liability, some secular and church-based development groups were engaged in promoting the issue of debt relief in Southern countries where many of them were missionaries. The missionaries upon return to their countries of origin urged various NGOs to bring up the issue and many of them founded initiatives, such as Peru Solidarity under the leadership of Rev. Thomas Burns in the late 1970s, to lobby for US policy change. They pressed for softening IMF policies to lessen pressure on poor people of LICs as they had experienced firsthand the economic crisis' impact on their parishioners and friends in debtor country shantytowns (Donnelly: 1999). Initially, the efforts were sporadic and limited to the staging of protests at the joint IMF/WB annual meetings, visits to congressional offices to elicit support, and attempts at popular education through talks and newsletter briefings. The targets were principally commercial banks, the IMF, the main NGOs and church-affiliated groups, with relatively little coordination among them. Debt Crisis Network (DCN) as the major organization emerged with active support of Washington and New York based NGOs with the intention to facilitate information sharing and coordination of strategy in 1985. DCN was almost entirely funded by progressive Protestant denominations, Catholic religious orders, and Catholic Relief Services. DCN experienced some difficulties in its journey when conflict regarding its working approach emerged and many leading figures left in 1990. But the

DCN Britain chapter launched a landmark round-Britain tour in February 1995 involving African leaders, ex-President Kenneth Kaunda of Zambia and Archbishop Makhulu of Central Africa, to put the case for debt cancellation to the British people. The tour helped open the door to meetings with politicians and officials, including a critical meeting with the IMF, involving Cardinal Hume, that led to the IMF agreeing to discuss a comprehensive debt relief program with the World Bank (Jubilee Debt Campaign: n.d.).

Contemporary to DCN was the Forum on Debt and Development (FONDAD) established in 1987/88 by four Dutch foundations and NGOs, including ICCO (the Interchurch Coordinating Committee on Development Projects) and NOVIB (the Netherlands Organization for International Development). The major objective of FONDAD was facilitating contact between Dutch and Latin American NGOs. In early 1990s more organizations and networks emerged to carry forward fighting the debt issue. 50 YEARS IS ENOUGH was such a group that ran various grass roots activism to bring profound transformation of the WB and the IMF. The coalition resulted from discussions among six leading organizations – International Rivers Network, The Development Group for Alternative Policies (Development GAP), and Friends of the Earth, Environmental Defense Fund, Global Exchange, and Oxfam America. The network, a coalition of over 200 US grassroots, women's, solidarity, faith-based, policy, social and economic justice, youth, labor, and development organizations, was founded in 1994 on the occasion of the 50th anniversary of the founding of the institutions (www.50years.org).

Oxfam-UK's autumn 1986 "Hungry for Change" Campaign directly impacted the early debt relief initiatives. While Oxfam was engaged in poverty relief and development projects for a long period of time, in 1984 it decided to launch a new "Hungry for Change" Campaign in order to address the more structural roots of poverty and promote policy change in Britain. After analysis Oxfam determined five factors, which were linked to Britain's policy with world hunger. The factors were Debt, Aid (not enough and the wrong type), Trade (the weighted scales), Agriculture (EEC policies of surplus and manipulated world markets), and Arms (the extravagant trade in weapons) – DATAA. It decided to organize special week-long programs in each fall on any of the five factors and debt was featured in 1986. The 1986 initiative came on the heels of an outburst of public concern over the African famine (e.g., the LiveAid concert). Oxfam hit upon a campaign theme linking the infusion of aid monies to Sub-Saharan Africa with the concomitant drain of debt servicing. They blanketed the 800 Oxfam shops around Britain with posters decrying, "THE SCANDAL OF THE MONEY AFRICA GAVE TO US! For every £1 we all gave for famine relief in Africa in 1985 the West took back £2 in debt payments. DON'T STOP THE GIVING … STOP THE TAKING … Join Hungry for Change".[5]

Oxfam also staged events around the country dramatizing the crisis, and approached radio and TV celebrities. Disc jockeys on Radio One , the major pop music channel, explained the 'scandal' on the air. Radio and TV talk shows and TV comedians took up the theme. A BBC weekly satire program did a skit about it, and articles were written in popular newspapers and magazines. All that activism eventually led to bringing the debt crisis into popular culture. People in the thousands wrote to the government and visited their Members of parliament, leading to a rash of parliamentary questions and activity. Earlier while in government circles, the debt crisis previously concerned commercial banks and Latin America, now it had become an African issue too, and most importantly, an issue of public concern. Something had to be done. In the campaign Oxfam activists used information gathered from their overseas work. Over the next several years, Oxfam increasingly collaborated with other British NGOs organized in the UK DCN, and exchanged information with the US DCN. The 1986 campaign helped spur the then Thatcher government to call for more generous bilateral debt reduction for the Severely Indebted Low Income Countries (SILICs) by the Paris Club countries (Donnelly: 1999).

Debt issue: bilateral responses through the Paris Club

In the 1980s the Paris Club (Boxes 1.2 and 1.3) and London Club[6] emerged in the scene while the LICs had negotiated with them for debt rescheduling or cancellation. Moreover, by then in various parts of the world, mainly in Southern countries, voices against 'odious'[7] debts were emerging. The bilateral and official debt negotiations were with the Paris Club while negotiations concerning commercial debt or money owed to private creditors were with the London Club (Mutume: n.d.). With persistent debt crisis, major bilateral lenders switched from non-concessional rescheduling to concessional rescheduling and finally to debt stock reduction actions through the Paris Club. The bilateral intervention was clearly motivated by political considerations in the hot environment of the cold war, which is why despite the lack of ability of repayment, resource transfers to the LICs were never stopped. Apart from addressing the liquidity crisis since the 1980s, the creditor countries of the Club wanted to assist the debtor countries by reducing the burden of debt on the debtors' economies. Initially rescheduling terms were applied on a strictly case-by-case basis but after the crisis occurred in the 1980s, that exposed the difficult economic situation of many LICs, the Club began to grant more long-term rescheduling to reduce debt burden.

Box 1.2 The evolution of Paris Club terms – Pre-HIPC

Toronto Terms

Decided in 1988 in the G7 Summit held in Toronto, only LDCs with debt service payments equivalent to at least 30% of their export earnings were eligible for these terms. The terms offered three options for non-ODA debt. The first is to write off one third of the consolidated debt with the outstanding balance rescheduled at market rates over 14 years with an 8-year grace period. The other two options open to creditors called for rescheduling over 25 years with a 14-year grace period or a consolidation of debt due at a concessional interest rate. Toronto Terms were the first such initiative by the Paris Club.

London Terms

The G7 leaders in their Summit held in December in London decided to deal with debt issue going further than the previous Toronto Terms. The London Terms were also known as the Enhanced Toronto terms.

The four options offered under these terms included writing off 50% of consolidated non-ODA debt and rescheduling the remainder over 23 years. For the first time, these Terms also offered the possibility of converting debt into local currency for investment in the debtor country and introduced a goodwill clause, which opens up the possibility of eventually obtaining a reduction in the debtor's stock of debt.

Naples Terms

Agreed by G7 leaders in the Naples Summit in 1994. It increased reduction to 67% of the consolidated non-ODA debt due. The remainder was rescheduled over 23 years with a 6-year grace period. The goodwill and debt-conversion clauses introduced by the London Terms still applied.

Adapted from: Béranger-Lachand: 2001

However, this did not resolve the problem and so in 1987 the Paris Club agreed, for the first time, to reschedule debt on concessional terms, by offering longer grace and maturity periods to the poorest countries in Sub-Saharan Africa. Subsequently, more debt relief, including an element of debt cancellation, was provided to the poorest countries (Vilanova and Martin: 2001). Since 1988 it has announced various terms – the Toronto Terms in 1988, the London Terms in 1991, the Naples Terms in 1994–5 and the Lyon Terms in 1996 – to inject some flexibility and relief into poor country debt rescheduling (Aggarwal: 2003).

A country wanting to restructure its debt with Paris Club creditors had to carry out some terms and the country had to conclude an agreement with the IMF to implement a structural adjustment program. The IMF acted as the independent expert on behalf of Paris Club creditor countries to assess the viability of the economic adjustment program. The debtor countries wanted the creditor countries to carry forward in exchange of IMF loans, the compulsion of complying with IMF conditionality that underlie Paris Club's relations with the IMF and WB (Béranger-Lachand: 2001).

Debt issue: multilateral responses

Box 1.3 The Lyons Terms

Non-ODA Debt

80% reduction in the present value of repayments during the consolidation period. Creditor countries can chose between the following options:

1. Debt Reduction Option (DR/Option A)

80% of debt service which is accrued during the consolidation period is written off. The balance (20%) is refinanced with a maturity of 23 years, including 6 years of grace, at the market rate.

2. Debt Service Reduction Option (DSR/Option B)

Debt service is reduced by 80% by refinancing 100% of the service with a reduced interest rate over 40 years maturity with an 8 year grace period.

ODA Debt

Concessional debt is refinanced with a 40-year repayment period, including 16 years' grace.

Previously Refinanced Debt

Any loan that has been previously refinanced under other terms, must be treated with special terms to ensure that the total debt relief (including what was previously granted) reaches 80%.

Source: Vilanova and Martin: 2001

The debt issue was not recognized by the WB/IMF as a problem even in the mid-1990s. WB officials, in a seminar paper titled "Toward Resolving the Debt Problem of Severely Indebted Low-Income Countries (SILICs)" in an international seminar held under the aegis of Sweden and Switzerland in May 1994, asserted that debt was not the most important development problem. Though some of them acknowledged that it was an issue, they thought multilateral debt was not a large and growing problem. The same view was expressed in a joint paper in March 1995 where they argued that the multilateral debt crisis had not been until then a problem and was not even expected to be a future problem. The WB's position was underpinned by the fact that the Bank believed that multilateral debt was a small portion of total debt liability of SILICs. Moreover, they held that the mechanisms of Paris Club rescheduling and more lending by all major creditors were adequate to cope with the crisis. While the management was very optimistic about the debt situation, analysis did not count the debit liability as major development threat. However, the WB Board members did not appear to be in line with management's interpretation of the crisis. In the discussion of the paper in March 1995, the UK and Netherlands made it very clear that the problem was much more serious than the paper indicated. Switzerland, Sweden, and India expressed similar views (Callaghy: 2004).

Meanwhile global pressure against debt cancellation was seriously mounting across the world by the NGO networks and BWIs also acknowledged that SAPs helped LIC economies very marginally. It was even endorsed that SAPs contributed to the deterioration of economic conditions in LICs. Thus, policy reforms as suggested by the WB/IMF remained no more a solution to the crisis. The continued lobbying by NGO networks had already been able to influence G7 leaders to consider the debt issue. As an outcome of NGO movement the issue of multilateral debt emerged in the 50th anniversary meeting of the WB/IMF held in Madrid in 1994 where the US and Britain suggested a study be conducted to draw a clear exit strategy with regard to multilateral debt. Eventually, as the result of increasing public pressure on a variety of fronts, the G7 at its summit in Halifax in June 1995 called upon the IMF and the WB to develop a comprehensive approach to assist countries with multilateral debt problems through the flexible implementation of existing instruments and new mechanisms where necessary (Callaghy: 2004).

While the G7 summit was held in June 1995 the World Bank changed its leadership. The new president, James Wolfensohn, was much appreciative of the concerns of NGOs regarding the debt crisis of the LICs, particularly those of Africa. To address increasing concerns about LIC debt, especially the rapidly increasing multilateral debt, the WB finally established a working group to assess the magnitude of the multilateral debt problem and develop possible mechanisms to deal with it. By July 1995 the working group had produced a draft paper acknowledging the existence of a multilateral debt problem. They proposed a set of mechanisms to deal with the debt problems of 20 to 24 poor countries in a comprehensive manner. The central recommendation of the proposal was the creation of a Debt Reduction Fund that would help to pay multilateral debt after all other debt mechanisms – private and public – had provided maximum debt relief (Callaghy: 2004; Gautam: 2003).

Complex birth of a recipe – Highly Indebted Poor Country (HIPC)[8]

The issue of debt relief received great momentum by the activism of various NGO networks working for cancellation of the debt burden of poor countries by the early 1990s. The resultant change in the mindset of G7 leaders and the WB/IMF stewards was reflected both in the WB/IMF joint meeting held in

Madrid in 1994 and the G7 Halifax Summit in 1995. The formation of a working group in the WB to draw together a comprehensive proposal to deal with the debt issue was also reflective of new posture of the multilateral body. In mid-September 1995 the draft proposal of the working group was leaked to the press and the *Financial Times* ran stories on the proposal with an editorial. The proposal suggesting the establishment of a Debt Reduction Fund to coordinate action for reducing the entire debt burden of the indebted countries to a sustainable level drew mixed reactions among the Northern rich countries. While in the Executive Session of the Board of the WB on 21 September 1995 in a discussion on a revised version of the leaked paper, the UK, the Netherlands, and Sweden extended strong support to WB/IMF efforts to help the indebted countries. The UK appreciated the radical option of the proposal and suggested for broader efforts on the part of the creditors to settle the debt issue. While the Netherlands supported a new multilateral approach aimed at developing an exit strategy for the HIPCs, Japan and France expressed that they were not ready to accept such proposal. In the face of opposition of a number of G7 countries in WB/IMF annual meetings in early October 1995, the Development Committee of the WB asked the two institutions (WB-IMF) to have proposals on multilateral debt relief ready for discussion by the time of its next meeting in April 1996.

The WB and IMF by late January 1996 jointly developed two papers dealing with debt sustainability and its application to the indebted countries. An informal meeting of Executive Directors of the WB discussed the papers in late February 1996. By early March the WB and IMF had put together a basic proposal for HIPC debt relief; it was discussed at a meeting of the WB's Executive Directors on March 14, 1996. The UK, Switzerland, Belgium, and Canada expressed strong support for the proposal with a few suggestions to make it more realistic. They urged continued forward movement. While the US, Russia, China, and India provided support in principle in the spirit of supporting a consensus for more action, the Netherlands and Sweden in one group and, France, Germany, Italy, and Japan in another group expressed their hesitation over the proposal. For the Netherlands and Sweden the argument was that the initiative was not strong enough to contribute to debt settlement. The other group viewed the initiative much too strong. France expressed considerable skepticism indicating that the approach was unrealistic and unworkable. The WB's Development Committee welcomed the proposed framework in its April meeting. Meanwhile, a considerable amount of internal exercises by the staff took place and the Executive Directors of the WB discussed them on 10 September 1996. Finally, the HIPC Initiative was formally approved and announced at the September 1996 WB/IMF joint annual meeting.

Alongside the internal studies and recommendations in the WB/IMF, the 1996 Lyons Summit of G7 nations made significant advances in the nature as well as the scale of debt relief, extending agreements reached in earlier summits in Toronto, London, and Naples. For the first time in the history of a G7

Summit the President of the WB, James D. Wolfensohn, and the Managing Director of the IMF, Michael Camdessus, participated in the Summit. In the Summit Communiqué the leaders acknowledged the need for additional action to deal with multilateral donors and bi-lateral donors, who were not members of the Paris Club. According to a Summit decision, countries willing to receive debt reduction had to go with reform programs in two phases of six years and countries with good reform performances would receive a reduction in the stock of eligible debt of up to 80 per cent and further support through grants by multilateral institutions in order to reduce the country's debt to a sustainable level. They advised both the IMF and the WB to make an exit for unsustainable debt based on case-by-case consideration. The decisions taken in the Summit were later formally accorded in the HIPC initiative by the WB/IMF (Hein: 2001; Lyon Summit Communiqué).

The HIPC (Box 1.4) was virtually the outcome of the interactions of different actors: the NGO networks that generated huge pressure and drew popular support across the world against the debt; the ideas of epistemic economists in and out of the WB and the IMF; continued support of some small creditor states such as the Netherlands and Sweden; special leadership of the UK due to heavy influence by some NGOs based in UK; learning and leadership change at the WB; eventual acquiescence and serious negotiation on the part of the IMF; and a set of complicated political compromises between the major players of the international debt regime, particularly those of the major creditor states and the IMF and WB. This convergence of factors allowed, finally, the emergence of the initiative.

Box 1.4 Principles of HIPC Framework

- The objective is to target overall debt sustainability on a case-by-case basis, focusing on the totality of a country's debt;
- Actions should be envisaged only when the debtor has shown, through a proven track record, an ability to put to good use the exceptional support provided;
- The new measures should build, as much as possible, on existing mechanisms;
- Additional action should be coordinated among all creditors involved, with broad and equitable participation;
- Action by the multilateral creditors should preserve their financial integrity and preferred creditor status; and
- New external finance for the indebted countries should be on appropriately concessional terms.

Source: IMF: 1997, 18

Unlike the previous debt reduction under Paris Club arrangement, the initiative had two basic features. The Paris Club provided a uniform facility for all eligible countries. For example, the Naples Terms provided a uniform 67 per cent reduction for all countries that qualified. This (Naples) initiative linked debt reduction to debt sustainability, enabling each country to exit the process of constant rescheduling and resume normal relations with its creditors, where it serviced all its remaining debt. That is, where it achieved debt sustainability. That means debt would be reduced to a sustainable level.

The other important feature was that for the first time along with commercial and bi-lateral debt, multilateral debt relief was an issue. Multilateral debt relief was important because the switch from loans to grants by the bilaterals meant that a large and growing share of debt service was being paid to the multilaterals. However, partly to maintain this formal status of preferred creditors, the institutions were not willing to write off the debt owed to them on their own (Birdsal and Williamson: 2002).

Although the initiative was an achievement of activisms of various individuals and NGO movements, it was still not readily welcomed for various reasons (Callaghy: 2004, Lockwood: n.d.). Built on the existing very complicated mechanisms the initiative was only for those countries that demonstrated a strong commitment to the WB/IMF reforms for at least six years. Through the initiative the BWIs continued the earlier stringent macroeconomic policy reforms, liberalization and privatization, although they were severely criticized for their ineffectiveness and inappropriateness. Debts, particularly of multilateral sources, were tools for creating pressure on poor countries to initiate reforms. Arguably, the initiative was neither for poverty reduction nor debt sustainability but for liberalizing the economic structure in line with neo-liberal orthodoxy. It was equally applicable to both the WB/IMF. The background to the HIPC initiative was a crisis of multilateral debt servicing for as many years as the poorest countries had been in arrears with their commercial and bilateral debt, but had continued to service the debts of the preferred creditors. However, by the early 1990s, a number of countries began to face difficulties so deep that the conventional rolling over of debts could not deal with them and repayments of multilateral debt were threatened. Thus, Lockwood (n.d.) argued:

> For the main beneficiaries of the debt relief plan at that point were definitely not the 41 impoverished countries on the HIPC list; rather, in the words of one of the Paris participants, the Initiative was there 'to protect the financial integrity of the international financial institutions' … The HIPC Initiative was therefore very clearly about debt relief for clearing arrears, and avoiding arrears in the future – that is, debt sustainability pure and simple. This purpose was built into its design. When challenged about the origins of the 200–250% present value of debt-to-exports threshold for sustainability, chief Initiative manager Axel van Trotsenburg pointed to 'previous experience' in Latin America. A recent paper by other World Bank staff confirms that this 'rule of thumb' is based on evidence from Latin American and other developing countries that

countries with debt-to-export ratios of under 200% tend to avoid rescheduling and arrears problems.

Quest for broader, deeper, faster and better debt relief, people's struggle, Jubilee 2000 and HIPC-II initiative

More critiques to HIPC initiative

As mentioned earlier the NGO networks did not spontaneously welcome HIPC and they were apprehensive of the impact of the initiative on the poverty reduction agenda of the LICs (Christiansen and Hovland: 2003; Caritas International and CIDSE: n.d.). The major arguments were that the initiative was not broad enough. In other words, the debt sustainability criterion would allow only a few countries to access the benefits. The condition of export–debt ratio was too high and eventually excluded many poor countries. Even a poor country like Nicaragua could not qualify for debt relief. Thus, too few countries were eligible.

There was disappointment that the debt relief was not deeper. Bilateral and multilateral creditors were not writing off debt; rather, they were raising money to pay for debt reduction. As a result, they wanted to minimize its cost. Some powerful G7 countries, as well as some middle-income countries that were unlikely to be eligible for HIPC debt relief, did not commit sufficient resources to bilateral debt relief. The IMF decided to provide multilateral relief only through an existing fund, the Enhanced Structural Adjustment Facility (ESAF). The WB, on the other hand, had set aside $2 billion for debt relief, an important commitment, but would release it only after bilateral creditors showed their financial commitment by contributing to a separate debt relief fund. Thus, it was too little.

The delivery of debt relief was not faster. Countries expecting relief had to follow complex procedures, processes, and stringent conditions for being awarded debt relief. Out of 41 HIPC countries the WB declared only seven could enter the initiative and more importantly only three reached the completion point.[9] Eventually, it was too slow to fulfill the commitments. The major problem with HIPC was that it had little impact on poverty reduction. While the debt overhang was partly reduced, with consequent benefits in future investment growth, governments saw little immediate impact on reducing domestic resources allocated to debt servicing. The definition of what the money relieved by the initiative should be spent on was not clear but it was generally linked to social sectors. Thus, the impact was not stronger.

Making debt relief an agenda and Jubilee 2000 in post HIPC-I initiative

The HIPC-I was obviously a major step forward in international development cooperation particularly with the opening up provision for the first time of multilateral debts. However, it failed to provide a deeper, faster, better and broader initiative. Only one country reached the completion point in three years since the initiation in 1996. Global voices through various NGO networks were intensifying against the multilateral debt burdens and for greater relief for poor countries. Moreover, it appeared that the initiative was geared toward bringing the countries back to debt sustainability instead of poverty reduction. At a time in the early 1990s whilst across Latin America, the US, the UK, and Africa the debt cancellation movement was growing and enjoying huge popular support. Support came from celebrities and faith leaders like Bono, Jeffrey Sachs, even Pat Robertson, and Pope John Paul II. Martin Dent, a professor at Keele University in the UK, came up with the idea for a "Jubilee year". Dent's knowledge of the Bible and his ethical commitment to the third world led him to formulate the plan for an end of the millennium campaign. The reference to Jubilee came from the Biblical notion in the Book of Leviticus of a time to relieve the debts of the poor. Dent's advocacy began with his students but soon attracted Christian Aid, the World Development Movement, and other UK charities, which formally launched the campaign in April 1996. The movement blossomed, galvanizing millions worldwide to participate in letter-writing campaigns and protests (Busby: n.d.).

In October 1997, the earlier Debt Crisis Network transformed itself into the Jubilee 2000 Coalition, with a broader base of membership that for the first time included black refugee groups, the trade unions, and organizations like the Mothers Union and the British Medical Association (Greenhill et al: 2003). Once small, Jubilee 2000 achieved international visibility through citizen advocacy. Its activities included popular education, media work, mass mobilization, legislation and lobbying, petitions, sign-on letters and the Jubilee 2000 trademark, and mass demonstrations at the annual G7 economic summits.

The popular global demand for debt cancellation was expressed through the human chain built around Birmingham at the 1998 G7 Summit. Mobilized by Jubilee 2000 the demonstration involved 50,000 people. The mass mobilization was very focused on the debt issue. In Birmingham, the Churches were particularly visible. The slogan was to "break the chains of debt", and people were wearing chains as symbols for debt dependency of the poor countries. According to some estimates, 70,000 people formed a human chain – as opposed to a chain of debt (Busby: n.d.). The Birmingham demonstration was the major success of Jubilee 2000 and also the major popular resistance to WB-IMF unjust policies that brought economic carnage to poor countries. The movement gathered a substantial number of signatures, an estimated 24 million people worldwide in favor of "breaking the chains of debt". In numbers, this could only be compared to the worldwide demonstrations against the US attack on Iraq on 15 February 2003. Again at the 1999 G7 Summit in Cologne, Germany, 70,000 people joined in a human chain symbolizing the bondage of foreign debt. Over 400 NGOs supporting debt relief handed over petitions with more than 17 million signatures to German Chancellor Gerhard Schroeder (Greenhill et al: 2003).

The movement impacted the debt relief issue in various ways (Collins: 1999; Busby: n.d.). After the Birmingham human chain, Jubilee 2000's political impact grew dramatically and it forced the G7 leaders to include debt relief in the Summits' agendas in Birmingham in 1998 and in Cologne in 1999 (Box 1.5). The uproar created by the network influenced the then UN Secretary General, Kofi Annan, to take a stand for quick debt relief. The Secretary General wrote in a letter to leaders of the G7 prior to the Cologne Summit that bold measures should be taken quickly to relieve the debt burden of the poorest countries. He stressed that further action was needed and cautioned that such relief should not come at the expense of official development assistance (ODA). He also called for a commitment to reverse the decline in ODA and to explore innovative ways to mobilize additional resources for development. He cautioned that there was a grave risk that the bulk of the world's population would be left on the margin of today's liberalized global economy, living in abject poverty. He underscored his statement by adding that it was the responsibility of all of us to redouble our efforts to ensure that this did not happen.

Box 1.5 The Cologne Terms 1999

Non-ODA debt

90% reduction (or more if required) of the actual value of payments falling due during the consolidation period (flow) or of the stocks. The creditor countries can choose from the following options:

Debt Reduction Option (DR/ Option A)

Debt is reduced by 90% or more. The remaining amount is rescheduled over a period of 23 years, with 6 years grace, at market interest rates with the same repayment profile as the Naples/Lyons Terms. Countries that cannot cancel debt can adjust this option to reschedule the part of the debt which would be cancelled with low interest rates (0.0001%) and a single bullet of maturity between 60 and 350 years with the maturity depending on the level of the appropriate market interest rates).

Debt Service Reduction Option (DSR/Option B) Debt service or stock is rescheduled over a period of 125 years, with 65 years' grace, and appropriate market interest rates as utilized under the Lyons Terms.

ODA debt

The Cologne Summit recommended that all creditor countries cancel 100% of ODA debt before and after the cut-off date).

Previously refinanced debt

Under the Cologne Terms, any loan that has been previously refinanced under other terms must be treated with special terms to ensure that the total debt relief (including what was previously granted) reaches 90%.

Source: Vilanova and Martin: 2001

It drew huge global popular support for debt relief that ultimately inflicted pressure on the rich countries. The WB/IMF began to address more seriously the growing public critiques of the HIPC initiative on grounds of poor policy, undemocratic process, and meager results. In March 1999, representatives of 10 Jubilee 2000 national campaigns met in London with officials of the IMF, WB, Paris Club, and G7 governments concerning Jubilee 2000's critique of current debt relief programs. By April, each G7 government had made its own proposal for debt relief of poor countries. Immediately prior to its joint spring meetings with the WB, the IMF also issued a 65-page review of criticisms of the current HIPC initiative, extensively quoting analyses by various Jubilee 2000 national campaigns, Oxfam, and other debt relief proponents. The important factor behind the remarkable mobilization of popular support was that the network successfully involved the faith-institutions in the process. In the Cologne Summit[10] in June 1999 the G7 nations took a fresh look at the debt relief issue to provide deeper, broader and faster debt relief through major changes to the HIPC framework. Following the Cologne Summit in September 1999 the WB/IMF emerged with a new framework for debt relief, Enhanced HIPC or HIPC-II. The WB claimed that it would cost about $30 billion, possibly more. Further, it would cut in half the approximately $90 billion in public debt of the 33 HIPC counties considered to be likely to eventually qualify for relief. However, they cautioned that funding was not ensured even for the first couple of years (Callaghy: 2004).

Towards policy change –proposal for a Comprehensive Development Framework (CDF)

The decade of the 1990s simultaneously experienced two different sources of impact on international development cooperation involving multilateral lenders such as the WB and the IMF. One impact was drawn from the massive popular resistance to and demonstration against policies of the BWIs, which had a genesis with the failed policies under SAP that ultimately caused the emergence of the financial crisis across the world. The debt cancellation movement thus was directly linked to the WB/IMF induced economic crisis. The other source of impact was the gradual shift of policy in IFIs. The IFIs were in response to the people's sentiment. Various research evidence points to the policy failure and then the attempt to bring a gradual change in development strategy. As part of change and an outcome of NGO activism the HIPC initiative emerged to deal with the debt crisis of the poor nations.

In the face of ever-growing criticisms in the 1990s, the WB refocused its development efforts. In a bid to promote a holistic approach encompassing structural, social, and human dimensions to development departing from the previous growth centric adjustment model James D. Wolfensohn (former WB president) proposed a Comprehensive Development Framework (CDF) based on his first approximately four years inside experience and extensive visits to a number of projects and countries, developed and poor alike. The CDF was presented to the Board, Management and Staff of the World Bank on 21 January 1999 (Wolfensohn: 1999; Blake: 2000; Hanna and Agarwala: 2000). The CDF (Box 1.6) was proposed "as a means by which countries can manage knowledge and resources to design and implement effective strategies for economic development and poverty reduction. It brings together many current trends in development thinking and is centered on a long-term vision – prepared by the country through a participatory national consultation process– that balances good macroeconomic and financial management with sound social, structural and human policies" (Wolfensohn and Fischer: 2000, 1).

Box 1.6 The prerequisites in CDF for sustainable growth and poverty reduction

Inclusive approach to development: It combines macroeconomic and financial dimensions with social, economic and human dimensions. It is a major departure from the previous adjustment centric approach.

Strategic: It appreciates local conditions and accordingly sequences policies, program, projects and pace of reforms.

Local ownership: Countries must be in the driver's seat and set the course. They must determine goals and the phasing, timing and sequencing of programs.

Structural institutions: The approach is contingent upon various structural institutions such as (a) good and clean government, (b) an effective legal and justice system, (c) a well organized and supervised financial system and (d) a social safety net and social programs.

Human institutions: It emphasizes overarching importance on (a) education and knowledge institutions and (b) health and population issues.

Physical institutions: These are (a) water and sewerage, (b) energy, (c) road, transportations and telecommunication and (d) sustainable development, environmental and cultural issues.

Developing special strategy: Building special strategy on (a) rural, (b) urban and (c) private sector.

Source: Wolfensohn: 1999

It was indeed an attempt to move beyond the current fragmented, short-term, and project-based development framework to one that emphasized the interactions among policies, investments, and institutions and their dynamics over the long term (Hanna and Agarwala: 2000). Wolfensohn's thinking provided indication of some plausible shifts in development strategy and also a stocktaking of previous approaches. The important aspect of his thinking was that it was the insight of an insider who at that point had already spent approximately four years at the helm of the affairs in the WB and visited a number of countries. As he said, "... during recent months I have been considering what I have learned in my first three and a half years as President of the World Bank Group ..." (Wolfensohn: 1999, 1).

The stocktaking was important as it suggested that despite the contribution of billions, people were deprived of a minimum standard of life. Three billion people lived on less than $2 a day and 1.5 billion people were deprived of access to clean water and sewerage. In the area of education 130 million children were deprived of access to education. In the shadow of the SAP failure CDF was premised on the balance sheet approach – an approach that viewed both sides of the coin as equally important. The failure to consider both sides, indeed, could be attributed to the previous failure. The balance sheet approach was the novelty of the framework. Regarding the balance sheet approach Wolfensohn (1999, 4–5) stated:

> When I think of a development framework for a country and for regions, I think of a balance sheet with two sides. On the left is the macroeconomic presentation including the Article IV reports of the IMF, the National Income Accounts, the Balance of Payments and Trade Statistics, and all the other financial and economic analysis which are at the core of our current appraisal system. All of us are used to quoting GDP statistics, interest rates, reserves statistics, percentage growth statistics, and so on as a basis for monetary and fiscal policy. Based on analysis of the information, we can decide whether a country is Part I or Part II, IDA eligible, or HIPC eligible. It is the language that Finance Ministers find comfortable, and we all use it to make decisions.
>
> There is however, a clear need for a second side which reflects more adequately an analytical framework that presents the structural, social, and human aspects. It must go beyond the familiar statistics of infant and maternal mortality, unemployment and children in school, to address fundamental long-term issues of the structure, scope and substance of societal development.

Thus, development needed to be holistic in considering the two parts: macroeconomic aspects on the one side and the social, structural, and human on the other. Integration of both aspects was essential and any wrong move in the macroeconomic side would result in dire consequences in the structural, social, and human dimensions of development.

The framework clearly advocated for and gave huge value to strategic thinking about the sequencing of policies, programs, and projects and the pacing of reforms. In the SAP regime various pieces of literature argued that the poor economies failed to profile strategies based on national priority and development in administering reforms and in effect, most of the reforming countries plunged deep into a vicious debt crisis. Wolfensohn, as an insider, although late, finally succeeded in capturing the previous strategic failure. He (Wolfensohn) appropriately recommended

> … privatization prior to establishing an effective regulatory or competition framework can be a recipe for a disaster; the benefits of lower prices for consumers may well not be achieved. We know, at least from hindsight, that part of the failures in Russia were due to paying insufficient attention to the preconditions for a market economy. Too often in the past, we have gone after the 'easy' targets, saying that we would attack the more difficult (often institutional) issues later on. In doing so, we have failed to recognize the essential complementarities.
>
> (1999, 9)

Another plausible development in the framework was that government was responsible to comprehensively review all elements to lead the national development agenda and that the country must be in the driver's seat to set the course. Different stakeholders such as civil society, NGOs, and the private sector in the country must be provided the opportunity to express their voice to make development as a national agenda. Previous experience here also might have led the past WB leader to accept the truth that reforms could not work as means of conditionality. The reforming countries must develop their own agenda independently with the obvious involvement of various stakeholders.

The overall analysis put forward that CDF incorporated some plausible policy shifts in the discourse of international development cooperation. The major shift was the introduction of a down-top approach in agenda setting rather than the previous stiff top-down approach. The traditional hierarchical relationship in development cooperation, where the loan receiving countries stood at receiving end with little choice and the lenders, both multilateral and bilateral, stood at the giving end with huge influence and authority, was criticized and challenged to make development inclusive. The qualitative progress in development thinking was that development was not one sided that only dealt with macroeconomic issues; it should now consider social, cultural, and human dimensions. Sustainable development thinking brought both dimensions together because parting the two might seriously backfire. The growth centric approaches of previous strategies failure could be attributed to the failure of developing a multidimensional development strategy. The previous approach led to promoting an uneven development, inequality, and social fragmentation.

Despite indications of shifts in development cooperation, Lie (2016) argued that they were rhetorical and did not happen in reality because of the asymmetrical power-relations implied in the mode of administration of partnership. While previously the lenders provided the lists of actions, the loan receiving countries now did the actions on their own based on their knowledge of the choice of actions preferred by the lenders.

Poverty reduction strategy paper (PRSP): emergence of the new agenda

Emergence of the agenda

The entire decade of the 1990s experienced huge global resistance to the neoliberal economic model. In response, the BWIs plus the G7 countries started changing their policies, particularly in bilateral and multilateral development cooperation for benefits of the poor countries. In 1999, in the face of the continuously changing dynamics, two major developments worked as tipping points to put a new agenda – the poverty reduction strategy paper (PRSP) – in place to tackle global poverty. While the first event was that the (former) president of the WB proposed a comprehensive development framework (CDF), the second one was the introduction of enhanced highly indebted poor countries (EHIPC)[11] initiative. The CDF being simultaneous with EHIPC initiative was geared toward enhancing loan receiving countries' independent thinking in strategizing a development roadmap. Upon retrospection, Wolfensohn recommended, unequivocally, that the governments of the aid receiving countries must be in the drivers' seats in managing their development effort. In other words, policy ownership and consultation with various stakeholders were the landmark developments of the CDF. He also attributed the failure of the SAP to the lack of ownership in reform initiatives that emerged as part of loan conditionality (Wolfensohn: 1999).

The failure of the previous "technocratic, incomplete and ineffective" model (WB: 2002, 2) necessitated the creation of the provision of HIPC in 1996 as part of debt relief of the LICs. The initiative experienced marginal impact on poverty reduction and debt sustainability. Within three years the new initiative, termed as EHIPC, was recommended by both the G7 nations and BWIs to provide deeper, broader, and faster debt relief. Debt relief this time through the EHIPC became firmly and transparently linked to poverty reduction (Godfrey: n.d.; IMF: 2000). Within the EHIPC agreement all low-income countries receiving debt relief under the HIPC initiative or concessional lending from the WB, through the International Development Association (IDA), or the IMF through the Poverty Reduction and Growth Facility (PRGF) were required to develop a PRSP (WB: 2002; IMF: 2000).

Initially, CDF appeared to have lacked operational content (Christiansen and Hovland: 2003) but at the end it appeared that PRSP was premised on the CDF principles. Thus, the PRSP was an operational vehicle of CDF principles intending to translate a country's poverty reduction strategy into a focused action plan (Wolfensohn and Fischer: 2000). While CDF provided theoretical underpinnings of a PRSP to hit back at poverty, EHIPC indicated the provision of funds, as countries receiving debt relief needed to spend the relief money in social development that aimed at contributing to poverty reduction (Malaluan and Guttal: 2003).

Finally, in September 1999 PRSPs emerged as the basis for concessional loans both from the WB and the IMF. Although it began as a HIPC requirement, a PRSP is today synonymous with the overall development strategy that the WB and the IMF are propagating globally (Hermele: 2005). Moreover, all major bilateral donors expressed their eagerness to align their activities in line with the PRSP approach. According to the WB, a PRSP defines a country's macroeconomic, structural, and social policies and programs that a country will pursue over several years to promote growth and reduce poverty, as well as associated external financing needs. A PRSP is supposed to be prepared by the government through a participatory process involving civil society and development partners, including the WB and the IMF.

Notes

1 (1) Fiscal policy discipline, with avoidance of large fiscal deficits relative to GDP; (2) redirection of public spending from subsidies ("especially indiscriminate subsidies") toward broad-based provision of key pro-growth, pro-poor services like primary education, primary health care, and infrastructure investment; (3) tax reform, broadening the tax base and adopting moderate marginal tax rates; (4) interest rates that are market determined and positive (but moderate) in real terms; (5) competitive exchange rates; (6) trade liberalization: liberalization of imports, with particular emphasis on elimination of quantitative restrictions (licensing, etc.); any trade protection to be provided by low and relatively uniform tariffs; (7) liberalization of inward FDI; (8) privatization of state enterprises; (9) deregulation: abolition of regulations that impede market entry or restrict competition, except for those justified on safety, environmental and consumer protection grounds, and prudential oversight of financial institutions; (10) legal security of private rights.

2 Olivier Blanchard, Guillermo Calvo, Daniel Cohen, Stanley Fischer, Jeffrey Frankel, Jordi Galí, Ricardo Hausmann, Paul Krugman, Deepak Nayyar, José Antonio Ocampo, Dani Rodrik, Jeffrey D. Sachs, Joseph E. Stiglitz, Andrés Velasco, Jaime Ventura, and John Williamson.

3 The excess of a country's debt liability over its long-term capacity to pay.

4 The forum of creditor governments belonging to the Development Assistance Committee of the OECD to negotiate the rescheduling of the debts owed to them – mainly aid loans and guaranteed export credits. Rescheduling is actually put into effect by a series of bilateral agreements negotiated separately by each individual creditor some time after the Paris Club agreement (Teunissen and Akkerman: 2004).

5 The poster featured a central figure of a bearded young Briton dressed up like a Horn of Africa nomad with his arms crossed in front, receiving one coin dropped on his left palm by a blue-jean-clad British teen. From his right hand the "African" is dropping two coins onto the surreptitiously outstretched palm of a Western

banker/civil servant type who is partially concealing his face behind a bowler hat (Donnelly: 1999).

6 ***Paris Club***: The forum of creditor governments belonging to the Development Assistance Committee of the OECD to negotiate the rescheduling of the debts owed to them – mainly aid loans and guaranteed export credits. Rescheduling is actually put into effect by a series of bilateral agreements negotiated separately by each individual creditor some time after the Paris Club agreement.
London Club: An informal grouping of commercial banks who meet to determine a common approach to rescheduling commercial bank debt to a country. The London Club does not have a secretariat comparable to the Paris Club.

7 Odious debts are those contracted against the interests of the population of a state, without its consent and with the full awareness of the creditor. Thus, these debts cannot be enforced against a debtor State (Khalfan: 2006).

8 Much of this section draws on Callaghy: 2004, 26–39.

9 Completion Point: The date at which a country completes the key structural reforms agreed at the HIPC decision point, including implementation of its poverty reduction strategy. The country then receives the bulk of HIPC debt relief without further policy conditions. As of January 2004, 10 countries reached completion point: Benin, Bolivia, Burkina Faso, Guyana, Mali, Mauritania, Mozambique, Nicaragua, Tanzania, and Uganda (Teunissen and Akkerman: 2004).

10 In the G7 Finance Ministers Conference held on 18–20 June 1999 in Cologne specific debt relief terms were determined and subsequently endorsed in the Cologne Economic Summit. [See Report of the G7 finance Ministers on the Cologne Debt Initiative to the Cologne Economic Summit, 18–20 June 1999]

11 In response to the continued pressures to make debt relief broader, faster, and deeper, the enhanced HIPC (EHIPC) initiative was crafted and approved by the WB-IMF in 1999.

References

Abugre, Charles. "Still Sapping the Poor: A Critique of IMF Poverty Reduction Strategies", World Development Movement, London: 2001.

Aggarwal, V.K. "The Evolution of Debt Crises: Origins, Management and Policy Terms" in Aggarwal, V. and Granville, B. (eds) *Sovereign Debt: Origins, Crises & Restructuring*, pp. 11–35. London: The Royal Institute of International Affairs: 2003.

Béranger-Lachand, Sophie. "Paris Club: A Strategic Instrument within the International Financial Community", *Banque de France Bulletin Digest* No. 86, February 2001.

Birdsall, Nancy and Williamson, John. "Delivering on Debt Relief: From IMF Gold to a New Aid Architecture", Center for Global Development, Washington DC: 2002.

Birdsall, Nancy. "Why It Matters Who Runs the IMF and the World Bank", Working Paper No: 22, Center for Global Development: 2003.

Blake, Richard Cameron. "New Development – The World Bank's Draft Comprehensive Development Framework and the Micro-Paradigm of Law and Development" in *Yale Human Rights and Development Law Journal* Vol. 3, No. 159, pp. 159–189: 2000.

Blanco, Masaya Llavaneras. "Asking the Iceberg to Save the Titanic: The HIPC Initiative as a Locus of the International Financial Regime's Underlying Rationale" in *Undercurrent*, Vol. II, No 1: 2005.

Broad, Robin. "The Washington Consensus Meets the Global Backlash: Shifting Debates and Policies" in *Globalizations*, , Vol. 1, No. 2, pp. 129–154: December, 2004

Busby, Joshua William. "Bono Made Jesse Helms Cry: Jubilee 2000, Debt Relief, and Moral Action in International Politics", Center for Globalization and Governance, Woodrow Wilson School, Princeton University: n.d.

Callaghy, Thomas M. *Innovation in the Sovereign Debt Regime: From the Paris Club to Enhanced HIPC and Beyond*, The World Bank Operations Evaluation Department: the World Bank: 2004.

Caritas International and CIDSE. "The Highly Indebted Poor Countries (HIPC) Debt Forgiveness Initiative": n.d. Available at: https://www.worldhunger.org/articles/global/debt/caritas3.htm Last accessed on 8 December 2017.

Christiansen, Karin and Hovland, Ingie. *The PRSP Initiative: Multilateral Policy Change and the Role of Research*, Working Paper 216, Overseas Development Institute, London: 2003.

Collins, Carole. "'Break the chains of debt!'" in *Africa Recovery*, Vol. 13, No. 2–3: 1999.

Donnelly, Elizabeth A. "Proclaiming the Jubilee: The Debt and Structural Adjustment Network", *UN Vision Project on Global Public Policy Networks*: 1999 [Available at: https://www.worldhunger.org/articles/hn/debtcrisisnet.pdf; last accessed on 8 December 2017].

Easterly, William. "What did structural adjustment adjust? The association of policies and growth with repeated IMF and World Bank adjustment loans", Working Paper No: 11, Center for Global Development: 2002.

Forum BARCELONA 2004, [Available at: http://www.barcelona2004.org/www.barcelona2004.org/esp/banco_del_conocimiento/docs/CO_47_EN.pdf; last accessed on 8 December 2017].

Gautam, Madhur. *Debt Relief for the Poorest: An OED Review of the HIPC Initiative*, World Bank: 2003 Available at: https://openknowledge.worldbank.org/handle/10986/15164 [Last accessed on 8 December 2017].

Gélinas, Jacques B. "The Reform of All Reforms: Structural Adjustment and Reforming Health Care in the Third World", presented in the second Canadian Health Conference, Ottawa, November 12–15: 1995.

George, Susan. "Down the Great Financial Drain: How Debt and Washington Consensus Destroy Development and Create Poverty", in *Development*, Vol. 50, No. 2, pp. 4–11: 2007.

Girvan, Norman. "The Search for Policy Autonomy in the South Universalism, Social Learning and the Role of Regionalism", Overarching Concerns Programme Paper Number 9, United Nations Research Institute for Social Development (UNRISD): 2005.

Godfrey, Steve. *Civil Society Participation in Poverty Reduction Strategy Papers (PRSPs)* –Report to the Department for International Development, Vol. I: Overview and Recommendations, SGTS & Associates, 20 Gladstone Court, 97 Regency Street, London SW1P 4AL: n.d.

Greenhill, Romilly et al. *Did the G8 Drop the Debt? Five years after the Birmingham Human Chain, what has been achieved and what more needs to be done?* Jubilee, CAFOD, Jubilee Debt Campaign: London: 2003.

Hanna, Nagy and Agarwala, Ramgopal. *Toward a Comprehensive Development Strategy*, OED Working Paper Series, No. 16, The World Bank: 2000.

Hanna, Nagy. *Implementation Challenges and Promising Approaches for the Comprehensive Development Framework*, OED Working Paper Series, No. 13, The World Bank: 2000.

Hayami, Yujiro. "From the Washington Consensus to the Post-Washington Consensus: Retrospect and Prospect" in *Asian Development Review*, Vol. 20, No. 2, pp. 40–65: Asian Development Bank: 2003.

Hein, Wolfgang. "Global Governance and the Evolution of a New Role of International Financial and Economic Institutions for Sub-Saharan Africa", Deutsches Übersee-Institut: 2001.

Hermele, Kenneth. *The Poverty Reduction Strategies – A survey of the literature*, Forum Syd, Stockholm, Sweden: 2005 [Available at http://citeseerx.ist.psu.edu/viewdoc/download?doi=10.1.1.605.109&rep=rep1&type=pdf; last accessed on 8 December 2017].

IMF. "Overview: Transforming the Enhanced Structural Adjustment Facility (ESAF) and the Debt Initiative for the Heavily Indebted Poor Countries (HIPCs)": 2000 [Available at: https://www.imf.org/external/np/esafhipc/1999/index.htm; last accessed on 8 December 2017].

International Monetary Fund (IMF). "Debt Relief for Low-Income Countries and the HIPC Initiative" Working Paper 97/24: 1997.

Jubilee Debt Campaign et al. The Asia-Pacific Movement on Debt and Development (Jubilee South). "The Competitiveness Report: What WEF & other economic elites have done to the world lately" Statement of the Asia-Pacific Movement on Debt and Development: 2001 [Available at: http://www.jubileesouth.org/news/EpFVuVpFlEtbrIzkOE.shtml; last accessed on 5 June 2007].

Jubilee Debt Campaign. "A brief account of the origins of the debt movement, and early campaigning against poor country debt burdens": n.d. [Available at: http://www.jubileedebtcampaign.org.uk/?lid=279; Last accessed on 12 May 2007].

Juichi, Inada. "Evolution of International Development Assistance Regime – Harmonization of Aid Policies among Major Donors and Its Structure": n.d. [Available at: http://www2.jiia.or.jp/pdf/asia_centre/h15_japan/5_inada.pdf; last accessed on 7 December 2017].

Khalfan, Ashfaq. "From Illegitimacy to Responsibility: Transforming Development Finance Odious Debt: Definition, Application and Context" presented at EURODAD Annual Conference, 30 October 2006 [Available at http://probeinternational.org/library/wp-content/uploads/2011/02/ODashfaqEURODAD.pdf; last accessed 15 March 2018].

Lapeyre, Frédéric. "Globalization and structural adjustment as a development tool", Working Paper No. 31, Policy Integration Department, World Commission on the Social Dimension of Globalization, International Labour Office, Geneva: 2004.

Lie, Jon Harald Sande. "Reproduction of Development's Trusteeship and Discursive Power" in *Consilience: The Journal of Sustainable Development* Vol. 15, No. 1, pp. 77–100: 2016 [Available at http://www.jstor.org/stable/pdf/26188759.pdf; last accessed on 8 December 2017].

Lockwood, Matthew. "From Washington to Koln: The struggle for debt relief": n.d. [Available at: http://www.twnside.org.sg/title/matthew-cn.htm. last accessed 5 June 2007].

Lyon Summit Communiqué, [Available at: http://www.g8.utoronto.ca/summit/1996lyon/communique.html; Last accessed on 8 December 2017].

Malaluan, Jenina Joy Chavez and Guttal, Shalmali. 'Poverty Reduction Strategy Papers: A Poor Package for Poverty Reduction'. Focus on the Global South: 2003 [Available at http://www.cadtm.org/Poverty-Reduction-Strategy-Papers; last accessed on 8 December 2017].

Mavroudeas, Stavros D. and Papadatos, Demophanes. "Neoliberalism and the Washington Consensus": 2005 [Available at: https://www.academia.edu/21879048/Neoliberalism_and_the_Washington_Consesus; last accessed on 7 December 2017].

McCutchan, Andrew. *Understanding the Inefficacy of Structural Adjustment Programs in Latin America,* Master's Thesis, School of Economics and Management, Lund University: 2010.

Mutume, Gumisai. "Backgrounder: Debt Relief and HIPC", *Initiative for Policy Dialogue*: n.d. [Available at: http://www2.gsb.columbia.edu/ipd/j_ debtrelief.html; last accessed on 12 June 2007].

Oberdabernig, Doris A. "The Effects of Structural Adjustment Programs on Poverty and Income Distribution": 2010, [Available at: http://economics.soc.uoc.gr/macro/docs/Year/2011/papers/paper_2_114.pdf; last accessed on 8 December 2017].

Öniş, Ziya and Şenses, Fikret. "Rethinking the Emerging Post-Washington Consensus: A Critical Appraisal" ERC Working Paper in Economic03/09, Economic Research Center, Istanbul: 2003.

Pramono, Siswo. "The Genocidal Global Politics and Neoliberalism", *Journal of Economic and Social Research* Vol. 4, No. 2, pp. 115–138: n.d. [Available at: http://citeseerx.ist.psu.edu/viewdoc/download?doi=10.1.1.202.903&rep=rep1&type=pdf; last accessed on 8 December 2017].

Rodrik, Dani. "Goodbye Washington Consensus, Hello Washington Confusion? A Review of the World Bank's Economic Growth in the 1990s: Learning from a Decade of Reform" in *Journal of Economic Literature*, Vol. 44, pp. 973–987: December 2006.

Sobhan, Rehman. "The Incapacity of Structural Adjustment Reforms to Eradicate Poverty: An Agenda for Change", Centre for Policy Dialogue [CPD], Dhaka: 2002

Stiglitz, Joseph E. "Towards a New Paradigm for Development: Strategies, Policies, and Processes" – the Prebisch Lecture 1998, October 19, 1998 at UNCTAD, Geneva: 1998.

Stiglitz, Joseph E. "Participation and Development: Perspectives from the Comprehensive Development Paradigm" in *Review of Development Economics*, Vol. 6, No. 2, pp. 163–182: 2002.

Stiglitz, Joseph E. "Democratizing the International Monetary Fund and the World Bank: Governance and Accountability" in *Governance: An International Journal of Policy, Administration, and Institutions*, Vol. 16, No. 1, pp. 111–139: January 2003.

Tagle, Yovana Reyes and Patomäki, Katarina Sehm. "The Rise and Development of the Global Debt Movement: A North–South Dialogue", Civil Society and Social Movements Programme Paper Number 28, United Nations Research Institute for Social Development (UNRISD): 2007.

Teunissen, Jan Joost and Akkerman, Age (eds). *HIPC Debt Relief Myths and Reality*, FONDAD, The Hague: 2004.

UNRISD. "Structural Adjustment in a Changing World", Briefing Paper No. 4, World Summit for Social Development: 1994.

Vilanova, Juan Carlos and Martin, Matthew. *The Paris Club*, Publication No. 3, Debt Relief International Ltd. London: 2001.

Williamson, John. "What Should the World Bank Think about the Washington Consensus?", *The World Bank Research Observer*, Vol. 15, No. 2, pp. 251–264: 2000.

Wolfensohn, James D. "A Proposal for a Comprehensive Development Framework" – A Discussion Draft to the Board, Management and Staff of the World Bank Group,

January 21, 1999 [Available at http://web.worldbank.org/archive/website01013/WEB/IMAGES/CDF.PDF; last accessed on 8 December 2017].

Wolfensohn, James D. and Fischer, Stanley. "The Comprehensive Development Framework (CDF) and Poverty Reduction Strategy Papers (PRSP)" – a joint note: 2000 [Available at: https://www.imf.org/external/np/prsp/pdf/cdfprsp.pdf; last accessed on 8 December 2017].

World Bank (WB). *Economic Growth in the 1990s Learning from a Decade of Reform*, Washington, DC: 2005.

World Bank (WB). Klugman, Jeni (ed.), *A Sourcebook for Poverty Reduction Strategies (Vol. I and II)*, Washington, DC: 2002.

2 Policy ownership and development agenda

An analytical framework

Introduction

The political economy of Bangladesh's development suggests that since independence Bangladesh has been strongly intertwined with policy influences of foreign actors and more particularly, of international financial institutions (IFIs). Domestic political actors hardly played a role in development policy formulation. Policies were never exposed to critical public debate or parliamentary discussion. It was always the prerogative of the ruling elite to formulate development agendas unilaterally with the blessings of foreign masters. Thus, the reform agendas often proved counterproductive. In such a situation Sobhan (2002a, 2002b) argues that if Bangladesh is to re-establish its legitimacy in the eyes of its citizens it has to assume charge over its own policy agendas. To qualify for true ownership such an agenda must start off through political dialogues in parliament with the opposition as well as across the country, and with the citizens of Bangladesh who are most likely to be affected or benefited by public policy. Moreover, such a policy agenda will have to be implemented through effective governance. Bangladesh policy establishment needs to shift its posture from being accountable to donors in the form of policy dependence to being accountable to the people who elect the political minders who can solve the myriad of problems by attaining policy independence that is backed by domestic policy action.

This chapter, while primarily making an effort to conceptualize the term 'policy ownership,' aims to illustrate the linkages of various stakeholders in ensuring ownership, particularly in a PRSP. This will capture the participating stakeholders ranging from general citizens to bureaucracy to parliament to civil society in the perspective of Bangladesh's PRSP. Moreover, at the end it illustrates the features and strategies of true ownership which any aid recipient country rather should pursue to ensure its ownership over development agenda.

Conceptualizing 'policy ownership'

Defining ownership

By the early 1990s the marginal impact of the WB-IMF development strategies was looming large to the BWIs. Various CSOs recognized the failure and demanded reversal of the BWIs' approaches much earlier than the WB-IMF findings. In reference to the failures, James D. Wolfensohn, the former president of World Bank, suggested a Comprehensive Development Framework (CDF) in 1999 where he categorically elucidated the notion of policy ownership that appeared as the cornerstone in his analysis of the failure of earlier economic reforms.

> It is also clear to all of us that ownership is essential. Countries must be in the driver's seat and set the course. They must determine goals and the phasing, timing and sequencing of programs. …In some countries the long and short-term goals will be set by a process of public debate and consensus building led by the government with all sections of society ….What is new is an attempt to view our efforts within a long-term, holistic and strategic approach where all the component parts are brought together. Such development should, in our judgment, be a participatory process, as transparent and as accountable as possible within the political climate prevailing in each country … It is a holistic and strategic approach to development based on country ownership and partnership.
> (Wolfensohn: 1999, 9, 30–31)

CDF seems the first formal discussion at the WB on the necessity of country ownership in development agenda. Sobhan (2002) argues that the reform process needs to be domestically owned, through the use of indigenous expertise, consultation with stakeholders, and drawing upon consensual political support within the country. In view of Bangladesh's huge policy exposure to donors, he mentions that the past record suggests that the government's commitment either remained shallow or insincere to reforms orchestrated by expatriate consultants and eventually all major reform agendas proved counterproductive. Referring to his personal experience as an adviser (minister equivalent) in charge of finance and planning to the caretaker government of Justice Shahbuddin in Bangladesh in 1991, he emphasizes the political intention to carry forward indigenous thinking and initiatives. During the regime he formed 29 taskforces on various issues of the socio-economic development of Bangladesh involving 250 of the best available professionals to prepare policy recommendations to assist the newly elected government and parliament in establishing domestic ownership over the policymaking process. Unfortunately the subsequent elected political regimes preferred listening to the sermons of donors rather than the independent thinking of the taskforce reports which later appeared in four volumes. However, in capturing ownership issues Sobhan (2003) further stresses the study of the aid relationship between the donors and the recipients rather than the policies associated with aid. Understanding the relationship is important because it impinges on the political economy of developing countries, which determines the distributive outcomes of policy.

Helleiner (2000) defines ownership as the widest possible participation of beneficiaries in development actions that are essentially the process of planning, design, implementation, monitoring, and evaluation which have to be driven by the recipients. On the other hand, the recipient should be highly committed and try to seize ownership, as it cannot be given. Country ownership develops the quality of a State such that people can understand that their representatives have freely chosen the strategies or programs to be implemented. The country then seems confident to risk the failure of a program and strategy and thus acts consistently with this belief and acceptance of responsibility (Johnson: 2005).

Stiglitz (1998) provides a comprehensive view of development strategy with special reference to the past few decades of global development pursuit. While a development strategy must be aimed at facilitating the transformation of society by identifying the barriers as well as potential catalysts for change, it requires being more ambitious. The strategy needs to set out a vision of the transformation of society rising beyond the nominal role of accumulation of capital and the deployment of resources to that of what the society will look like ten to twenty years now on.

> This vision may embrace certain quantitative goals, such as a reduction in poverty by half, or universal primary education, but these are elements in or targets for the transformation process, not the vision of the transformation itself. … This vision needs to include a view of the transformation of institutions, the creation of new social capital and new capacities, in some cases to replace traditional institutions that will inevitably be weakened in the process of development. In other cases, the new institutions will contain within them elements of the old; there will be a process of evolution and adaptation (underline mine).
>
> (Stiglitz: 1998, 13)

He argues that such a transformative development strategy calls for a transparent and participatory process to ensure ownership, policy consensus and to reach and motivate all stakeholders. Ownership is important because Stieglitz says,

> … effective change cannot be imposed from outside. Indeed, the attempt to impose change from outside is as likely to engender resistance and give rise to barriers to change … At the heart of development is a change in ways of thinking, and individuals cannot be forced to change how they think. They can be forced to take certain actions. They can be even forced to utter certain words. But they cannot be forced to change their hearts or minds.
>
> (Stiglitz: 1998, 16)

He is highly critical of policy imposition. Policy conditionality not only undermines the interest of the recipient country to acquire capacity but also the confidence to exploit the ability for development. If policies are accepted in view of aid conditionality it is obvious that they are going to be superficial and equally be implemented half-heartedly. Eventually, such policy generates a counterproductive result. He views "thus, key ingredients in a successful development strategy are ownership and participation" (Stiglitz: 1998, 17). While successful social transformation demands policy ownership, greater degree of ownership can be achieved only when the strategies and policies are developed by the major stakeholders of the country, and when the country itself is in the driver's seat.

Thus in the end, as development is a transformative process to influence every institution and individual of the society, so a macro involvement of institutions is imperative. Institutions that must be involved are political institutions such as the parliament and the bureaucracy and citizens, civil society organizations, and other major stakeholders. They must all be involved in the process of analysis of local situations, identifying adaptive strategies in case of exogenous models in view of local needs, determining strategies and goals and equally so in implementation. While partnership, as imbued with the definition of the WB-styled ownership, may provide space for policy influence to key international actors, true ownership that negates partnership on ground of developing countries' inability to frame their own development model is more applicable to underwriting homegrown development strategies. The success of the Southeast Asian nations endorses the defiant attitude of the countries regarding external policy advocacy. True ownership gives opportunity to local institutions to prove their quality and ability, as the country does not opt for external support in managing development that usually happens in donor-supported interventions. The ability of local institutions is important because incapacity of institutions in many poor countries inhibits the development process from running independently and eventually paves the way for donor influence.

The Paris Declaration, the first formal high-level conference on aid effectiveness, sets country ownership as one of the major principles that should guide aid management for greater effectiveness. It defines country ownership thus "Partner countries exercise effective leadership over their development policies, and strategies and co-ordinate development actions" (OECD: 2005/2008, 58). The core argument of this definition is that there should be effective leadership by the aid recipients over development agenda. However, effective leadership requires an enabling environment at both the supply and demand side. The scope of country ownership was expanded in the Accra Agenda for Action, 2008 where participation of and dialogue with different stakeholders including the parliament, CSOs etc. were seen important in ensuring ownership at the national level (OECD: 2005/2008). The Busan Partnership Document further refined the definition of country ownership by saying that "countries should define the development model that they want to implement" (The Busan Partnership for Effective Development Cooperation: 2012, 1). It unequivocally demands that it would be the prerogative of the country to define its development model. It should not be the business of donors. NGOs further argue that country ownership should be more than government ownership; it means non-state stakeholders should have space in dialogue and discussions while setting up national development strategies (Xaxás and Vogel: 2007).

Participation as condition of ownership

The dominant development approaches of 1960s and 70s emerged following top-down pathways and undermining local actors and realities by consultants of the developed countries. These approaches failed to generate the promised trickledown effect to the local poor. The failure of the approaches to improve lives of the poor necessitates the engagement of the stakeholders in the process of development agenda setting (Willems: 2003; Cornwall and Gaventa: 2001). In fact, by the late 1970s, 'popular participation' entered the dictionary of many development experts and was endorsed in various United Nations declarations and resolutions (Stiefel and Wolfe: 1994). In the face of the citizens' growing demand for involvement in the decision-making process, consultative mechanisms in the form of participation emerged. However, the impact was enormous as people were engaged in many projects aimed at community development. But initially, participation was often limited to users groups. Through strengthened participation of the clients of social services, it was hoped that providers would be better able to understand their needs and perspectives.

Box 2.1 Participation is important ...

It is the right of the people; it enables people to interact with policy process and eventually ensures people's ownership;

It captures political dialogue and promotes political consensus on broad issues and eventually ensures policy continuity meaning major policy guidelines may survive regime change;

It gives local actors chance to contribute to the policy process and in effect develop professional ability and lessen dependence on donors and consultants;

It involves people and eventually strengthens government and other state actors to withstand donor leverages;

It encourages political government to involve various constituencies to have diversified approach and agenda of national development.

Participation in administering change is very important (Box 2.1). Earlier experiences suggest that policy conditionality may get the governments around the reform agendas but unless a consensus is reached or ownership achieved through dialogue or discussion, the continuity of policy change may be dismantled once government changes. Moreover, development is linked to the change in mindset of the greater society rather than a select group in the society to create an internal urge for change. Without internal motivation for development even good policy imposition may not work and the motivation comes through involvement of the stakeholders in open and extensive discussions (Stiglitz: 2002, 2003; Williams: 2006).

Although over the last approximately four decades there have been experiments regarding participation, it was in various forms and nature and was done in isolation. Participation in development projects was essentially different from political participation and, again, political participation was limited to exercising the right to vote only.

Box 2.2 Levels of participation (from low to high)

Information Sharing: It is a one-way flow of information from primarily the government to the stakeholders. The purpose is to keep the actors informed, ensure transparency in the process and gain legitimacy Various mediums are used to reach the public with information such as print and electronic media. Documents must be understandable to people either by translation where it is written in a foreign language or in a native language and information uploaded on websites. Local administration or local government institutions may be used to disseminate information.

Consultation: It is the two-way flow of information and gives an opportunity to stakeholders to share their reactions and feedback. It can be translated through participatory assessments, field studies with stakeholders, focus groups, parliamentary hearings, roundtables, participatory poverty assessments, etc.

Collaboration: On the surface it seems that it is a multiparty process, i.e. the initiator and the other groups together participate in various stages. But the bottom line is that the initiator retains the final decision-making authority. It moves beyond feedback or reaction gathering as in the case of consultation. Examples could include: public reviews of draft government documents such as legislation, government-led working groups, and government convened planning process, etc.

Joint decision-making: It enables parties to exercise shared control over the decision-making process. Examples may be: participatory planning, joint committees, working groups, taskforces with stakeholders' representatives, public–private partnerships, etc.

Empowerment: It is the highest level of stakeholder participation. The stakeholders instead of the initiator establish control over decision-making, resources, and activities. Eventually the stakeholders gain control over their own lives. It is a process that fosters power (that is, the capacity to implement) in people, for use in their own lives, their communities, and in their society, by acting on issues that they define as important.

Adapted from Brinkerhoff and Crosby (2002); Willems (2003); Page and Czuba (1999)

In recent years, there has been a convergence of concern with citizen engagement in policy formation and implementation and with 'good governance', broadening political participation to include a search for new, more direct, ways through which citizens may influence governments and hold them accountable. Both of these shifts contribute to new discussions of participation as citizenship and as a social, as well as a political right (Cornwall and Gaventa: 2001, 3).

Institutionalization of participation has brought a significant shift in the approach to participation, while earlier it involved people as members of user groups, now it is argued as "an approach to social policy that sees citizens not only as users or choosers, but as active participants who engage in making and shaping social policy and social provisioning" (Cornwall and Gaventa: 2001). Active involvement brings commitment to the lessons being learned and ownership of the results. Apart from government officials or managers, participation and involvement needs to reach deeper to include those who are often excluded and who are key to strengthening social and organizational capital. Greater ownership can only be ensured by involvement of those who carryout policies in the process of shaping and adapting (Box 2.2).

Reforms that are imposed as aid conditionality may not only fail to produce lasting change but also tend to undermine people's incentives to develop their capacities and weaken their confidence in using their own resources. Failure to ensure participation for greater ownership in the development process may give external agencies the leverage to short-circuit learning activities and reinforce feelings of impotence instead of acting as a catalyst or midwife that empowers change (Stiglitz: 2002).

Participation and poverty analysis: showcasing a pathway and the need to get closer to the people in the development agenda

The previous predominant approaches to development were counterproductive and brought compelling shifts in strategies in international financial institutions (IFIs). In the 1990s, a few years ahead of Wolfensohn's *Comprehensive Development Framework* (CDF), the World Bank conducted the *Voices of the Poor* (Narayan et al.: 2000) series. It was a phenomenal academic exercise involving the poor themselves in understanding poverty. Across 60 countries the team collected interviews of 60,000 poor women and men. These women and men shared their views, experiences, and aspirations. In collecting data for the series the participatory poverty assessment (PPA) tool was used. PPA being an iterative, participatory research process sought to understand poverty from the perspective of a range of stakeholders, and to involve them directly in planning follow-up action.

The most important stakeholders involved in the PPA research process were poor men and women. It also involved decision-makers from all levels of government, civil society, and the local elite, to uncover different interests and perspectives and increasing local capacity and commitment to follow-up action. The important aspect of PPA was that it endeavored to understand poverty in its local social, institutional, and political context (Narayan et al.: 2000).

A contemporary of the *Voices of the Poor* was the *World Development Report* 2000/2001, which was another landmark work in capturing the many facets of poverty. While the report exclusively focused on poverty, it indicated that poverty was a complex phenomenon. Poverty was more than inadequate income or human development. Poverty was also vulnerability, a lack of voice, power, and representation. The report advocated for dealing with the complexity of poverty reduction through empowerment and participation at local, national and international levels. It recognized the right of the citizenry to hold their governments accountable for development paths the government pursued. Moreover, participatory mechanisms could provide voice to women and men, especially those from poor and excluded segments of society. Further, international institutions should listen to and promote the interests of poor people. The report stated that the poor were the main actors in the fight against poverty, so they must be brought to the center stage in designing, implementing, and monitoring antipoverty strategies (World Bank: 2001).

While clearly the leadership of citizens in general and the aid recipient countries in particular is acknowledged in both these landmark documents to make antipoverty interventions successful, yet many in developing countries question whether this will in fact occur. The Bank must allow the recipient countries to be really in the driver's seat. It must go beyond rhetoric. As Stiglitz (2003, 125) mentions:

> Does the Bank have in mind a 'dual control' car or a car in which the true driver is the instructor, with the pupil's steering wheel, brakes, and accelerator for little more than show? The real test will come when the country proposes doing something different from what the Bank wants. How much leeway will the Bank provide? Will it be able to distinguish between cases where its fiduciary responsibilities – its responsibility to those that provide the funds to make sure that they are reasonably well spent – are at issue and those where reasonable people might well differ about the desirability of alternative policies?

Apart from 'dual control' as epitomized by Stiglitz (2003), understanding the complex interplay of power, knowledge and agency in poverty policy processes is equally important. The dynamics of participation needs to be understood through understanding the complexity of poverty policy process by understanding what was the scope for engagement, whose voices were privileged, and how the framework to define, measure, and tackle poverty was determined (Brock, Cornwell, and Gaventa: 2001).

PRSP and Participation

The World Bank (2002) dedicates a chapter in *A Source Book for Poverty Reduction Strategy* (*Volume 1*) to illustrating participation in PRSP. The *Sourcebook* is a guide to assist countries to develop PRSP following a participatory process. Chapter 7 of the *Sourcebook* deals with multi-dimensional aspects of participation in regard to PRSP and argues that participation is the process by which stakeholders influence and share control over priority setting, policy making, resource allocations, and/or program implementation.

Suggested to be outcome oriented, it narrates the different stages of participatory process in a PRSP: information dissemination, dialogue, collaboration in implementing programs, and in participatory monitoring and evaluation. It advocates the involvement of various stakeholders in the participatory interactions. The stakeholders are the general public, poor and vulnerable groups, organized civil society, private sector, government, representatives of parliament, and donors.

The *Sourcebook* model provides five stages of the PRSP process:

Stage 1: ***Analytical and diagnostic work*** – deepening the understanding of poverty and reflecting the diversity of experiences according to gender, age, ethnic, or regional groups, and so forth.
Stage 2: ***Formulation of the strategy*** – analysis of the poverty reduction impact on a range of public expenditure options and identification of public actions that will have the most impact on poverty.
Stage 3: ***Approval*** – initial approval at the country level, then formal approval by the World Bank and IMF boards.
Stage 4: ***Implementation*** – agreement on roles and responsibilities with government and service provider at the local level and monitoring implementation.
Stage 5: ***Impact assessment*** – retrospective evaluation of the PRS to derive lessons for subsequent versions.

Apparently, the Bank in qualifying participation does not maintain any stiff definition as it argues, "… there is no blueprint for participation because it plays a role in many different contexts and for different purposes" (WB: 2002, 237). In the analytical stage it also advocates capturing diverse experiences to deepen the understanding of poverty.

However, in contrast, stiff limitations to participation are candid and loom large in the same document. It openly explains (WB: 2002, 240) "the first step entails negotiation among the government, civil society, and World Bank and

International Monetary Fund (IMF) staff to clarify and define participation and the role it can play in the poverty reduction strategy." The opportunity for participation with the aim to develop a national development strategy independently appears to be farcical. National authority appears totally undermined and by-passed. Eventually, the WB-IMF would take control of the entire process and it may not, however be necessarily open. Because, once the recipient countries agree on broad principles laid down by the Bank-Fund their presence carries little purpose. As put by a finance minister (WDM: 2005, 8):

> We do not want to second-guess the Fund. We prefer to pre-empt them by giving them what they want before they start lecturing us about this and that. By so doing, we send a clear message that we know what we are doing – i.e. we believe in structural adjustment.

Another distinctive point to note is that PRSPs are meant for receiving concessional loans from the WB, through the International Development Association (IDA), or the IMF, through the Poverty Reduction and Growth Facility (WB: 2002). In view of the ground reality, how can one expect that participation in a PRSP would be genuine? It is true that countries may seize the opportunity of participation provided for the first time by IFIs, but not necessarily that it is sure to happen.

Ownership in PRSP and the role of the parliament

Parliament is the major political institution in national governance systems and plays the functions of legislation, oversight, and representation. By playing these roles effectively, parliaments can contribute to ensuring elements of effective governance – state capability, accountability, and responsiveness (Hudson and Wren: 2007). It articulates the aspirations of their constituents in national policy, and provides subsequent oversight of the implementation of the poverty reduction strategy. Central to good governance are transparency and accountability, which can be ensured by the oversight role of parliament. As the most representative organization it can ensure the integrity of participation in development policies and make people's voices heard (Sharkey, Dreger, and Bhatia: 2006). Intervention by political institutions such as particularly parliament in economic strategies has been proved useful and beneficial to development and it not only establishes checks and balances on the decisions of the executive organ of the state but also ensures that the national economic development agenda is generated, implemented, and evaluated through national institutions with adequate political legitimacy to ensure ownership and sustainability (Hubli and Mandaville: 2004; Sharkey, Dreger, and Bhatia: 2006; UNRISD: 2004).

A development strategy addresses issues of national interest from a long-term perspective and thus, requires major political forces reaching a level of consensus that ensures continuity of the strategy. Discussion of a development agenda in parliament, the politically representative major institution, may well serve the national consensus or ownership over it. Sharkey, Dreger and Bhatia (2006, 5) rightly argue, "a broad-based consultative process in the formulation of the poverty reduction strategy that cuts across (political) party lines is more likely to survive a change in regime". On the other hand, given the geographic spread, political composition, and sector-specific committee structure of national parliaments, legislatures (and legislative structures) offer a potential space to capture a nationally comprehensive view of poverty and the impacts of poverty reduction initiatives through debates and deliberations (Hubli and Mandaville: 2004).

Hubli and Mandaville (2004) very critically further argue that parliamentary involvement can help capture non-quantitative aspect of poverty, which is very critical to address the factors that produce poverty. They aptly put:

> Poverty diagnosis is the first step in any country's development of a full PRSP; before determining the most appropriate strategies to reduce national poverty levels, efforts must be made to understand which factors create or reinforce conditions of poverty. To understand how parliamentary involvement could improve the accuracy of a country's poverty diagnosis exercises, one must view legislative involvement in light of a multidimensional definition of poverty. For purposes of PRSPs, a person living in poverty lacks: opportunity (due to low consumption or income); capability (due to poor health or education levels), security (due to exposure to economic shock); and empowerment (due to inhibited access to power). The representative responsibilities of national assemblies mean that MPs have a role to play in the empowerment of citizens and citizen groups. In these instances parliamentarians may provide the only political representation for larger numbers of citizens from specific geographic or demographic constituencies; thus, an accurate diagnosis of the roots of poverty in a country could include parliamentary input regarding poverty's non-quantitative aspects.
>
> (Hubli and Mandaville: 2004, 6)

Thus, to qualify for the major condition for the PRSP to be homegrown, the involvement of the national parliament is more than essential. Let us be clear that involvement of the individual MP is not similar to the involvement of the parliament as a unit. While government may confer governmental stewardship to a PRSP but without thorough discussion or, for that matter, an effective political dialogue on the entire issue of a PRSP in parliament, it would be hard to convince anyone that the PRSP is nationally owned. The statement given by the Bangladesh finance minister (WDM: 2005) aptly underscores the importance of parliamentary debate on strategies that readily may not be palatable. He mentioned a parliamentary debate might not give blanket support to 'one-size fits all' policies. Here lies the strength of the involvement of parliament as a unit. Whereas, on the contrary, he argued that in a regimented regime it was possible to have approved whatever policies the government thought fit.

In addition to an oversight role, the major role a parliament plays is that it passes the national budget. A budget is obviously the reflection of activities that a nation chooses to promote national development. Unless the parliament is aware of the major economic strategies of the state, how does it take a position in a budget discussion? How does it decide priorities? The involvement of parliament in the articulation stage of policies is critically important. However, it is more so because the previous policy intervention by WB-IMF in the name of structural adjustment was totally counterproductive in many developing countries and research reveals there is no major policy shift in WB-IMF development discourse. While debate in the house is highly expected, ministry-wise critical review in the standing committees can be immensely useful, because they can give time and attention to critically analyze a strategy *per se.*

Ownership in PRSP and the role of the civil service

The Cambridge University economics professor Ha-Joon Chang (1998) illustrates the role of institutions in economic development with special reference to Asian countries. He argues pure market economies cannot explain the success of Southeast Asian nations' economic progress. That success needs to be looked through the contribution of institutions. He identifies three types of institutions:

- i institutions of coordination and administration;
- ii institutions of learning and innovation; and
- iii institutions of income redistribution and social cohesion, which contributed to the economic development of the nations.

While he argues that many non-state institutions such as business corporations, industrial associations, labor unions, government–private sector consultation bodies, and so on, are all important institutions of coordination, he acknowledges the importance of non-market, non-state institutions of coordination. He focuses upon two state institutions whose importance has been emphasized in recent debates on the East Asian experience. They are the government bureaucracy, which is the central institution that makes up the state, and the institutions that provide state–business links. He states "in the case of certain East Asian countries such as Korea, Taipei, China, and Singapore the high quality of general administration and the proactive role of the elite bureaucracy in designing and implementing effective national and sectoral developmental plans have been identified as crucial factors behind their economic successes" (Chang: 1998, 69).

According to Chang (1998), central to bureaucratic contribution is to provide entrepreneurial vision, going beyond popular belief of running productive enterprise. The vision needs to articulate the new economy that it wishes to forge out of the developmental process and to encourage investments in those activities that will help it realize that vision.

> What is more important in this connection is the provision of 'focal points' for private sector investment decisions through continuous policy dialogue with the private sector and through encouragement of cooperation among private sector firms. The best example is the encouragement of information technology industries by the Japanese government since the early. The Japanese government attracted the private sector decision-makers to a single vision through a series of White Papers envisioning the 'information age' and encouraged their cooperation by supporting the formation of consortia for technological development (this involved only a very limited amount of public sector money).
>
> (Chang: 1998, 72–73)

In providing entrepreneurial vision he suggests some objective conditions for bureaucracy based on experiences of successful East Asian countries. The first condition is the availability of a highly competent bureaucratic elite who are not necessarily providing advanced training on economics, management, or some other technical subjects, but generalists who can make sensible judgments on the basis of given information. The second condition is that "this elite need to have a substantial degree of political insulation, which will enable them to retain a degree of 'autonomy' that is essential in long-range planning" (Chang: 1998, 73). The third condition is to establish a high-prestige career bureaucracy, where political appointments are checked through a competitive recruitment system and thus politically motivated hiring and dismissal is made difficult. However, while he highlights the political insulation of bureaucracy in the light of successful East Asian nations, he shares the downside of the insulation. He understands that the overarching influence of neoliberal orthodoxies may itself become a threat. In order to have a balance between the neoliberal pressures and political insulation of bureaucracy he suggests an engagement of dialogues with private sectors.

Chang's (1998) insights fit well into the context of Bangladesh. The contribution of the generalist civil service to economic development is a necessity on various counts. While recent literature strongly advocates active involvement of parliament and civil society in the economic agenda, the role of bureaucracy is again purposefully bypassed. But the ground realities are that from independence in 1971 until 11 January 2007, the nation encountered various interventions by military and survived only 15 years of continued democratic governance. The parliament is yet to be a strong political and representative organization in the face of confronting political culture between two major political parties. However, the immediate impact of democratic rule is the rise of a vibrant civil society and free press. But there are some valid arguments in place in respect of civil society regarding who constitutes and by what terms and most importantly how the organizations are run.[1] Reality suggests that most of them are embedded with Western countries for funds. In such a situation, the contribution of a career civil bureaucracy to the making of and implementing development strategies can hardly be overemphasized.

With special reference to a PRSP one may search for the answers to two fundamental questions: how bureaucracy was involved in the process to determine a roadmap for poverty reduction in Bangladesh and how the PRSP itself focuses on further development of an efficient bureaucracy to spearhead national economic development. In the absence of a particularly actively engaged parliament and independent civil society it is only logical that an efficient bureaucracy can overcome the policy leverage through multilateral and bi-lateral development cooperation.

Making ownership real: towards a 'true ownership' approach

Box 2.3 Basics of true ownership

- Strong will and commitment of national leaders to build a self-reliant economy.
- Based upon a concrete vision and realistic measure economic strategies and policies should indicate an exit plan from aid.
- Independent execution of development, i.e. agenda setting, implementation strategy and timetable, should be done without donor influence.
- Mapping development strategies in line with local conditions and in doing so a trial and error approach may be practiced to reach the best option.
- Using indigenous expertise, holding consultation with stakeholders, and drawing upon consensual political support within the country.
- Avoiding a 'blue print' approach in pursuing development strategies.
- Giving local institutions opportunities to prove and excel in ability.

While Wolfensohn (1999) defines ownership as saying that the country must set an agenda through a fruitful public debate where stakeholders participate and the entire process of agenda setting is transparent, Shimomura and Ohno (2005) move further stressing on 'true ownership' (Box 2.3). Their argument of 'true ownership', a three-dimensional phenomenon, is qualitatively much more comprehensive than that of Wolfensohn's definition of ownership. The first dimension of true ownership is the ***goal of aid***. Ownership should be translated through strong will and commitment of national leaders to build a self-reliant economy. Development strategies and policies should assume eventual 'graduation' (or an 'exit plan') from aid, be supported by a concrete vision and realistic measures for growth promotion, and domestic resource mobilization (Shimomura and Ohno: 2005). Policies, being beyond mere slogan, also should be truly imbued with equitability and growth sustainability.

The second point is the ***scope of ownership***. It is expressed by two distinct capacities of aid receiving countries: (i) donor management and (ii) policy autonomy and content (referring to the substance of national development strategies and policies). Donor management refers to the capacity to own the relationship with the donor community and requires leadership in policy dialogue. The leadership needs to coordinate diverse requests, selectively adopt donor advice, handle friction with diplomatic grace, and more. Policy autonomy requires the government to set national development goals and implement strategy and timetable independently. It is in other words the carrying out of development by the country itself – a far broader vision than donor management. In this type of development cooperation

> the government is capable of managing the entire development process and hence coordinates aid as part of its own coherent development effort. The government initiates and formulates a national development strategy, identifies specific needs to be financed by aid, presents its aid requests and negotiates with donors, matches aid programs and projects with its own internal resources, implements various developmental activities, and monitors and evaluates results.
>
> (Shimomura and Ohno: 2005, 4)

There exists another kind of donor management where the donors assume joint responsibility to guide the development process and they intervene in the process in the plea of capacity constraints of loan receiving governments to formulate and present policy content. In this type of management they set goals together, allocate money, and monitor activities. Eventually, it becomes a process of donor coordination rather than government coordination of aid resources.

The East Asian development 'miracle', for example, is of the first category of donor management where the aid receiving East Asian countries led their development activities – from inception to implementation. Under strong political leadership, governments tried to build their own institutions to compensate whatever institutional incapacity they might have had. For these governments, the aid relationship was just one component of development management, a means to achieve a national goal of promoting growth and establishing wealth-sharing mechanisms on a nationwide scale (shared growth).

Referring to the present aid relationship in most developing countries where donors enjoy substantial authority and constrain genuine autonomy of the countries, Shimomura and Ohno (2005) stress that government must be at the center of the development process to establish true ownership. Developing vision for promoting shared growth, building national systems for mobilizing financial and human resources, and nurturing local expertise in managerial and technical skills are also recommended to attain true ownership.

The third dimension of true ownership is the ***creativity of ideas***. It is the ability of the countries to make development strategies in line with their own situations. The countries should not implement the copying of particular strategy(s) floated by donors. Even if exogenous models are considered, it should be 'translative adaptation'. This means the relevant elements in any exogenous model should be reinterpreted ensuring that the locus is situated in the country where the strategy would be implemented. True ownership eventually should mean the capacity of a developing country to choose from alternative policy prescriptions – even if they are not recommended by the international aid community. Indeed it is precisely the point that differentiates true ownership from "nominal ownership" (Shimomura: 2005). When a country decides to rely on external advice or foreign models, policymakers and technocrats must conduct a thorough assessment of alternatives and carefully adapt the policy content and sequencing to the country-specific context in both the design and implementation stages.

Ishikawa (2003) identifies four determinants to explore the actual 'ex ante' processes of a specific socio-economic system transforming itself to another: (1) economic issues (trigger), (2) exogenous models, (3) *Koku-jo* (study of local scenarios), and (4) scenario. Economic issues deal with the motivation of leaders or the main group of people of a country to change the regime – 'emergence of a change trigger'. However, the outcome of the change or the scenario of regime transition may not be foreseen. At this stage they may opt for analyzing exogenous models and their relevance to local reality. It requires a thorough evaluation and study of local scenarios (*Koku-jo*). The repeated interaction following a 'trial and error' method between exogenous models and *Koku-jo* contributes to the emergence of an effective scenario for new regime. The implementation of this scenario may further produce a new series of economic issues, but they should be dealt with as second-generation issues.

The determinants provide clearly an autonomous scenario in development strategy setting. In other words, the motivation for change occurs first in the mind of national leadership and it is not an outcome of any external actors. The local reality should motivate the leadership for a change and a copy of exogenous model is not required, rather its relevance as a guideline may help local situation. The important issue is that there may be some trial and error processes by which developing countries arrive at the point of identifying an effective reform scenario. The second-generation issues suggest that development scenario may not be constant and it may travel through different experiences. Capturing the local need and situation, adaptation relevant to local scenarios and trial and error are important aspects to ensure true policy ownership in international development cooperation rather than having the donors set the scope for policy choice and interpretation.

The other contrast is that while at the heart of participation lies policy ownership, the formal approval of the PRSP would be in the hands of WB-

IMF. But true ownership in development, as argued by Ishikawa (2003) and Ohno et al. (2005), disapproves of the interaction of donors in the entire process. In the approval stage, though non-binding, consultations with civil society representatives and their constituencies are indicated but national parliament is not mentioned. Without parliamentary involvement per se how could a strategy be called nationally owned? Civil society involvement, dubbed as civic engagement, is also a condition. It means that only selected people and organizations may be invited and at the same time the topics of discussion are also previously selected (WB: 2002).

How does true ownership make a difference?: Learning from Korea

Korea is an important example of aid success and could be a good lesson for many of the developing countries. Much of the initial conditions of Korea were similar to many of other poor countries. Moreover, the economy was ravaged by two wars – the war of independence from Japan and the civil war. But within a period of five decades after the independence, the country transformed itself from its borrower or recipient identity to donor identity being an OECD-DAC member in 2010. Korea was not blessed with natural gifts as the countryside was denuded, arable land was scarce and mountainous, and the climate was harsh. Due to the extreme environment, multi-cropping was not feasible. At today's value, per capita income in 1964 was only USD 80. Infant mortality was as high as 90/1000 live births; life expectancy was also low at 57 years of age and over 60 per cent of people were stricken by absolute poverty (Adelman: 2007). The formative years of Korea (until 1964) with regard to foreign aid represents a situation of business as usual, is similar to many countries dealing with aid. Aid did not assist in reducing the challenges facing the country and the detrimental policies adopted resulted in the need for more aid. The country became extremely dependent on aid creating crony capitalism within government and business. The country became known to the aid establishment as "the hell-hole of foreign assistance", a "bottomless pit", a "hopeless case or a "basket case" (Adelman: 2007; Ministry of Strategy and Finance and KDI School: 2012). But the situation changed dramatically during the regime of President Park Chun Hee. The magic was nothing new beyond an expression of true ownership of development reforms. Korea, during this time, adopted some strategic reforms with a long-term economic vision in mind. It expanded its manufacturing and export capacities; created effective institutions to spearhead development; invested in education for sustainable human development and increasing productivity; and expanded its strategic relations with Japan, minimizing its high dependence on the US (Ministry of Strategy and Finance and KDI School, 2012). These all impacted highly positively on the well-being of the country. The major lesson from the Korean case is that government has to take charge of development and reforms, and development is possible when the government takes the charge. The Korean examples also challenged the Washington Consensus orthodoxy of the minimalist role of the state (Adelman:

2007). In Korea government was the prime mover of undertaking development policies and strategies. Finally, the Korean case exemplifies that if government shows commitment and undertakes a needs-based development policy, aid can play big role in development; in fact, serious commitment can only ensure country ownership.

Conclusion

Policy ownership is not a straightforward phenomenon. National leadership and institutions need to be willing to ensure ownership and core political institutions such as parliament and administrative organs of government such as the bureaucracy have to play a large role. Thus, it is not just enough that 'ownership' is tied in with the PRSP approach. Any country receiving concessional loans either from the IMF or World Bank or any donor should be able to ensure independence in her development agenda. Precisely, the degree of policy independence or ownership should be examined in terms of greater participation and interactions of core state and non-state actors vis-à-vis the will of the political regime. In analyzing ownership in Bangladesh's PRSP, this project aims to examine the evolution of the policy package vis-à-vis the nature and degree of participation of different stakeholders in the formulation process of the PRSP in Bangladesh. Evolution at country level will unravel the genesis of the package, whether it has emerged as an independent initiative by the state or came as a policy prescription of the donors.

Note

1 In many instances it was noticed that many well-known members (of civil society) questioned the existence of true civil society in Bangladesh. They tried to hint at the embeddedness of the CSOs with powerful Western countries as far as the fund is concerned. Many even questioned the validity of the urban elite in the name of civil society to represent the people and thus, many people believe that they are engaged in proxy representation. Without donor funds they hardly undertake any program.

References

Adelman, Irma. "From Aid Dependence to Aid Independence: South Korea": 2007 [Available at: http://www.un.org/esa/ffd/wp-content/uploads/2007/11/20071116_Irma Adelman.pdf; last accessed on 10 December 2017].

Brinkerhoff, D.W. and Crosby, B.L. *Managing Policy Reform: Concepts and Tools for Decision-makers in Developing and Transitioning Countries*, Kumarian Press: Bloomfield, CT: 2002.

Brock, Karen, Cornwell, Andrea and Gaventa, John. "Power, knowledge and political spaces in the framing of poverty policy", IDS Working Paper 143, Institute of Development Studies, Sussex: 2001.

Chang, Ha-Joon. "The Role of Institutions in Asian Development" in *Asian Development Review*, Vol. 16, No. 2, pp. 64–95: 1998.

Cornwall, Andrea and Gaventa, John. "From Users and Choosers to Makers and Shapers: Repositioning Participation in Social Policy, IDS Working Paper127, Institute of Development Studies, Sussex: 2001.

Helleiner, Gerry. "Towards Balance in Aid Relationships: External Conditionality, Local Ownership and Development", Munk Centre for International Studies, University of Toronto: 2000 [Available at: http://ibrarian.net/navon/paper/Towards_Balance_in_Aid_Relationships__External_Co.pdf?paperid=35005; last accessed on 10 December 2017].

Hubli, K. Scott and Mandaville, Alicia P. "Parliaments and the PRSP Process", World Bank Institute, World Bank: 2004.

Hudson, Alan and Wren, Claire. "Parliamentary strengthening in developing countries", ODI: London: 2007.

Ishikawa, Shigeru. "Ex Ante Determinants of Regime Transition: China, Vietnam, and Russia Compared": 2003 [Available at: http://www.grips.ac.jp/forum/pdf02/Ishikawa_ex_ante.pdf; last accessed on 10 December 2017].

Johnson, Omotunde E.G. "Country Ownership of Reform Programmes and the Implications for Conditionality", UNCTAD, G-24 Discussion Paper Series, No. 35: 2005

Ministry of Strategy and Finance and KDI School. *Miracle on the Han River*: 2012

Narayan, Deepa et al. *Voices of the Poor. Can Anyone Hear Us?*, The World Bank: 2000.

OECD. *The Paris Declaration on Aid Effectiveness (2005)/Accra Agenda for Action (2008)*. [Available at http://www.oecd.org/dac/effectiveness/34428351.pdf; last accessed on 10 December 2017].

Ohno, Izumi et al. *True Ownership and Policy Autonomy: Managing Donors and Owning Policies*, National Graduate Institute for Policy Studies and GRIPS Development Forum: 2005.

Page, Nanette and Czuba, Cheryl E. "Empowerment: What Is It?" in *Journal of Extension*, Vol. 37, No. 5: 1999.

Sharkey, Katrina, Dreger, Theodore and Bhatia, Sabina. "The Role of Legislatures in Poverty Reduction Experience and Future Directions", The World Bank Institute: World Bank: 2006.

Shimomura, Yasutami and Ohno, Izumi. "Introduction and Overview" in Ohno, Izumi et al. *True Ownership and Policy Autonomy: Managing Donors and Owning Policies*, National Graduate Institute for Policy Studies and GRIPS Development Forum: 2005.

Shimomura, Yasutami. "Export Capacity Building in Thailand: Managing Donors and the Development Process toward a Self-Reliant Economy" in Ohno, Izumi et al. *True Ownership and Policy Autonomy: Managing Donors and Owning Policies*, National Graduate Institute for Policy Studies and GRIPS Development Forum: 2005.

Sobhan, Rehman. "Aid, Governance and Policy Ownership in Bangladesh". CPD: Dhaka: 2003.

Sobhan, Rehman. "Policy Independence and Political Accountability", Centre for Policy Dialogue, Dhaka: 2002a.

Sobhan, Rehman. "The Incapacity of Structural Adjustment Reforms to Eradicate Poverty: An Agenda for Change", Centre for Policy Dialogue [CPD], Dhaka: 2002

Sobhan, Rehman. "The Political Economy of the State and Market in Bangladesh", Centre for Policy Dialogue, Dhaka: 2002b.

Stieflel, Matthias and Wolfe, Marshall. *A Voice for the Excluded: Popular Participation in Development – Utopia or Necessity?*, Zed Books: London and New Jersey in association with the United Nations Research Institute for Social Development (UNRISD), Geneva: 1994.

Stiglitz, Joseph E. "Towards a New Paradigm for Development: Strategies, Policies, and Processes" – the Prebisch Lecture 1998, October 19, 1998 at UNCTAD, Geneva: 1998.

Stiglitz, Joseph E."'Challenging the Washington Consensus' – An Interview with Lindsey Schoenfelder" in *The Brown Journal of World Affairs*, Vol. 9, No. 2, pp. 33–40: Winter/Spring/Winter/Spring 2003.

Stiglitz, Joseph E. "Participation and Development: Perspectives from the Comprehensive Development Paradigm" in *Review of Development Economics*, Vol. 6, No. 2, pp. 163–182: 2002.

The Busan Partnership for Effective Development Cooperation: 2012 [Available at https://www.oecd.org/dac/effectiveness/Busan%20partnership.pdf; last accessed on 10 December 2017].

UNRISD. "Research and Policy Brief 3", Geneva: 2004.

Willems, Sonja. *Participation Without Power? Civil Society Participation and Political Influence in the Bolivian Poverty Reduction Process*, Master Thesis, Development Studies, Centre for International Development Issues Nijmegen, University of Nijmegen, the Neherlands: 2003.

Williams, David. "'Ownership,' Sovereignty and Global Governance", Global Economic Governance Programme, Department of Politics and International Relations, University College, Oxford: 2006.

Wolfensohn, James D. "A Proposal for a Comprehensive Development Framework" – A Discussion Draft to the Board, Management and Staff of the World Bank Group, January 21, 1999 [Available at http://web.worldbank.org/archive/website01013/WEB/IMAGES/CDF.PDF; last accessed on 8 December 2017].

World Bank (WB). Klugman, Jeni (ed.), *A Sourcebook for Poverty Reduction Strategies (Vol. I and II)*, Washington, DC: 2002.

World Bank (WB). *World Development Report 2000/2001: Attacking Poverty*, Oxford University Press, New York, 2001.

World Development Movement (WDM). *One size for all: A study of IMF and World Bank Poverty Reduction Strategies*, London: 2005.

Xaxás, Mercedes Mas de and Vogel, Carolyn Gibb. "Making Country Ownership a Reality: An NGO Perspective", *Population Action International*, Vol. 2, No. 3: 2007 [Available at: https://pai.org/wp-content/uploads/2012/01/CountryOwnership.pdf; last accessed on 10 December 2017].

3 Development agenda and Bretton Woods Institutions

Revisiting Bangladesh's engagement

Introduction

Bangladesh could be a good example for those interested in the political economy of developing countries and in particular, how a country with a huge spirit of independence chose its own developmental path to become a top adherent of multilateral financial institutions. The chapter draws on first-hand accounts of some witnesses closely involved in the formative years of the creation of the country's political economy. The chapter is dedicated to presenting the shifts that occurred in Bangladesh's political economy over the last three decades from a historical perspective. A special focus is on the initial few years that were so crucial for subsequent developments. The strategic shifts in the development agenda mark broadly that Bangladesh failed to withstand both internal confusion and external pressures to march on its own path to development. The failure, in fact, determined Bangladesh's future in regard to a persistent and overwhelming engagement with the Bretton Woods Institutions [BWIs] in the broader area of development strategies. Although the early days seemed a bit uncomfortable and encountered some resistance, it did not take much time to smooth out the engagement with the BWIs. Initially, there was political resistance and also resistance from the Planning Commission to the creation of a rapport with the BWIs. However, we do not find any such resistance in the later phases of the history of Bangladesh. Thus, though Bangladesh was exposed to BWI tutoring with reluctance in the beginning, the relationship was transformed afterwards into an obedient and persistent engagement.

The chapter shows that initial internal confusion was mainly due to the lack of participation by both the people and political institutions in determining national development strategy. This lack of participation was so much so that Bangladesh opted for a development strategy with a huge gap in understanding of the process among the leadership and no practical preparation. Members in the Planning Commission, the organization bestowed with the responsibility of preparing national development strategy, were totally frustrated noting the gap between words and commitment for a planned economy after independence. On the other hand, the issue of foreign assistance appeared very crucial and there were even debates in public spheres between the Prime Minister and the finance minister with regard to receiving foreign assistance. With the considerable damage that occurred during the war of liberation the internal imperatives for assistance were high, but the threat to be exposed to external pressure also loomed large. In such a significant scenario sensible leadership was critically needed. Bangladesh failed to experience that leadership and eventually encountered a messy situation beset with deep economic and political problems as witnessed in the early stages of the 21st century. The spirit of a planned economy faded away. Thus, the nation increased its engagement with the BWIs, accepting humiliating conditions. It continued for decades and is still continuing. Thus, the issue of crisis in policy ownership in Bangladesh indeed has historical roots.

Looking at the situation from another perspective, it appears that the BWIs tried to totally exploit Bangladesh's internal chaotic situation – the lack of coordination among leadership and the great need for reconstruction of a war-ravaged economy. They imposed many stiff conditions forcing the economy into further deterioration. Many of these issues are discussed in subsequent sections. The first country director of the World Bank [WB] in Bangladesh did not try to hide his uneasiness as to how fiercely the WB was trying to capture the Bangladesh economy. Eventually Bangladesh succumbed to pressures of the Bank-Fund and the knot has been so tight for decades that according to Sobhan (2002a) the Bangladesh state lost its legitimacy in the eyes of its citizens.

This chapter is split into two major parts: the first focuses on the institutions, process, and intricacies of the initial attempts to construct a development policy that would be independent of external pressure and based on national hopes and aspirations. The second part makes a rapid review of the evolution of Bangladesh's engagement with the BWIs. This part also presents very briefly the implications of IFIs' reform measures on Bangladesh.

Part 1: The setting of development strategy of a new country: understanding the institutional process and politics

The establishment of the Planning Commission

During the Pakistan regime the Planning Commission was under the leadership of the President of Pakistan with himself as Chairman. He played a vital role in economic decision-making and the founding leaders of Bangladesh were exposed to that experience. The Bengali leadership also saw the Commission negotiate with the central government of Pakistan for an adequate share of financial resources for the development of the then East Pakistan. Thus, in light of historical exposure, the founding leadership in Bangladesh became convinced of the need to establish a commission at the earliest opportunity after independence to form proper guidelines for the economic development of a new country (Islam: 1993). Although the Commission was formally established in January 1972, it had its practical genesis during the time of the liberation war with some economists playing a crucial role in advising the government in exile. Many of the founding members of the Commission had contributed significantly during the fateful days of the 1970 elections and subsequent negotiations with Pakistan. Thus, the war-time rapport of those economists[1] with the political leadership established confidence in the Commission with the higher political authorities of Bangladesh's emergence. The Commission was given the best support that the government could provide at that time (Alamgir: 1986; Islam: 1993, 2003).

The structure and organization of the Commission matched the functions it was bestowed upon it to perform. It had ten divisions, each division headed by a chief enjoying the status of a secretary to the government – the highest position of administrative hierarchy. The divisions were: General Economics, Programming and Evaluation, Industry, Agriculture, Water Resources, Rural Institutions, Physical Infrastructure, Socio-economic Infrastructure, External Resources, and Administration. The Commission was chartered to perform ten specific functions that could be segregated into three broad sets.

Planning, feasibility study and development plan preparation: This category included preparation of annual and longer term plans (including five-year and perspective plans); assisting ministries in preparing development projects; undertaking feasibility studies, and coordinating preparation of projects in cases where several ministries were involved in a large development plan; and conducting technical and economic appraisal and evaluation of projects for their inclusion in plan.

Policy recommendations: This was another broad function of the Commission. Apart from the intra and inter sectoral financial allocations in a plan, it also required recommendations on a whole range of policies and institutional changes for implementation and realization of the objectives of the plan; thus the Commission was expected to have made recommendations as well as being involved in the process of deliberation on these matters.

Coordination and secretariat role: Another major function of the Commission was to coordinate economic policies, both short term and long term, to be undertaken by various ministries. It also was to serve the secretariat roles for the National Economic Council (NEC) – the mini cabinet consisting of major economic ministers in the cabinet and led by the Prime Minister for deliberations on economic policy issues and for the approval of development projects and programs.

Planning Commission and the politico-administrative dynamics

Dealing with politicians

The initiation of the Commission took little time and deliberation by the political leadership. After the second meeting of the cabinet immediately after independence, the organization and functions of the Commission were approved. Surprising enough, the responsibility to delineate the functions and responsibilities was left to the Commission and the Deputy Chairman. Therefore, arguably since its formation, the Commission enjoyed a high level of authority and status. Except for the first year or so, the Commission was headed by the Prime Minister, thus making the Commission a super ministry. On the other hand, the Prime Minister had a very positive impression of the understanding and capability of the members of the Commission. The Prime Minister had to assume that the Deputy Chairman and members were fully aware of the hope, aspirations, and objectives of the ruling party and of the limitations in a political process where differing and sometimes opposing interest groups had to be accommodated in order to preserve the unity of the ruling party and its continuance in power (Islam: 1993).

The members of the Commission were not political elements but professional economists who had little exposure to direct political activism, whereas, the politicians, especially the ministers, had little interaction with the Commission under the given policy-making culture. The Commission members were also not involved in the political process and in the ruling party's deliberations. Thus, in effect, they could not fully appreciate the political feasibility constraints on economic policy-making and political costs-benefits of decisions they were offering (Islam: 1993). This is all in view of the fact that there was no prospect of any fruitful political dialogue in parliament on development decisions as parliament was predominantly controlled by a single party. The authority of the Prime Minister appeared the key to all decision-making and the ministers tried to survive by being in the confidence of the Prime Minister. The centralization of power in the hands of the Prime Minister resulted in the erosion of the prospect of the institutionalization of the collective decision-making process. Eventually, the Commission did not have a political leader in the cabinet to support the policy deliberations. The Commission had eventually to convince the Prime Minister by having separate and private dialogues as means of influencing decision-making. This special favor by the Prime Minister to the Commission increased the tension between the Commission and the ministers. It was widely believed that the Commission exercised appreciable influence on decisions of the Prime Minister in economic matters (Islam: 1993).

The higher status of the Commission members, such as the Deputy Chairman with the status of a cabinet minister and the members with state minister status, was not welcomed by the politicians. This was in view of the fact that the Commission members were not the members of parliament (MPs) but mere bureaucrats coming from the academic arena. However, the Commission argued that their higher positions were deemed essential in view of their inter-ministerial coordinating role. The Commission viewed that under the prevalent bureaucratic tradition unless the members had a status higher than that of the secretaries, the former would not have the authority to require the participation of secretaries for consultations to expedite the process of decision-making (Islam: 2003). A systemic planning process also was considered to have appeared as a threat to the independence of the minister (s). Ministers were used to making pledges for particular projects in their constituencies. However, in the course of subsequent examination by the Commission on the validity and feasibility of the projects pledged by individual ministers, many projects could not be entertained and thus the tough scrutiny was not appreciated by the political elements (Islam: 1993, 2003).

Working with bureaucracy

During the Pakistan regime, the civil service of Pakistan (CSP), the elitist regular civil service, used to contribute tremendously to the formulation of national policies and used to assume positions with highest authority and responsibility. After independence, the civil service encountered several challenges that posed a threat to their previous authority and superiority. The setting up of the Administrative and Services Reorganization Committee (ASRC) under the leadership of Dr. Muzaffar Ahmed Chowdhury, the then vice-chancellor of the University of Dhaka, was a clear cut message to the civil service about the dismantling of bureaucratic elitism[2] in the administrative machinery (Rahman: 1997; Ahmad: 1998). Apart from the ASRC, new tensions were added to the civil service between those who participated in the war of liberation and worked with the government in exile and those who continued with the Pakistani regime (Islam: 1993). Beneath this backdrop, the Planning Commission emerged on the scene with more authority and status. During the Pakistan period, the senior level secretaries, mostly from the CSP, used to staff the Commission, but this time, breaking with previous traditions, academics from the university were posted to run the Commission. Moreover, they were given the status of a cabinet minister or a state minister.[3] So naturally, the set up of the Commission was not well received by those in the civil service (Islam: 1993, Ahmed: 1991). The Commission posed a threat to the mainstream civil service, generalist in nature, by becoming an active party to the recommendations of the Services Reorganization Committee for the unification of different types of services. The Commission, being an ally to the political authority, also advocated for inclusion of technical professionals in the higher positions (Islam: 1993). In effect, the interference of the Commission in the interests of the civil service resulted in creating discomfort between the two groups. However, Rahman[4] argued that this perception about the Commission was the major reason for making the Commission an isolated organization and leading to its ultimate failure (Rahman: 1993).

However, since the beginning the Commission had to work in a situation where cooperation from both politicians and civil service was not readily available. The politicians wanted their pet projects approved and did not like technical arguments raised by the Commission while they were evaluating the projects. The Commission's inter-ministerial coordination also gave the Commission a virtual super ministry role which also became a major source of resentment for the politicians and civil service. The relationship with the

Commission was also misunderstood due to the lack of a collective decision-making culture. The parliament unfortunately was not in a position to give space for debate on the socio-political issues and absorb grievances of the members for their constituencies, and thereby, give room for reaching decisions based on consensus. Had there been sufficient debates there would have been congenial relations among the contending groups of governance. The Commission decided to counter the resentments by heavily depending on the Prime Minister who was the major source of strength for the Commission from the beginning. However, in the wake of a situation of deteriorating law and order and abnormal price hikes in 1974, the decision of the Commission was challenged and the role of the Commission was greatly reduced. Under the backdrop of deterioration on all fronts of governance, the frustrated Deputy Chairman of the Commission took long-term leave for treatment abroad and left the Commission in early January 1975 for Oxford (Islam: 2003).[5]

The First Five-Year Plan (FFYP)

The FFYP was the landmark event of the Planning Commission. Within a year and a half, the Commission was able to prepare the document. While the statistical data and empirical investigation into various aspects of the economy were not sufficiently comprehensive and reliable to meet the full needs of planning, the nation needed the plan urgently so as to provide a sense of direction and determine the order of priorities within the framework of which coherent and consistent policies and programs could be formulated. Another important reason for preparing the plan in a hurried manner was to exploit the plan to get foreign assistance. Donors expected the recipient country to have a plan setting out a consistent framework of investment priorities and policies, which would enable them to assess the needs for assistance and the form it should take (Islam: 1993). Thus, it was obvious that the Commission had to work under tremendous pressure and limitations.

Imbued with the aspirations of democracy, nationalism, secularism, and socialism, the then four state ideals, the FFYP was a road map for planned development. Whereas the major focus of the plan was to go in line with the spirit of the then political leadership for transforming society with the ideals of socialism, the Commission was aware of the limitations of the socio-economic conditions of the country. The Commission argued that the ideal of socialism merited rigorous exercise to be translated into reality. The Commission valued firm political commitment as crucial for transformation of the society. They understood that without this political commitment the process might falter midway and end up with an authoritarian social order instead of political and economic emancipation of the masses (GoB: 1973). The Commission, before setting the development agenda, wanted to have objectively studied the conditions prevalent in the country. The Commission categorically stated the importance of an objective assessment of local conditions for a planned economy. It argued that without an objective assessment programs and priorities might be misleading. Underscoring that planning is more a political process than an economic device it gave importance to the will of the political leadership and human beings as the agents of change for the execution of policies (GoB: 1973).

The Commission, based upon the critical evaluation of the socio-economic conditions prevalent at that time, came up with some suggestions and concerns. While they suggested for gradual removal of the capitalist system of income distribution, of private ownership, of means of production and of pre-capitalist mercantile or feudal forms of production relations to create the precondition for socialist development, they were aware of the obligation to fulfill the necessities. As more than 80 per cent of economic activities were dependent on agriculture so bringing changes, as part of making the precondition for socialist development, in land ownership was a vital point to think over.

Production and austerity was another important issue to take into consideration. While an increase in productivity or the growth of productive forces and egalitarian distribution of social income was needed, it was also imperative that government convince the people of the determination of the leadership to ensure that a minimum living wage was available to all workers. Further, poverty and deprivation would be shared by all until such time as income had risen sufficiently before it could expect responsible behavior from different classes of income earners.

Objectives of the plan

The plan envisaged an egalitarian society as the ultimate objective with an assurance of every citizen's right to work and with limits imposed by law on the private ownership of the means of production (Islam: 2003). However, the major specific objectives of the plan were as follows:

1 *Poverty reduction*: Indeed poverty reduction was the foremost objective of the plan and to that end it focused on creating employment opportunities for the unemployed and the underemployed. It also aimed to accelerate the rate of growth of national income, as well as effective fiscal and pricing polices for equitable distribution.
2 *GDP growth acceleration and employment generation*: Increase in the rate of growth of GDP to at least 5.5 per cent per annum was targeted. While the target of increase in full time jobs was 4.01 million, the plan also aimed to reduce underemployment. Apart from this target, the plan also expected to put in efforts to mobilize labor in the unorganized non-monetized sectors, with a view to expanding output and employment.
3 *Increase in per capita income*: 2.5 per cent per annum increase in per capita income was targeted in the plan. The plan also envisaged ensuring better access to increased per capita income for the poorer section of the population and in this connection, imposition of ceilings on income

and wealth and introduction of redistributive fiscal measures were employed.

4 *Reduction of dependence of foreign aid:* This was a major target of the plan. While mobilization of domestic resources and promotion of self-reliance were deemed to be important factors in achieving the goal of minimizing foreign aid dependence, the plan targeted to expand and diversify exports, and achieve an efficient pattern of import substitution for reducing the foreign exchange gap.

The plan envisaged generating a rate and pattern of income growth that, besides meeting basic consumption standards, would expand employment opportunities and ensure a socially desirable pattern of income distribution. The plan was considered to have concentrated on increasing output in the labor intensive sectors. Reduction of dependence on imports of food grain and improvement in the balance of payments through import substitution and export promotion were major factors in the plan strategy.

The setting of a development vision for a new country: towards understanding the dilemma

Crisis in ideology

Bangladesh opted for socialism as a strategy for development after independence. Socialism had been one of the four state principles laid down in the constitution. The constitution also contained some other provisions for creating the path to socialism. The constitution promised to establish planned economic development. The constitutional commitments were the expression of spirit of the national independence movement of that time and people expected quick development (Muhammad: 1998). Economic emancipation of the common people became the major focus because the economic exploitation of Bangladesh by West Pakistan featured strongly in the struggle for liberation (Rahman: 1993). Premised on the constitutional commitments, the FFYP was considered a first step towards the progressive achievement of a socialist economy (Islam: 2003).

Making socialism the choice as the means of rapid economic development and ensuring an egalitarian society (Rahman: 1993) was subsequently challenged on various counts. The ruling party Awami League (AL) and its leadership took the role of a nationalist party, being in the forefront in the emergence of Bengali nationalism through the movements of 1950s and 1960s. The promise of emancipation from the economic exploitation and political domination of Pakistan was the core agenda for its mass appeal (Islam: 1993). The major thrust of its struggle was to ensure a larger share in the benefits of economic progress and a larger share of resources for the development of East Pakistan. They also sought a larger share of East Pakistan in the process of political and economic decision-making. The movement in the late 1960s took to shaping the demand for autonomy in the management of financial and foreign exchange resources of East Pakistan on the basis of what came to be popularly known as the *six points program for autonomy* (Islam: 1993).

However, the AL, a middle class party in terms of the composition of economic interest, with the passage of time had been tremendously ideologically influenced by radical elements among the workers and students. This had been so, partly because while the nationalist movement in the late 1960s gathered momentum, students and workers became an increasingly important force in the struggle for autonomy. Moreover, during the movement, most of the top leaders of the AL were imprisoned and responsibility for the movement, to a major extent, was carried out by students. During 1968–69 all major students' organizations including the student front of AL became united to spearhead the autonomy movement and declared an eleven-point action program that also rendered support to the six-point program of AL. The war of liberation witnessed the increasing role of radical elements. In the mean time, the leftists joined the labor organization of AL. In effect, it appeared that the leftists could capitalize a greater degree of influence over the AL after independence and AL had to respond to their pressure by accepting socialism as the major principle for social and economic development (Islam: 1993, Maniruzzaman: 1988). The trial of Sheikh Mujib following the false 'Agartala Conspiracy Case' was a turning point in terms of getting popular support for the six-point cause. The Students Action Committee (SAC) during this time radicalized East Pakistan's politics and injected socialist slogans through the eleven-point plan. With the acquittal from the conspiracy charges on February 22, 1969, Sheikh Mujib on February 23, 1969 at a reception held in the Race Course Field, feeling the pulse of the people, declared that his party would work for the realization of both the six-point program of Awami League and eleven-point plan of the student community (Maniruzzaman: 1988, 2003). Therefore, it appears that socialism did not emerge as a natural phenomenon of AL's political discourse and thus, the AL leadership accepted socialism through the pressure of the student communities, greatly dominated by the leftists. According to Khan (1996), Mujib had a very simple understanding about socialism and thought socialism, when applied to Bangladesh, would acquire unique qualities in conformity with the requirements of Bengali culture, history, and economy. Mujib wanted a special type of socialism not necessarily compatible with the phenomena developed and practiced in the then socialist countries. Islam (1993, 2–3) pictured the issue of ideological vagueness in the following way.

> The general qualification to the formal commitment of the political leadership to economic development was that the statements of objectives and policies were of a very general nature; even when they referred to specific programmes and projects, they were often not the result of systematic and careful examination by the political leadership … By the

> time of independence there was not set of widely shared convictions or a consensus within the party or among the leaders of opinion at large, either about the character and nature of the future economic system of independent Bangladesh or about the strategies and policies of development. Whatever analysis was undertaken on the objectives and policies of development planning in Bangladesh was done in the context of successive Five-year plans of Pakistan. Moreover, socio-political circumstances as well as economic policy choices were very different in Bangladesh compared to what they were before independence. As a consequence, the economic principles of the new constitution formulated in 1972 or the economic components of the election manifesto in 1973 were in the nature of broad declarations of intent, which were not formulated as a result of serious and extensive debates and dialogues among the competitive groups and divergent opinions in society, on the contrary they most often marked the beginning of debates, examinations, scrutiny, and analysis as years went by. Even the formulation of the Five-year plan did not become nor was it treated by the political leadership as an occasion for hard policy choices on specific issues; it was treated more as a guideline or a framework for decision-making in subsequent stages, specially at the time of preparation of Annual Plans.

While the strategy of mixed economy as a transitional course in the Five-Year Plan was a decision of the Commission, the political leadership had no firm convictions in this respect. Within the political leadership it was not unanimous as to whether a mixed economy would be a transitional stage or whether it was going to be the permanent long-term pattern of the economic system. Moreover, the Commission had to even set the size and priorities of the Plan based on its interpretations of the preferences of the political authorities, as revealed in public pronouncements and in discussions of a general nature with the highest political leadership (Islam: 1993). The Commission virtually played two-pronged roles of a preacher and a theoretician of the party (Islam: 2003). The political leadership also appeared to have been vacillating as to deciding on the role of private sector. Based on their previous unpleasant memories of private capitalism in Pakistan with its concentration of economic power, its inequalities, and its control of the political and economic decision-making process, they opted unequivocally not to support the private sector or introduce incentives and concessions to enable it to expand and gain in strength. On the other hand, the political leadership was apprehensive that the policy of limiting private investment might limit the growth prospects of the economy. Surprisingly, while the debate on the role and limit of private sector continued, no effort was made to improve the working and efficiency of the public sector enterprises (Islam: 1993).

The political leadership reiterated their reluctance to receive foreign aid; Tajuddin Ahmed, the first Prime Minister of Bangladesh soon after independence declared that Bangladesh would not seek foreign assistance for her development (Ahmed: 1991). Arguably based on the prevalent euphoric political milieu, the FFYP set an objective to reduce foreign aid and realize self-reliance (GoB: 1973). However, the subsequent heavy dependence on foreign aid, particularly that from non-socialist countries (specially the big powers) created a political dilemma and inconsistency for Bangladesh (Alamgir: 1986; Islam: 1993). The rigidity against foreign aid was also reflected in the behavior of Tajuddin Ahmed, the then Finance Minister, while he was visiting Delhi in February 1972 and invited to *Son et Lumière*. Mr. McNamara, the then president of World Bank was also present on the same occasion and more surprisingly, they were seated together but did not exchange a single word. The Indian government skillfully wanted to give them (Tajuddin and McNamara) a common space to interact but Tajuddin appeared to have been not amenable to such tactics (Parkinson: 1981).

There seems to have been a rift within the top leadership, Sheikh Mujibur Rahman, popularly known as Bangabandhu and also officially regarded as the Father of the Nation, and Tajuddin Ahmed, in relation to foreign aid. Upon contemplating the reality Mujib evidently became convinced for a higher amount of foreign aid irrespective of the political views of the source country and also he did not like the staunch opposition of Tajuddin to aid particularly coming from the capitalist west. The rift even was taken to the public spheres.

> The ideological difference between Mujib and Tajuddin on the question of foreign – in particular United States –'assistance' again surfaced openly in the first week of January 1973. On 3.1.73 Mujib in his address at Patuakhali referred to the 'conspiracy to deprive Bangladesh of foreign assistance' (*The Daily Azad*, 4.1.73); the very next day Tajuddin said in an address on the occasion of the 50th anniversary of the formation of the Unions of the Soviet Republic, 'It is never possible to construct socialism taking assistance from capitalist countries. For construction of socialism assistance can be taken from countries believing in the same ideology, at the same time with an attitude of self-reliance' (*The Daily Azad*, 5.1.73). These two opposite statements revealed also Mujib's attitude of dependence on foreign assistance vis-à-vis Tajuddin's philosophy of self-reliance.
>
> (Rahman: n.d)

A letter written by one of the members of the first Planning Commission to the Chairman, Deputy Chairman, and the members of the Commission highlighted the policy toward foreign assistance. The mood in the Planning Commission was also against receiving aid from a country that did not support Bangladesh's struggle for independence and the Commission was aware of the leverage of foreign assistance, which Bangladesh could not readily afford. There was dilemma also with regard to the approach to establishing socialism. Parliamentary democracy that was enshrined in the constitution of Bangladesh seemed to have been an unrealistic method in which to establish socialism. On the other hand, applying force was also not the solution because the party itself could split due to no firm conviction or consensus within the party on the nature, time path, and the manner of establishment of socialism (Rahman: 1993; Islam: 1993). Looking back, the then Deputy Chairman of the Commission now evaluates the ideological vacillation that the socio-political policies and objectives contained in the FFYP as pious exhortations rather than serious recommendations for action by the political leadership. The highest political leadership wanted a limited or populist version of *Fabian Socialism* where government would have a significant role to play (Islam: 2003).

Crisis in process

Another major contradiction was the lack of consensus about the development strategy. The priorities or goals of the nation were not set in the FFYP. Nor was the strategy of creating a socialist economy debated in the political forums. There was no effective and continuous dialogue between the Planning Commission and the political leadership and it virtually resulted in keeping both sides unaware of the aspirations and limitations of each other (Islam: 1993, 2003). Despite desperate attempts and intentions, the Commission failed to illicit public opinion, opinion of different interest groups and professionals to make the plan a nationally owned document. Upon approval of the plan by the cabinet, the members of parliament were provided with copies of the plan for perusal and not for debate (Islam: 1993, 2003; Rahman: 1993). Moreover, the approach to establishing socialism, particularly economic agendas, did not draw upon a consensus among the leadership of the ruling party and the members of parliament (Islam: 1993).

Apart from the lack of dialogue between different stakeholders, Rahman (1994) also raised the issue of a 'consciousness gap' between revolutionary intellectuals and the 'masses'. Rahman (1993) argued that the planning commission, being monopolized by the professional economists, remained as an isolated organization. They had to work in a compartment of their own, secluded both from the regular civil service and from the ruling party. He was against the proposition of professional economists spearheading the Commission. He argued that in a parliamentary democracy the representatives of the people would decide the future of a nation.

He was apprehensive that under that given political atmosphere, the professionals (economists) were likely to compromise their commitments. However, he suggested that it would be prudent on the part of the intellectuals "to stay out and advise if advice would be sought, from an independent forum. But circumstances, including impulses of the exciting hour, pushed the intellectuals in" (Rahman: 1993).

The scope of participation of the stakeholders in developing a development strategy such as the FFYP was so poor that even a member of the Planning Commission was deliberately bypassed. While there were elevated discussions of self-reliance everywhere in the political arena, the Planning Commission could not work together. The member who was most vocal about self-reliance was ignored. Upon critical evaluation it appears the leadership was obsessed with rhetoric instead of capturing the prevalent socio-political environment. Rahman (n.d, 82–83) very poignantly expresses his frustration of that period.

> … By that time the draft of the Five Year Plan had been completed. I knew that the Plan had been framed within the conventional development planning paradigm … I gave an official letter to the Deputy Chairman of the Planning Commission saying that I would like to see the draft of the Five-year Plan before it was sent to the Cabinet. I knew that the draft plan document would not be shown to me, as I had already given enough evidence that I was a rather 'troublesome' member!
>
> After about two weeks Member One called me in his room. He seated me with great affection, held a hand of mine, and said, 'Brother Anis, we had to do something without informing you. Cabinet was in a great hurry to get the draft Plan, so it had to be sent there without showing it to you. Please do not mind, brother.'
>
> I returned to my room and sent a note to the Deputy Chairman, saying that it was unfortunate that the draft Plan had been sent to the Cabinet without being shown to me. Under this circumstance I was no longer available to the Planning Commission from 1 October (1973). … The Five-year Plan had been prepared, and there was not much value in it of my 'rural' recommendations …
>
> The Planning Commission gave me a very respectful and affectionate formal farewell on 4.10.73.

Summing up

The underlying dynamics of the development agenda setting in the beginning clearly implies that there were huge gaps of understanding as to what would be the strategy and how the issue of development assistance would be negotiated among the leadership. The then ruling elite, without much thought and commitment, incorporated socialism as the economic strategy partly because of pressure from leftist organizations that dominated the autonomous movement and partly because of the nature of opposition against the Pakistani establishment.

While the elitist Pakistani establishment was not a popular platform for the common people, the major political parties in opposition to the ruling elite opted to couch their political discourse in the voice of the public which primarily suited socialistic principles. Thus, socialism was deemed the major strategy to meet the needs of the common people. With the independence earned through a populist struggle the major concern that arises from discussions and evidence of the closest witnesses is why neither of the political parties nor the political institutions such as parliament was given the opportunity to take a lead in the development agenda setting. Does this imply that the ruling elite suffered from a lack of confidence? The immediate impact of the lack of the people's participation was that Bangladesh missed the opportunity to promote the political culture of policy debate thus recognizing the people's right to development. The country even today continues with the same lack of the participation of stakeholders in development agenda setting.

Part 2: A revisit of Bangladesh's engagement with Bretton Woods Institutions: understanding the politico-economic dynamics

The tie in the making

The issue of foreign aid, especially from multilateral sources like the BWIs, became very delicate after independence. The BWIs found it difficult to win support from the founding leadership of Bangladesh to play a leading role as a useful proxy for Western interests in the economy of Bangladesh. The blanket support by the BWIs for the ruling elite of the Western wing of Pakistan in the 1960s; as well as their overwhelming influence in development agenda setting; and the opposition of the Western ruling establishment, particularly the then Nixon administration, to the movement for Bangladesh liberation influenced post independence decisions regarding BWIs. The founding goals, to make Bangladesh a socialist country, also contravened with the notion of seeking aid from capitalist establishments. In addition, the urge to maintain policy independence in the development agenda was another major issue that made the leadership reluctant to approach the BWIs (WB-IMF) for aid (Hossain: 1996). The first Prime Minister of independent Bangladesh was in such a euphoric mood that he declared immediately after independence that Bangladesh would not seek foreign assistance for development (Ahmed: 1991). However, contrary to the political high spirit of self-reliance and policy independence, the war-devastated country was in dire need of foreign assistance in order to rebuild the economy. Under such a contradiction of ideology and sentiment developed through the unparallel peril and ignominy of the liberation war, and the need that was well substantiated by the prevalent wreckage and carnage caused by the war, the engagement of Bangladesh with the BWIs was taking shape. The step towards establishing official cooperation between Bangladesh and the Bank started with the visit of Robert D. McNamara, the then president of the World Bank. While on a tour to India in February 1972 he expressed his desire to visit Bangladesh in order to discuss the possible contribution by the Bank to rebuilding the war-ravaged economy of the country. However, until his arrival, Bangladesh was not a member of the WB. In other words, the sovereignty of the new country was not recognized by the Bank authority and this contributed to developing some reservations in receiving the Bank's President in his first ever visit to Bangladesh. Moreover, the Bank was primarily conjectured as the extension of the US establishment. The president of the Bank was viewed as a card-carrying member of the Washington power elite who deliberately stood against the liberation movement of Bangladesh and supported the atrocities of the Pakistani ruling military junta. Thus, the entire political milieu was not at all receptive to the Bank's presence in Bangladesh. The visit of Robert McNamara revealed a clear lack of consensus among the top leaders of Bangladesh. While the Prime Minister Bangabandhau Sheikh Mujib and the Deputy Chairman of the Planning Commission were agreeable to providing McNamara all official protocol and courtesy, the Minister for Finance and Planning appeared to have opposing views. With the insistence of the Minister for Planning and Finance, McNamara was received at the airport by the Governor of Bangladesh Bank accompanied by the Chief of Protocol instead of the Deputy Chairman or for that matter any member of the Planning Commission. An official lunch with the Deputy Chairman also was ruled out, although the Prime Minister wanted to make the lunch happen (Sobhan: 1982; Islam: 2003). The meetings between McNamara, Prime Minister Sheikh Mujib and Finance Minister Tajuddin were very remarkable. Two different political postures regarding the cooperation with the BWIs emerged through the meetings. While the Prime Minister was his natural self and polite, the Finance Minister was seemingly reluctant and offensive. The Finance Minister's reluctance was expressed while he asked McNamara for support for bullocks and bull sheds instead of infrastructure development (Islam: 2003). Sobhan (1982) rationalizes Tajuddin's offensive behavior towards McNamara as saying that it was an attempt to convey to the Bank the political mood in Bangladesh and the awareness that Bangladesh at that phase was averse to concede to the Bank and the hegemony it had traditionally enjoyed over the development agenda of Pakistan. However, the persistent deterioration in governance and economy and west-led international political configurations took the country to a point of suffocation such that the liberation war pledges and bravado of the leadership faded away. In the words of Parkinson (1981, 148):

> … Bangladesh was eventually drawn into the Bank's orbit. Initially relationships with the Bank … were strained, but economic necessity and accommodation of the attitudes on both sides eventually enabled a smoother working arrangement to be established.

With Bangladesh becoming a member of the Bank by August 1972,

> a spate of missions began coming out with a view to reactivating ongoing projects and initiating new lending programs. By this time Bangladesh had already been hooked onto the aid narcotic so that there were few inhabitants against encouraging the Bank to step up its aid program in Bangladesh.
>
> (Sobhan: 1982, 173)

While in 1973 Bangladesh was first exposed to policy dialogue with the IMF, Bangladesh had negotiations between 1972 and 1975 for borrowing from the Bank, the Fund, and other bilateral donors (Islam: 1991). By mid-1974 Bangladesh sent aides-memoire to all donors drawing attention to the magnitude of the food and balance of payment crisis and stressing the need for immediate assistance to meet payments on past commitments. Missions from Bangladesh also approached donor countries and agencies to explain the desperate need for assistance (Faaland: 1981).

Bangladesh's dealing with the BWIs: initial hard negotiations

Appointment of the bank representative

After Bangladesh became a member of the WB, the first task was to appoint a resident representative of the Bank in Bangladesh. The choice was not simple. Being profusely predisposed to a strong nationalist mood of that period, the Planning Commission was particularly reluctant to let the Bank resume its role as philosopher and guide to policy-making for development (Sobhan: 1982). Therefore, the Deputy Chairman of the Commission, in view of the immediate past history of the independence war when Bangladesh was caught in the crosscurrents of the cold war and big power rivalries, emphatically suggested that the representative should be from a small, preferably neutral country.

However, the suggestion was not immediately palatable to the Bank,[6] as they did not like anyone other than a career Bank staff member to represent the Bank. However, eventually in an unusual manner, the Bank had to succumb to the pressure of the Deputy Chairman and Just Faaland from Norway, a member of Harvard Advisory Group but not a career staff member of the Bank, became the first country representative of the Bank (Islam: 2003). The reason behind the surrender of the Bank to the leadership of the Planning Commission can be construed that the Commission took a hard line as to giving the bank any kind of royal treatment they previously enjoyed during the Pakistan regime. Moreover, the Commission was also very much determined to ensuring policy independence. Thus, the country representative was expected to be free of the imperial pretensions inherited by the representatives of the Bank in their dealings with the lesser breeds. The strategy by the Commission to recruit someone like Faaland from a politically less ambitious country proved useful in later years. Faaland, being less committed to the Bank's political ambition, used his position to ease the confrontation of interests between the Bank and Bangladesh vis-à-vis the Commission. He even took the side of Bangladesh in the issue of the Pakistan debt settlement, which is thought to have caused his premature termination with the Bank in Bangladesh (Sobhan: 1982).

Pakistan debt crisis

The settlement of the debt liability to Pakistan incurred before the independence in 1971 emerged as a central issue to the evolution of relations between

Bangladesh and major Western bilateral donors as well as the World Bank. With the gradual shifting in the nature of support to Bangladesh from giving grants for rehabilitation and reconstruction to development assistance of the donors, the creditors raised the issue of Bangladesh's share in the previous debt liability of Pakistan in early 1972. The bilateral donors such as the USA, the then Federal Republic of Germany, and France joined the World Bank to ask Bangladesh for the settlement of the debt liability.

The issue of debt settlement served to uniquely illustrate the weight and modes of pressures of external interests, including in particular the WB, on an economically weak developing country (Faaland: 1981). At a time when the issue of debt settlement was gaining a stronghold in the agenda of the western bilateral and multilateral donors, Bangladesh applied for membership to the WB and IMF. This gave the Bank an opportunity to take the lead in raising the issue of past liability with Bangladesh and to act as a spokesman for all creditors. However, as Bangladesh's independence was not recognized by Pakistan until then, Bangladesh officially took the position that it was by no means responsible for foreign debts acquired by the Pakistan government during unity with the then East Pakistan until 1971. Moreover, Bangladesh opted for taking a comprehensive approach to settling all assets and liabilities of a United Pakistan upon recognition of Bangladesh's sovereignty by Pakistan. Indeed Bangladesh wanted the matter to be resolved between her and Pakistan bilaterally (Faaland: 1981, 128; Sobhan: 1982, 174; Islam: 2003).

In the debt issue, the Western donors including their spokesman – the World Bank – took Pakistan's side ignoring the reality of what Bangladesh endured during that time and the essence of international justice. In this war of liberation Pakistan unjustly caused unfathomable human and asset loss for Bangladesh. Under applicable international law, Bangladesh was under no compulsion to accept Pakistan's debt liability. Simply put, Bangladesh did not have any contract with the creditors. Moreover, it is conventional that a state, when faced with a loss of a major part of her territory, is still liable for all debts that were contracted before the loss. There are examples, Jordan paid debt service on projects located in territories occupied by Israel and further, Malaysia paid debt services on loans in public utilities located in Singapore. So was the case between India and Pakistan when the two nations emerged in 1947, consequent to the dissolution of united British India. So most cases of debt succession in the past were settled by agreement between the countries concerned (Faaland: 1981). The World Bank and other Western bilateral donors tried to put pressure on Bangladesh to accept Pakistan's debt liability. The BWIs knew of Bangladesh's heavy dependence on foreign aid thus seeing an opportunity to exploit the difficulties of Bangladesh. Bangladesh by that time started negotiations for aid to activate projects abandoned during the war and also to start fresh projects to resume socio-economic development of the war-damaged country. While the donors pressed Bangladesh to negotiate debt liability, they rescheduled Pakistan's debt several times to provide concessions.

Even though Falaand served as the country director of World Bank, he could not hide the unjust and extremely partisan treatment of Western donors dealing with the Pakistan debt crisis and their desire to establish control over Bangladesh's struggling economy and faltering politics. Donors sought to impose a burden of debt service on Bangladesh, which they had no legal right to do. Donors were not prepared to insist on the resolution of their affairs in other ways. Intense leverage was exercised in the process in an effort to force one of the poorest countries in the world to accept obligations that it had not incurred and could not readily afford to take on. The major instrument of leverage was the World Bank and pressure was exerted by threatening to refuse assistance unless the terms that the donors wished to impose were accepted. The handling by the World Bank and other creditors of the conflict on the debt issue undoubtedly set back Bangladesh's development. Moreover, ill-informed and unsympathetic handling of the situation by the Bank strained political relationships and made it difficult to establish conditions of mutual confidence in which international relations can best work (Faaland: 1981).

By mid-1974 Bangladesh entered into an acute economic crisis concerning foreign exchange and food supply. Bangladesh very urgently needed foreign assistance on most concessional terms. It requested the World Bank to convene an emergency meeting of donors to secure assistance for Bangladesh. Donors took full advantage of Bangladesh's difficulty, expecting Bangladesh to accept the liability of Pakistan's debt. In the end Bangladesh had to bow down to donor leverage by accepting a compromise deal of the Pakistan's debt liability for projects that were "visibly located in Bangladesh" (Faaland and Parkinson: 1976; Islam: 2003). However, the compromise deal put the sovereignty and dignity of the nation and people of Bangladesh at real risk by creating a sense of a "superior-creditor/inferior-debtor" relationship in development cooperation (Faaland and Parkinson: 1976).

Postscript: The issue of division of assets and liabilities of united Pakistan until 1971 between Bangladesh and Pakistan as of today remains unsettled. In the words of Prof. Nurul Islam, "this issue has effectively disappeared from the agenda for serious negotiations with Pakistan, as it has been caught in the maze of political changes at home and geopolitical developments abroad" (Islam: 2003, 299).

Dhaka Conference on the Bangladesh economy

The international conference on the Bangladesh economy in 1973 was another landmark event in the formative phase of relationships between Bangladesh and bilateral and multilateral aid donors under the leadership of the World Bank. The conference also serves to provide the understanding of the hegemony of donors for a newly independent country with a fragile economic record, and of the misunderstanding between Bangladesh and the donors or vice versa.

By the end of 1972/early 1973 Bangladesh's aid negotiations with both bilateral and multilateral donors went into full swing and the World Bank suggested convening a consortium of donors. The suggestion was not readily accepted by Bangladesh in fear that a forum of donors would provide scope to exercise collective pressure by donors on a weak and poor country (Islam: 2003; Faaland: 1981). With pressures mounted by donors on Bangladesh to build up a consortium of donors to coordinate aid negotiations, Bangladesh took the initiative to hold an international conference on the economy involving all bilateral and multilateral donors to give a fresh picture of Bangladesh's economy and the need of foreign assistance. The initiative received the same response as Bangladesh expressed to the WB's proposal of convening of a consortium of donors. The World Bank, as the leaders of the Western donors, did not want the conference held in Dhaka going beyond the norm of that time in which aid consortiums were normally held either in Paris or Washington. The Bank raised many questions about the efficiency of holding such a conference almost similar in status and content to the Paris or Washington consortiums. They argued Bangladesh would not be able to provide the standard logistics and secretarial services for holding such a conference. More importantly, the Bank was rigid on the grounds that holding a conference in a loan-receiving country may create arguments for other loan-receiving countries to hold consortium meetings in their own countries. Donors including the Bank were also fearful for the organization of such a meeting in Dhaka because "it would be more subject to leakage to the local press and that this would inhibit free and frank discussion as well as expose Bangladesh Government to political attack and accusation of bowing to pressure from donors" (Faaland: 1981). In the face of the stubborn attitude of the Bangladesh government to hold the meeting with the donors, and valid arguments against the feeble and intentional reservations of the donors, the WB sounded a note of warning that the donors would not send high-level delegations to Dhaka. The warning had the tacit implications that non-participation of senior officials from the donor side would cause the lack of realization of objectives of the meeting in facilitating discussions for the first time between top officials and ministers of the government of Bangladesh and high level policymakers or aid administrators of donor counties (Islam: 2003). Following the warning by the Bank, the Bangladesh government contacted the high officials of the donor countries. They gained the impression that most donors did not see any difficulty to meeting in Dhaka and further, did not think that the composition of the delegations would suffer because of the venue. Finally, the meeting termed as the International Conference on the Development of Bangladesh was held in Dhaka in 1973. The conference was chaired and managed by the Bangladesh government on the basis of documentation prepared by both the Bank and government.

In the meeting, the Scandinavian countries were in favor of soft loans and grants and more importantly they stressed the need for providing assistance to Bangladesh within the context of the socio-political goals decided by the government. Their stance was so heartening that a Nordic country made a very revealing statement that as follows: "We the donors, are a very dangerous crowd and we should be feared despite the gifts we bring or promise that we may convey. Too much foreign assistance has a tendency to distort priorities of the recipient country".[7]

The issue of Pakistan debt settlement appeared in the meeting very unusually; it was not on the agenda but more or less every delegate mentioned the issue on the first day and eventually it took a very serious turn.

> The crucial issue was whether, when and to what extent Bangladesh would accept a share of Pakistan's debt liability. Absence of the issue from the agenda made no difference to the delegations; it was raised nonetheless in a pre-determined and concerted move to impress upon the Bangladesh Government the serious view donors took to what they considered its unwillingness to come to terms. Although the reasons for this had been fully explained in bilateral discussions between individual donors and Bangladesh, they insisted on an answer satisfactory to them before they would pledge further development support. Bangladesh made it clear that it would rather go without pledges of assistance, than accept conditional ones. Nevertheless, practically all delegations persisted in announcing such conditional pledges.
>
> (Faaland: 1981, 110–11)

Bangladesh's first policy exposure to BWIs – the devaluation of currency

After independence, Bangladesh experienced a very hard start to the economy. Due to unsatisfactory rain, there were bad harvests in 1971–72 and 1972–73, which caused a food crisis. Agricultural output did not see any dramatic progress and continued at an earlier rate and Bangladesh remained heavily dependent on grain imports. In addition to the crisis in food grain production, input prices began to go up rapidly hitting Bangladesh severely from that last quarter of 1972. The price of wheat in the US rose from about US$ 60 per ton to over US$ 100 per ton in January 1973 and to about US$ 200 per ton by the end of that year. The price of other imported commodities also increased significantly (Faaland and Parkinson: 1976). Eventually, the economy, already ravaged by the impact of the liberation war, was exposed to a plethora of crises. They were chiefly high inflation and a crisis in the balance of payments during the period 1972–75. Under such adversity and uncertainty, the need for a stand-by arrangement with the IMF was felt by Bangladesh as a cushion against potentially adverse situations.

Bangladesh started policy negotiations with the IMF while an IMF mission was visiting Bangladesh in March 1973 with a view to drawing the first and possibly the second tranche of Bangladesh's quota in the IMF. While under the standard rules of the Fund, a first tranche could be withdrawn from the resources of the Fund without difficulty and without much conditionality just by demonstrating need and active concern to find appropriate solutions to its balance of payments problems. A stand-by arrangement would involve the acceptance to increasingly onerous conditions as well as higher rates of interest (Parkinson: 1981). As Bangladesh decided on a stand-by arrangement, more than one tranche, therefore, policy negotiation was essential with the IMF team. While in earlier donor transactions, conditionality and policy issues were very nominal in number, at the same time they were mostly attached to efficient and timely implementation of development projects. Indeed, the negotiation with IMF appeared as the first critical policy interaction to address the prevalent macro-economic issues (Syeduzzaman: 2004).

In the negotiation, Bangladesh provided measures and decisions already taken to correct financial imbalances but failed to convince the Fund delegation. The delegation in the face of Bangladesh's constant opposition based on national economic interest, pushed for currency devaluation. However, the discussion on devaluation remained deadlocked between the government of Bangladesh and the Fund until early 1974. The government was willing to take other measures such as improvements in budgetary and public sector performance, raising interest rates, restricting credit, taxing imports, and removing subsidies on food and agricultural inputs but was not willing to consider devaluation (Islam: 1991).

With further deterioration in the balance of payments in 1974, dialogue between Bangladesh and the Fund, at the request of other donors, resumed in July 1974 and the issue of devaluation further became prominent in the discussion. However, finally Bangladesh became amenable to the instructions of the Fund for devaluation. The Bangladesh negotiators raised different views on the magnitude of the devaluation, on the nature and extent of accompanying measures, and most emphatically on the timing. Indeed, in the fear of losing total assistance from donor communities Bangladesh undertook devaluation measures.

In retrospect, the issue of devaluation can be attributed to the donors' collective pressure and their strategic thinking. Devaluation was not a sufficient condition for an improvement in the balance of payments; moreover, a dialogue on determining the timing of devaluation was very much essential (Parkinson: 1981; Faaland: 1981).

Bangladesh's exposure to structural adjustment policies and beyond

Change in BWI policies and emergence of SAP

After World War II, between the 1950s and 1970s economics saw the dominance of Keynesian ideas and state intervention by an import-substitution industrialization strategy (ISI). ISI promoted some variety of welfare economics through maintaining or enhancing the level of economic activities, correcting market failures, and securing more equitable distribution of income

(Rahman: 1994; Hayami: 2003). While conversely, the rising deficit, inflation, and unemployment in industrialized countries beginning in the 1970s caused disillusionment with these policies and led to a search for new economic paradigms and policies popularly called as *structural adjustment* policies (Dasgupta: 1988; Holsen: 1991; Taylor: 1996). Stiglitz (2002) however, argued that the most dramatic change in the BWIs occurred in 1980s with the preaching of an open market economy strategy in both the USA and the UK by Ronald Reagan and Margaret Thatcher. The IMF and WB became the new missionary institutions, through which these ideas were pushed on the reluctant poor countries that often badly needed their loans and grants. The Ministries of Finance in poor countries were willing to become converts, if necessary, to obtain the funds. However the vast majority of government officials and, more to the point, the people of these countries often remained skeptical. The dramatic change brought the twins (IMF-WB) together while previously they had different distinct missions and eventually their activities became increasingly intertwined. In the 1980s, the Bank went beyond just lending for projects (like roads and dams) to providing broad-based support, in the form of structural adjustment loans. But it did only when the IMF gave its approval and with that approval the IMF imposed conditions on the countries. As the prime mandate of IMF was to look at the crises of a developing economy needing support, so the structural adjustment policies of the IMF became a permanent part of life in most of the developing world.

Structural adjustment policies had two objectives. Firstly, the receiving countries had to set their policies right, which meant adopting policies that conformed in essence to the economic paradigms of the BWIs. Secondly, appropriate lending modalities were required to permit fast disbursements to meet balance of payments and budgetary support was needed by the receiving countries (Rahman: 1994). The motivation behind IMF-WB structural adjustment policies was neoclassical economics and the belief that market forces were superior to state planning and/or intervention for resource allocation and output distribution. The IMF-WB relied on restrictive monetary and fiscal policies and currency devaluation to stabilize an economy in the sense of bringing internal and external equilibriums. As such policies could cause stagnation, stabilization measures were accompanied or followed by reform measures that aimed at removing controls and distortions in the factors and goods markets, strengthening external competitiveness, and mobilizing domestic resources to promote investment and growth (Hossain: 1996).

Bangladesh's engagement with the structural adjustment regime

In the beginning, Bangladesh was hesitant to approaching the BWIs for financial loans in fear of obvious policy conditionality linked to loans. However, subsequent socio-politico-economical reasons forced the country to live with, or experiment with, adjustment policies and structural adjustment efforts intermittently on a more or less continuous basis. In September 1974 the government approached the donors and the World Bank (as the coordinator of donors) for immediate external support. In response to Bangladesh's request the WB suggested Bangladesh to initiate dialogue with IMF for balance of payment support. In October 1974, at the request of Bangladesh government Bangladesh Aid Group was formed and the meeting was held in the same year in Paris (Syeduzzaman: 1991).[8]

The major initial policy conditionality was devaluation of currency, which had created huge uneasiness on the part of Bangladesh in the early 1970s. The other policy measures agreed upon were: liberalizing imports and reduction of the role of the Trading Corporation of Bangladesh (TCB), enhancing interest rates and limiting credit to the government, bringing economic efficiency into the SoEs, reviewing tax systems, incremental reduction of subsidies on food grains and agricultural inputs, cancellation of minimum prices of jute, and avoiding multiple currency practices.

In 1982 the economy was exposed to various vulnerabilities under the pretext of the crisis in the international economy following the second oil shock at the international level, and climatic difficulties at the local level. Prolonged drought caused a decline in food production while terms of trade deteriorated by around one third. Export earnings dropped by approximately 15%, oil import rate rose to nearly 70% of total export earnings, and the import of raw materials declined by around 20%. Further, deficit financing reached about 4% of GDP, inflation reached a level in excess of 16%, foreign exchange reserves reduced to about only two weeks of imports, and GDP growth was only 0.9%, resulting in a decline in per capita income. While every indicator of economy was at an alarming situation the IMF chose to terminate the Extended Finance Facility (EFF) which began in July 1980. Their action was based on the grounds of non-compliance with the policy reforms agreed upon. Thus, upon contemplating the economic crisis, the new government that emerged through a military coup opted for some reforms to show its compliance with IMF suggestions in order to get IMF support. The major reform agendas taken on a short-, medium- and long-term basis included reduction in the public investment program, measures to raise domestic resources through upward revision of public sector goods and utilities led by petroleum products, reduction of subsidies on the public food distribution system and agricultural inputs, adjustment of the exchange rate and expansion of credit to the private sector, and the expansion of distribution of agricultural inputs including agricultural credit. Under the second five-year plan the government initiated a New Industrial Policy (NIP) as part of the long-term measures. The major features of NIP were greater opportunities and credit facilities to the private sector, disinvestment of jute and textile mills, activation of export processing zones, and other measures to attract foreign private investment.

Since 1973 the World Bank International Development Association (IDA) had been providing assistance to Bangladesh through a number of Import Credit Programs (IPC) that more or less attached various conditions. In the mid-1980s, though there was no formal linkage, both the Fund and the Bank eventually came together to work on policy reforms through the Structural Adjustment Facility (SAF). Accordingly, aid was explicitly or implicitly made contingent upon reforms. Bangladesh was one of the first countries (among a total of 36) to resort to the SAF set up by the IMF in March 1986 to provide highly concessional but extremely conditional loans in support of bringing adjustments in the economic structure of developing economies. Bangladesh was also among the first movers (a total of 29) in making use of the Enhanced Structural Adjustment Facility (ESAF), which was launched by IMF in 1987. Later on, the economy of the country was guided by the conditionality and targets laid down in various Policy Framework Papers (PFPs), jointly written by the IMF-WB, with negligible input from Bangladesh (Bhattacharya: 1995).

In the SAF a tripartite new element, the PFP, emerged to work as the basis of cooperation between the IDA, the Fund, and the government. The PFP reflected medium-term development objectives and policy reforms with targets within a stable macroeconomic environment. There had been two strategic developments in SAF-PFP that contained a Priority Investment Program (PIP) and replaced the traditional Five Year Plan. The major policy reform agendas included: liberalization of the import and export systems, domestic resource mobilization, realistic public expenditure planning and improvement in project implementation, and beginning of a financial sector reform program.

The PFP, as the guiding principles of policy reforms, was supposed to incorporate the policy understanding of the loan-receiving countries in order to ensure country ownership but in effect it ignored the loan-receiving countries voice in the agenda. Though the Bank-Fund were eager to claim that it was the Government's own document, yet the Bank-Fund staff were very keen to draft it themselves (Syeduzzaman: 1991). Another finance minister, M. Saifur Rahman (1991, 286–89), echoed the same tenor:

> The IMF or the World Bank structural adjustment policy maker should have given more attention, to my mind, to the institutional reform policies rather than price rise policies. They are not much interested in institutional reforms. When it comes to institutional reforms suggested by them, it has been my experience that they do not see them through the end in the implementation stage. They insist in the earlier stages but give up when the implementation really begins … Structural adjustment in the agricultural sector in particular has been the most severe because of the abolition of subsidies on inputs e.g. fertilizer etc.

With the end of the cold war and apparent failure of SAFs across poor countries, a spectacular shift was noticed in the agenda of the international aid regime in the 1990s. In 1990 the World Development Report, the annual flagship publication of the Bank, drew special focus on poverty reduction while being adherent to reform measures. The IDA shifted its mandate to a 'broad-based framework for poverty reduction'. Poverty reduction became the overarching priority of IDA assistance and moreover, some new areas became prominent in the reform process such as social sector investment, private sector development, and environmental aspects of development, gender issues, and improving governance.

The impact of policy reforms under the structural adjustment on the poor in terms of employment was direct. It was obvious that the thrust of adjustment policy reforms in Bangladesh was mainly geared towards more privatization, more liberalization, and more austerity. The instant effect of privatization was a transfer of assets to the private sector but unfortunately the private sector could not work efficiently and it resulted in creating huge unemployment (Akash: 2004). Privatization of state owned enterprises (SOEs) resulted in large-scale retrenchments which contributed to enhancing poverty and the suffering of laborers. ILO mentioned that between 1995 and 1997 89,000 workers were retrenched (ILO: 1999).

On the other hand, trade liberalization also impacted employment in the industrial sector. The number of unemployed persons increased from 0.6 million in 1989 to 1.4 million in 1996. The increase in open unemployment occurred during the period when the process of import liberalization was accelerated. They reasoned that industrial restructuring to cope with import competition along with privatization of SOEs led to labor shedding in some large and medium enterprises in the manufacturing sector. Import liberalization also adversely affected the output growth of several large- and medium-scale industries that competed with imports (Bhattacharya and Titumir: 2001).

The other aspect of the reform measures was the incidence of the rise in inequality in wealth distribution and it was observed in both urban and rural settings. However, the incidence of inequality was higher in urban areas than rural areas (Ahmed: n.d.; Syeduzzaman: 2004; GoB: 2005). Inequality in the distribution of private per capita expenditures as measured by the Gini coefficient increased from 0.259 in 1991–92 to 0.306 in 2000. Most of the observed increase in inequality took place during the first half of the 1990s. Breaking down the national Gini coefficient by sector suggests that the increase in the national Gini was due not only to rising inequality within sectors, but also to rising inequality between the urban and rural sectors (Temple: 2002).

Muhammad (2006) observed a marked shift in the economy through the reforms that an agrarian economy transformed into a service sector-led economy ignoring the text book notion of the economic development path as the manufacturing sector failed to capture a dominant position in the economy. In the process he argued that shopping malls took over the mills that symbolized the collapse of the manufacturing sector. It is poignant to note that 'Bashundhara City', claimed to be one of the largest shopping malls in South Asia, emerged here while the largest jute mill 'Adamjee' closed down. During the last three decades the proportionate share of manufacturing in GDP marked little change. According to the old estimates of GDP, manufacturing was 7.90% in 1972–73; it increased to 8.47% in 2003, a less than 1%

increase in thirty years. According to the new estimates, the share of manufacturing in GDP was 15.43% in 1995/96; it decreased to 14.68% in 2000 and slightly increased to 15.97% in 2003. Thus when comparing the share of manufacturing from early 1980s with the figure in 2003, it shows a clear de-industrialization.

Muhammad (2007) also questioned the efficacy of the reform measures on poverty alleviation. Though poverty alleviation had always been the 'top objective' of successive governments in Bangladesh and global institutions, and foreign aided 'poverty alleviation' projects were in abundance, the poverty scenario had hardly changed then despite donor induced reforms and strategies. The size of population living under the income poverty line increased from 50 million in 1972 to 68 million in 2006, accompanied by steady inequality. The lowest 5% saw loss of decline of their share in national income (1.17% in 1983–84 came down to 0.67% in 2004) but the highest 5% experienced increase from 18.30% in 1983–84 to 30.66% in 2004. The poverty scenario and growing inequality could explain the reasons for rural–urban migration and the rise in number of slums in the country's major cities.

Beyond structural adjustment and the beginning of PRSP regime

Enjoined by the World Bank and IMF in 1999, as a condition to access foreign assistance provided in the form of concessional loans and grants from bilateral donors, Bangladesh with many other countries embarked on preparing a poverty reduction strategy paper (PRSP). Initially, Bangladesh chose to prepare an I-PRSP but finally it produced a full PRSP. The Bangladesh PRSP is titled as *Unlocking the Potential: National Strategy for Accelerated Poverty Reduction, 2005.* Although like many other different countries' PRSPs, Bangladesh's PRSP also drew serious criticisms from various sections of the people including civil society organizations, think tanks, and even ruling ministers for bypassing many issues and dwelling upon previous the Washington Consensus (Ahmad: 2005). However, the government claimed the PRSP was nationally developed without having conceded to aid conditions for access to concessional loans (GoB: 2005). PRSP in essence is the culmination of Bangladesh's longstanding development partnership with donors.

Conclusion

In the beginning Bangladesh rightly tried to go with the spirit and mood of independence to experiment its own way for development. However the devastation caused during the war and various other domestic issues compelled to opt for foreign loans and assistance. Unfolding the internal dynamics of Bangladesh's development process is instructive and relevant even after so many years. The limitations of consultations, dialogues, and participation continue to be a predominant deficit feature in Bangladesh's policy-making process. Although greater involvement of key actors is crucially needed to sustain development strategies and overcome pressures of donors, no sign of change is seen in that direction. There must be a consensus among the leadership, which evidently was missing over the previous decades. An analysis as to why successive governments have failed to carry out policy agendas autonomously may prove that neither rhetoric nor half-heartedness can work. How come that while the nation fought a repressive regime, it failed to practice democratic norms in setting its own development agenda. It was a complete failure of the successive ruling elite that neither the parliament nor political and administrative institutions were proactively engaged to contribute to setting the development agenda. Thus, the wreckage of war and lack of internal cohesion in thinking finally paved the path for foreign loans and assistance. Though initially it was a hesitant move, it finally became the dominant feature of Bangladesh's economic condition and all successive governments tried to become cronies of the international lenders or donors. This cronyism became so much so that according to Sobhan (2002b: 5):

> [T]his incapacity to restore sovereignty to Bangladesh's policymaking process has contributed to the erosion in the credibility and authority of the state. In the eyes of the public the state had some years ago surrendered its policymaking prerogative to the donors and was seen to be more accountable to the donors than it was to parliament or the voters. Today, as the influence of the donors has eroded the state is seen to have lost its moorings, remains directionless and has limited capacity to deliver either on its own commitments to the electorate or to honour its obligations to its external partners. Such a rudderless state is progressively delegitimising itself in the eyes of its citizens, who mostly see the machinery of the state as part of the problem rather than the solution to their daily concerns.

This leaves one with the impression that the ruling elite of Bangladesh considers the role of development agenda setting as their political prerogative and do not feel obliged to be accountable to the people through political institutions, particularly parliament. The political culture of unaccountability eventually has made the successive regimes vulnerable to the pressures and policy conditionality of the donors and Bangladesh's engagement with donors' policy prescriptions has continued to be pervasive. There have been changes in regimes and also apparent differences in ideologies among them. Yet irrespective of regimes, donors have successfully emerged to continue their influence on Bangladesh's economic development.

Notes

1 Professors Nurul Islam, M. Anisur Rahman, Mosharraf Hossain and Rehman Sobhan served on the Planning Commission as the founding members. While the

Prime Minister headed the Commission as Chairman, Professor Nurul Islam was the Deputy Chairman with the status of a Minister.

2 Now it is argued that the dismantling of elitism in bureaucracy as a populist response has been extremely counterproductive. Due to this reckless attempt, since independence the Bangladesh civil service has encountered extreme adverse situations at times and failed to contribute to national development effectively. The situation was further aggravated by military coups taking place at various times as they considered the bureaucracy the only threat to their self-interest seeking policies. While the experience of the economic development in East Asian countries enlightens us regarding the crucial bureaucratic contribution to economic development and leadership, Bangladesh bureaucracy truly was not given the opportunity to prove its excellence.

3 The vice chairman was accorded with the status of a cabinet minister while the members were equivalent to the rank of state minister(s).

4 Professor Muhammad Anisur Rahman was one of the members of the first Planning Commission who joined the Commission in early 1972 and, having been frustrated over the role and contribution of the Commission, left the Commission in 1973.

5 Shortly, after the departure of the vice-chairman from the Commission the country witnessed a very traumatic shift in the polity that murdered the founding leaders of the country with their family members and subsequently the constitutional commitment to planned economy was abandoned and the role of the Commission and the status of the members was formally relegated. However, the vice chairman, Professor Nurul Islam did not come back to his earlier position and preferred to stay abroad.

6 Even 20 years after the appointment of first country representative, Michael Wiehen, then in-charge of the Bangladesh Division at the Bank could not hide his dissatisfaction over the appointment. In a communication, April 12, 2002, with Prof. Nurul Islam – the then Deputy Chairman of Planning Commission wrote "You *(Prof. Islam – addition is mine)* made it quite clear that you would accept (!) only one person – Just Faaland. Faaland is/was (?) a very competent economist, but he knew little about the Bank, and making him the Bank's ResRep had high risk attached to it. I took your choice to Cargill and RSM and against my better judgement supported it. The rest is history. But my unhappiness with your choice of ResRep did not for one moment influence my professional judgement about Bangladesh, or my total commitment to doing the best possible for your country. And that is how most of my colleagues acted." The original letter is incorporated in Islam: 2003: 287–88.

7 Verbatim records of the conference, Planning Commission and the World Bank's Local offices, Dhaka: 1973 and quoted in Islam: 2003, 258.

8 For a detailed picture see Syeduzzaman: 2004.

References

Ahmad, Qazi Kholiquzzaman. "Poverty Reduction Strategy Paper: Repackaging Old Medicine" in *Journal of Bangladesh Economic Association*: pp. 111–118. Bangladesh Economic Association: Dhaka: 2005.

Ahmad, Salma. "Major Administrative Reforms in Bangladesh: A Historical Perspective" in Bayes, Abdul and Muhammad, Anu [eds] *Bangladesh at 25:An Analytical Discourse in Development*, pp. 283–304. UPL: Dhaka: 1998.

Ahmed, Moudud. *Bangladesh: Era of Sheikh Mujibur Rahman*. UPL: Dhaka: 1991.

Ahmed, Sadiq. "The Political Economy of Development Experience in Bangladesh" presented in the Seminar on Accelerating Growth and Poverty Reduction in

Bangladesh jointly organized by the World Bank and the Bureau of Economic Research, University of Dhaka: n.d..

Akash, M.M. "Aid and Poverty" in *Revisiting Foreign Aid: A Review of Bangladesh's Development 2003*, CPD and UPL: Dhaka: 2004.

Alamgir, Muhiuddin Khan. *Development Strategy for Bangladesh*. National Institute of Local Government: Dhaka: 1986.

Bhattacharya, Debapriya. "Bangladesh's Experience with the Structural Adjustment and Enhanced Structural Adjustment Facilities" in Grieve, Roy H. and Huq, Mozammel [eds.], *Bangladesh Strategies for Development*, UPL: Dhaka: 1995.

Bhattacharya, Debapriya and Titumir, Rashed A.M. *Bangladesh Experience with Structural Adjustment: Learning from a Participatory Exercise*. CPD: Dhaka: 2001

Dasgupta, Biplab. *Structural Adjustment, Global Trade and the New Political Economy of Development*. Vistaar Publications: New Delhi: 1988.

Faaland, Just and Parkinson, J.R. *Bangladesh: The Test Case for Development*. C. Hurst & Company: London and UPL: Dhaka: 1976.

Faaland, Just. "The Debt Liability of Pakistan" in Faaland, Just (ed.). *Aid and Influence: The Case of Bangladesh*. Chr. Michelsen Institute: Bergen: 1981.

Government of Bangladesh (GoB). *The First Five-Year Plan 1973–78*. Planning Commission, Dhaka: 1973.

Government of Bangladesh (GoB). *Unlocking the Potential: National Strategy for Accelerated Poverty Reduction*, General Economics Division, Planning Commission, Dhaka: 2005.

Hayami, Yujiro. "From the Washington Consensus to the Post-Washington Consensus: Retrospect and Prospect", *Asian Development Review*, Vol. 20, No. 2, pp. 40–65: 2003.

Holsen, John A. "An Overview of Structural Adjustment" in Sobhan, Rehman (ed.) *Structural Adjustment Policies in the Third World: Design and Experience*. UPL: Dhaka: 1991.

Hossain, Akhtar. *Macroeconomic Issues and Polices: The Case of Bangladesh*. Sage Publications India Pvt. Ltd: 1996.

ILO. *Retraining and Redeployment of Workers affected by Privatisation in Bangladesh*, Draft report, May 1999.

Islam, Nurul. "Economic Policy Reforms and the IMF: Bangladesh Experience in the Early 1970s" in Sobhan, Rehman (ed.) *Structural Adjustment Policies in the Third World: Design and Experience*. UPL: Dhaka: 1991.

Islam, Nurul. *Development Planning in Bangladesh: A Study in Political Economy*. UPL: Dhaka: 1993.

Islam, Nurul. *Making of a Nation Bangladesh: An Economist's Tale*. UPL: Dhaka: 2003.

Khan, Zillur R. *The Third World Charismat: Sheikh Mujib and the Struggle for Freedom*. UPL: Dhaka: 1996.

Maniruzzaman, Talukder. *The Bangladesh Revolution and Its Aftermath*. UPL: Dhaka: 1988.

Maniruzzaman, Talukder. *Radical Politics and the Emergence of Bangladesh*. Mowla Brothers: Dhaka: 2003.

Muhammad, Anu. "Actors, Victims and Rhetoric: A Deconstruction of 'Development' Exercises" in Bayes, Abdul and Muhammad, Anu (eds). *Bangladesh at 25: An Analytical Discourse on Development*. UPL: Dhaka: 1998.

Muhammad, Anu. "Development Strategy and Problems of Democratisation in a Peripheral Country: The Bangladesh Experience", in *Radical Notes*: 2007 [Available at https://web.archive.org/web/20101224084531/http://radicalnotes.com/content/view/25/39/; last accessed on 12 December 2017].

Muhammad, Anu. "Globalisation and Economic Transformation in a Peripheral Economy", *Economic and Political Weekly*, Vol. *41*, No. 15, 15–21 April. Mumbai, 2006.

Parkinson, Jack. "The Role of the World Bank" in Faaland, Just (ed.) *Aid and Influence: The Case of Bangladesh*. Chr. Michelsen Institute: Bergen: 1981.

Rahman, Anisur. *The Lost Moment: Dreams with a Nation Born through Fire*. UPL: Dhaka: 1993.

Rahman, Aminur. *Politics and National Formation in Bangladesh*. UPL: Dhaka: 1997.

Rahman, Masihur. *Structural Adjustment, Employment and Workers: Public Policy Issues and Choices for Bangladesh*. UPL: Dhaka: 1994.

Rahman, Md. Anisur. *Bangladesh '72–'75:Four intense years of struggle for development* (n.d.) [Available at: https://www.scribd.com/document/284676935/2005-Bangladesh-72-75-Four-Intense-Years-of-Struggle-for-Development; last accessed on 10 December 2017].

Rahman, Saifur. "Structural Adjustment Policies" in Sobhan, Rehman (ed.) *Structural Adjustment Policies in the Third World: Design and Experience*. UPL: Dhaka: 1991

Sobhan, Rehman. *The Crisis of External Dependence: The Political Economy of Foreign Aid to Bangladesh*. UPL: Dhaka: 1982.

Sobhan, Rehman. "Policy Independence and Political Accountability", Centre for Policy Dialogue, Dhaka: 2002a.

Sobhan, Rehman. "The Political Economy of the State and Market in Bangladesh", Centre for Policy Dialogue, Dhaka: 2002b.

Stiglitz, Joseph E. "Participation and Development: Perspectives from the Comprehensive Development Paradigm" in *Review of Development Economics*, Vol. 6, No. 2, pp. 163–182: 2002.

Syeduzzaman, M. "Aid and Policy Reforms in Bangladesh" in *Revisiting Foreign Aid: A Review of Bangladesh's Development 2003*, pp. 295–350. CPD and UPL: Dhaka: 2004.

Syeduzzaman, M. "Bangladesh's Experience with Adjustment Policies" in Sobhan, Rehman (ed.) *Structural Adjustment Policies in the Third World: Design and Experience*. UPL: Dhaka: 1991.

Taylor, Lance. "Finis to Laissez-Faire?" in Abdullah, Abu and Khan, Azizur Rahman (eds) *State, Market and Development: Essays in Honour of Rehman Sobhan*, pp. 65–87. UPL: Dhaka: 1996.

Temple, Frederick T. "Growth and Poverty Reduction in Bangladesh" Lecture presented in National Defence College, Dhaka, 27 May 2002.

4 Whose agenda is it anyway?

Bangladesh's policy ownership in the PRSP regime

Introduction

Bangladesh expressed commitment to prepare a poverty reduction strategy paper (PRSP) in the 2000 Bangladesh Development Forum (BDF)[1] meeting. The first meeting in this connection was held on 16 November 2000 under the leadership of the then Finance Minister Mr. Shah M. S. Kibria. The government decided to develop a PRSP drawing on the principles of a Comprehensive Development Framework (CDF) espoused by the former World Bank chief James Wolfensohn and Sector Wide Approach (SWAp) (Deb, Raihan and Ahmed: 2004: 74; Khan: 2005). Initially the government opted for an interim PRSP (I-PRSP) and finalized it by the end of 2003 entitled *Bangladesh: A National Strategy for Economic Growth, Poverty Reduction and Social Development*. The Economic Relations Division (ERD) of the Finance Ministry under the leadership of the Secretary coordinated I-PRSP preparation activities. By the end of 2005 the government prepared a full PRSP: *Unlocking the Potential: National Strategy for Accelerated Poverty Reduction, 2005* (GoB, 2005). In the preparation of the full PRSP the coordination role was shifted to the Planning Commission from the ERD. The preparatory activities for a full blown PRSP in Bangladesh was organized by National Poverty Focal Point (NPFP) in the General Economics Division of the Planning Commission and under the leadership of a National Steering Committee (NSC) headed by the Principal Secretary to the Prime Minister.

The primary goal of this chapter is to delve into the quality of national ownership in Bangladesh's PRSP as a development agenda. The chapter is split into two parts. The first part attempts to present an overview of Bangladesh's PRSP: targets, goals, key issues in building strategies, monitoring and evaluation features, Joint Staff Advisory Note, etc. The section, in order to unfold the progress of PRSP in Bangladesh, also highlights some key points of I-PRSP. It also presents the institutional provisions for PRSP preparation with particular focus on the participatory consultations in PRSP formulation to qualify national ownership as envisaged in the document. In essence, the first part reviews the official position in PRSP formulation. The second part analyzes the real scenario of ownership by examining various key issues. This part of the chapter aims particularly to assess the quality of engagement of various key actors in the process which should indicate the reality of national ownership.

1: Bangladesh's policy ownership and independence in PRSP: presenting the official point of view

Bangladesh PRSP: an overview[2]

From I-PRSP to PRSP

As mentioned earlier, Bangladesh first prepared an I-PRSP in 2003 which narrated five anti-poverty strategies. These were (1) ***pro-poor economic growth*** for increasing income and employment of the poor; (2) fostering ***human development*** of the poor for raising their capability through education, health, nutrition, employment-related skill training and social interventions; (3) supporting ***women's advancement and closing gender gaps*** in development; (4) providing ***social protection*** to the poor against anticipated and unanticipated income/consumption shocks and vulnerabilities to disasters through targeted and other efforts; (5) influencing ***participatory governance***, enhancing the ***voice*** of the poor and improving ***non-material dimensions*** of well-being including security, power, and social inclusion (GoB, 2002). The I-PRSP identified three challenges Bangladesh would face in the next decade to overcome poverty and realize MDGs and they included: *first* – the consolidation of the past successes occurred in 1990s that include improvements in child nutrition, expansion in primary and secondary education, reduction of gender inequality in education, decrease in chronic food shortage and insecurity, enhanced capacity for disaster management, and declining trends in income poverty; *second* – combating the negative tendencies unfolded over the past decade and they were law and order problems, deteriorating investment climate, economic mismanagement such as continual system loss and avoidable leakages, policy inconsistency and lack of coordination among the development agencies, poor quality of education, health, and public services, polarized politics, etc.; and *third* – risks and uncertainties stemming from a changing global economic environment specially in areas of trade, aid, and investment, new tensions in the wake of MFA (Multi Fiber Agreement) withdrawal, growing urbanization, deteriorating environment, new public health concerns, and security threats, etc. The I-PRSP again argued

> sustaining the past positive trends over the next decade while overcoming the accumulated negative trends and facing up to the new agenda posed by globalization would be the central task of the poverty reduction strategy. This task would dictate new ways of managing the development process, demanding a new mix of poverty reduction strategies and policy

> priorities, and inviting a new ensemble of change agents both within and outside the government. This would require taking initiatives on all fronts.
> (GoB: 2002, 27)

The reason behind preparing a PRSP from the I-PRSP was attributed to scanty opportunities for consultation and thematic review, and some strategic gaps in the I-PRSP as identified in the post preparation review and in Joint Staff Assessment (JSA) by the World Bank and IMF (GoB: 2005; IDA and IMF: 2003). The major gaps identified were: environment–poverty interface, strategy for water resources management, quality improvement in education, mainstreaming gender issues in agriculture, rural development and labor market, private sector development, medium-term plan for trade policy reforms, financial sector reforms, policies and institutions for rural non-farm activities, and medium-term framework on sectoral policy priorities.

PRSP: vision and targets

The vision set out in Bangladesh's PRSP is to substantially reduce poverty within the next generation. In realizing the vision it draws strength from the constitutional obligation of developing and sustaining a society where people enjoy their basic needs, can prosper in freedom, and cherish the ideals and values of a free society. In realizing the vision it made two overarching independent strategic goals: poverty reduction with special focus on the removal of chronic poverty and hunger, and social development with particular emphasis on gender equality. The vision is said to have proposed a comprehensive approach premised on the rights-based framework.

Box 4.1 PRSP goals to be realized by 2015

Remove poverty by eradicating hunger, chronic food-insecurity, and extreme destitution;

Reduce the proportion of people living below the poverty line by 50 per cent;

Attain universal primary education for all girls and boys of primary school age;

Eliminate gender disparity in primary and secondary education;

Reduce infant and under-five mortality rates by 65 per cent, and eliminate gender disparity in child mortality;

Reduce the proportion of malnourished children under five by 50 per cent and eliminate gender disparity in child malnutrition;

Reduce maternal mortality rate by 75 per cent;

Ensure access of reproductive health services to all;

Reduce substantially, if not eliminate totally, social violence against the poor and the disadvantaged groups, especially violence against women and children; and ensure comprehensive disaster risk management, environmental sustainability and mainstreaming of these concerns into national development process.

Source: GoB: 2005, 189

The road map for poverty reduction described in the PRSP (Box 4.1) rested on a policy triangle of: *pro-poor economic growth, human development*, and *governance*. The PRSP argued that on the poverty front there had been many successes in the last decade. Bangladesh managed to register a considerable success in income-poverty reduction since independence. The Household Income and Expenditure Survey (HIES) data suggested that there had been an around 10% decline in national poverty incidence between 1991/92 and 2000 from 58.8% to 49.8%. Thus, it was an indication of a 1 percentage point reduction per year. In the same period while the progress in terms of head-count index of poverty was better in urban areas, the rural areas showed progress in the declining depth and severity of poverty. The progress in human poverty was faster than income poverty in the same period. The human poverty index (based on deprivations in health, education, and nutrition) dropped from 61% in the early 1980s to 35% in late 1990s (1998/2000). In the areas of infant mortality, under-five child mortality, gender dimension in mortality, and nutritional status and enrolment in primary schools all witnessed a significant improvement. Infant mortality rate (IMR) declined from 94 deaths per 1000 live births in the 1990s to 53 in 2002. In 2002 the under-five mortality rate stood at 76 per 1000 live births after having declined from 108. The gross primary enrolment rate increased from 75.6% in 1991 to 105.7% in 2002. Achievements were also registered in the case of reducing child malnutrition and those were expressed through the drops in the rate of stunted children in the age group of 6–71 months (from 69% in 1985/86 to 49% in 2000), the proportion of underweight children of the same age-group (from 72% in 1985/86 to 51% in 2000), the rate of stunted children for the age group of 0–59 months (from 55% to 45% during 1996–2000) and that for underweight of the same group (from 56% to 48% during the same period). However, despite successes aggregate poverty continues to be pervasive with pockets of extreme poverty and growth inequality rising, thus becoming a major issue of concern. Moreover, it is argued in the PRSP that poverty is a pervasive issue that has many faces. It is about income level, about food security and quality of life. It is also about human resource capacities, vulnerabilities and coping, and human security. It has also a gender dimension (GoB, 2005). Thus, while the PRSP focuses on the robustness of the growth process, it includes policy goals, which would enhance the opportunities for the poor to be the participants. The PRSP summarizes that the strategic agenda around which the pro-poor growth challenge crystallizes most potently is the theme of employment. This is characterized as gainful employment for men and women sought in productivity enhancing and diversifying agriculture including critical sub-sectors such as fisheries, poultry, and dairy as well as through effectively reaping the potentials of the agro-processing, rural and urban services, ICT, manufacturing including ready-made garments, and overseas employment sectors (GoB, 2005).

As mentioned, the second element of the policy triangle is education. Over the past one and a half decades, Bangladesh progressed well through an obsession regarding enrolment. The success was translated through ensuring Bangladesh's entry to UNDP's medium human development league. The response was not only on the supply side but also on the demand side, while the poor families valued education and gave high priority to basic education for their children, boys and girls alike. However, despite achievements in enrolments, the issue of quality became the major challenge for the future. A paradigm shift towards a preoccupation with quality was needed.

The heath frontier, similar to education, witnessed significant progress on various access indicators but issues of quality and the burden of health-care expenditure emerged as the new strategic concerns. The PRSP argued that there had been successes in building awareness related to diarrhea diseases and breaking the cycles of secondary huge death tolls that usually followed natural disasters, developing infrastructure, and bringing about attitudinal change. However, there was another area where palpable successes were not noticed and that was maternal health. The PRSP advocated for a determined strategic push to realize the goal on maternal health without which the overall health sector gain would remain limited and vulnerable.

With governance being the third element in the triangle the PRSP argued that the good governance issue was critical to an effective growth and poverty reduction strategy. This was due to its pertinence to better articulation of priorities, creation of an enabling environment for public and private action, and optimum use of resources and distribution of benefits. Governance includes a number of issues such as checks and balances among various organs of the government, legitimacy and authority of state institutions, rules and norms that determine who holds power and exercises of this power, relationships of accountability among state functionaries and between these functionaries and citizens, the capacity of government to make policy, manage administrative and fiscal affairs of the state, and deliver goods and services, and the opportunities and efficacy of redress available to citizens. For Bangladesh two major agendas concerning governance that interfaced with poverty reduction were said to have emerged in the consultations carried out to underpin the analytical approach in the PRSP and they were local governance and criminal justice.

The importance of local governance was mentioned in a way that it was central to establishing local level accountability, decentralized service delivery, and the newer focus on regeneration of local economies through partnerships of government organizations, CBOs, NGOs, private sector, and local government organizations. On the other hand, the critical role of criminal justice was pointed out in relation to human security.

Thus, the policy triangle laid out in the PRSP set the medium-term strategic agenda for Bangladesh for the goal of accelerated poverty reduction on the following eight points: *employment, nutrition, quality education* (particularly in primary, secondary and vocational levels with strong emphasis on the education of girl's), *local governance, maternal health, sanitation and safe water, criminal justice*, and *monitoring.*

Bangladesh's PRSP identified eight specific avenues to define the poverty reduction strategy. They were divided into two groups: *four strategic blocks* and *four supporting strategies.* The strategic blocks were: (1) macroeconomic environment for pro-poor economic growth, (2) critical sectors for pro-poor economic growth, (3) effective social safety nets and targeted programs, and (4) human development, while the supporting strategies were (1) ensuring participation, social inclusion, and empowerment, (2) promoting good governance, (3) service delivery, and (4) caring for the environment and sustainable development (GoB, 2005).

Key issues in building strategies in PRSP

The PRSP stated that poverty is pervasive and prioritization of issues is required for a stronger engagement that is coupled with the political viability of policy. With that understanding it narrated some key issues required for construction of a road map for accelerated poverty reduction. They were (i) building on past achievements, (ii) preventing slippages, (iii) addressing implementation, (iv) bringing employment and the meso-economy to center stage, (v) strengthening the focus on women's rights and advancement, (vi) up-scaling micro credit, (vii) bringing the policy process into focus, (viii) making governance work for the poor, (ix) bench-marking for monitoring progress, (x) quality education, (xi) child rights issues, (xii) capturing 'spatiality' in the planning process, (xiii) land administration reform and land use policy, (xiv) urban poverty, (xv) critical infrastructure, (xvi) technology, and (xvii) risk, vulnerability, and social protection (GoB: 2005).

Monitoring and evaluation (M & E)

The World Bank made result orientation of a PRSP, as one of the major principles and Bangladesh's PRSP, as well, expressed monitoring as a cardinal point making it one of eight strategic agendas. The PRSP stated "an energised strategy for accelerated poverty reduction cannot but be result-oriented" (GoB: 2005, 48). Monitoring in the PRSP was linked to implementation, accountability, results-orientation, and progress assessment and thus focused on both the process and outcomes. It consisted of continuous assessment of the flow of inputs and policy changes for fulfillment of specific objectives and the appropriate utilization of inputs to achieve target outputs.

JSA comments[3] on Bangladesh's PRSP

The Joint Staff Assessment (JSA) in the form of a Joint Staff Advisory Note (JSAN) on the PRSP was issued in December 2005, two months after the final approval of the PRSP in the meeting of the Executive Committee of the National Economic Council (ECNEC) with the leadership of the Prime Minister. While the staff of both the World Bank and the IMF prepared the report, Steven Dunaway and Anthony Boote (IMF) and Praful C. Patel (IDA) on behalf of their respective organizations approved the note. The note was split into several sections. Given the massive incidence of poverty, the note acknowledged the broad definition of poverty. This definition involved deprivations in income, food security, quality of life, and vulnerability. The note also acknowledged the intention to address these issues through a strategically prioritized policy framework building pro-poor growth, human development, and governance as its main pillars. It was recognized that the PRSP could be an important step towards the achievement of MDG targets for Bangladesh by the year 2015. But the note commented that poverty diagnostic analysis lacked specific policy directions.

The note maintained that the medium-term macroeconomic framework was broadly under a high growth scenario and sustained high growth would be necessary to meet the MDG for poverty reduction. Terming the growth projection ambitious, it pointed out that a steadfast implementation of reform policies presented in the document would be needed, together with favorable economic conditions to achieve the growth. Keeping the challenges of realizing higher growth in consideration, the World Bank and the IMF staff recommended inclusion of two growth scenarios in future projection in the PRSP. These scenarios were a baseline scenario reflecting progress toward agreed objectives in line with past experience, and a more ambitious high-growth scenario. The note was highly appreciative of the government's commitment to maintain macroeconomic stability and support the thrust of macroeconomic policies. But it maintained implementation of policies including financing social expenditures targeted for poverty reduction would critically depend on the effective initiatives to improve revenue collection and to eliminate quasi-fiscal losses in the public sector enterprises. Implementation of the revenue administration measures identified in the NSAPR was highly recommended. The focus on a monetary policy geared toward price stability and the commitment to market-based instruments were also appreciated. The note advocated for further improving the functioning of the foreign exchange market and allowing the exchange rate to move continually in response to the changes in economic fundamentals.

The note questioned that the projected accelerated growth was not justified, especially when investment in physical and human capital was likely to be affected and policy reforms were not underpinned. Thus it was unlikely to have a higher growth scenario implemented. The World Bank and the IMF staff in the note welcomed the emphasis on prioritization in project selection to ensure that there was no case of under-funding leading to delayed implementation. In this regard, it viewed that the government's commitment to align the NSAPR to a medium-term budgetary framework (MTBF) is a step in the right direction. The new system under the MTBF encouraged allocation of resources for programs integrating recurrent and capital spending and medium-term expenditure plans in line with the PRSP priorities, which assured greater funding certainty to priority projects.

The note observed that the NSAPR focused less on the role of trade policy to project the need for ensuring globally competitive industrialization based on the country's comparative advantages. The joint note mentioned the lack of a future course to be taken to improving Bangladesh's export competitiveness and diversification. There was also no indication in the NSAPR of the future course to be taken in reforming the highly protective trade regime. Non-discriminatory trade liberalization polices in the future PRS medium-term trade reform strategy were recommended. The note opined that the post MFA challenges concerning the RMG sector were scantily discussed in the NSAPR. The note took the position that though speedy implementation of Nationalized Commercial Banks (NCB) reforms were recognized but it did not provide the government's own roadmap for financial sector reforms and thus it recommended that future PRS incorporate banking sector and capital market reform agendas.

Finally, the report (IMF: 2006, 11) said "on balance the staffs of the World Bank and the IMF believe that the poverty reduction strategy outlined in the NSAPR is comprehensive and contains critical policy actions that, over time, could help foster accelerated growth and poverty reduction. In particular, the poverty diagnostics contained in the NSAPR are of high quality as they come to grips with the multi-dimensional nature of poverty, recognizing both income and human dimensions, in making judgments on poverty trends and prospects".

Institutional framework for Bangladesh's PRSP preparation

Bangladesh government made special institutional provisions to create a full-blown PRSP. While the Economic Relations Division (ERD) of the Ministry of Finance prepared the I-PRSP, the main task of preparing the PRSP was bestowed upon the General Economics Division (GED) of the Planning Commission. The government designated the GED as the National Poverty Focal Point (NPFP) in July 2003 (Ahmed: 2004). Moreover, a high-powered committee entitled the National Steering Committee (NSC) was to guide and monitor the activities of the PRSP preparation. The NSC was formed on 18 September 2003[4] with the principal secretary to the Prime Minister as chair and the Member, General Economics Division (GED) as member secretary. In the beginning it had 17 members but later it was expanded to 22.[5] Secretaries of various ministries and divisions served as members on the committee.

In order to provide technical support to various ministries and the NPFP, the NPFP proposed constituting various sectoral thematic groups and finally formed 12 thematic groups (TGs) (Box 4.2) and in the fifth meeting of NSC they were reconstituted. Bangladesh Institute of Development Studies (BIDS) was formally awarded the consultancy to technically contribute to the preparation of the PRSP. In the sixth meeting of the NSC it was decided to recruit two full-time consultants[6] to work with NPFP and also to hire an international consultant under a TA (Technical Assistance) project of ADB.[7]

Box 4.2 Terms of References of thematic groups

Thematic Groups (TGs) would be formed comprising of the government sector, private sector, civil society and NGOs.

Each TG would prepare its own plan of action particularly in light of the description of the expected output given by the NSC.

The Plan of Action would contain, among others, the scope of work, the responsibilities of the relevant Ministry/Agency, the frequency, stages, and the spatial level of consultation, and the time frame for completion of the work.

Based on the scope of work, each TG would identify the need for consultancy services and arrange for securing those services.

The time frame for completing the task of the TGs would follow the roadmap adopted by the Steering Committee.

Issues relating to interfacing between the TGs, between the TGs and the NSC, and between the TGs and the NPFP would be addressed, as far as practicable, in accordance with the description provided by the NSC.

Each TG would decide/arrange to have, in consultation with the NPFP, a pre-determined time-slot to report back to the Steering Committee.

Source: Ahmed: 2004

Participatory consultation in PRSP formulation

Chapter III of NSAPR was dedicated to presenting the ownership aspect of Bangladesh's PRSP. The chapter dealt with the approach and methods, structure and process of participatory consultation, thematic groups, and consultation on the draft PRSP. However, it argued that the commitment of the government was critical to make the participatory consultation a key element in the preparation process to make PRSP country driven and nationally owned.

Approach and methods

In the beginning of that chapter it described the approach and method followed in the process of preparing the full-blown PRSP in Bangladesh. While it was claimed in the PRSP process that it opened up new spaces for dialogue on public policies, it followed an inclusive approach to cover all stakeholders. Members of the civil society and parliament members were claimed to have been covered. It further claimed that special attention was given to involve the women, children, the weak, and vulnerable groups in the consultation process. The PRSP building process did not follow a fully open-ended method in the consultations, rather it followed a combination of structured and open-ended methods. During the consultations two imperatives were considered: (1) ensuring participants' informed, active, and committed participation in discussions, and (2) ensuring an encouraging ambiance for participatory discussions.

However, in order to ensure a participatory approach in the process various methods of participatory consultation were adopted. They included: consultations with members of the parliament, participatory consultation meetings at national and regional levels, face to face consultations with the poor, interfacing with development partners[8] for their feedback and forming twelve thematic groups involving line ministries.

Structure and process of participatory consultation

As mentioned above, consultations were held at different levels, national and regional, and with different stakeholders. The national consultation and the regional consultations were held during March and April of 2004. The national consultation was held in Dhaka and the regional consultations in the divisional headquarters.

National level discussion

The National Poverty Focal Point (NPFP) in the General Economics Division of the Planning Commission selected the participants for what it claimed would make the consultation participatory. The stakeholders included a wide range of experts, subject-matter specialists, members of the civil society, ethnic minorities, IT experts, and physically disadvantaged people. Participants represented the issues such as environment, governance, health, education, agriculture, etc. Representatives of various professional organizations were invited as were representatives of the poor.

In the consultation there were thirteen topics set for discussion and the participants were also distributed into thirteen groups. The issues taken for discussion were:

- Macroeconomic stability and pro-poor growth, financial sector reform (banking, trade, and globalization) and domestic resource mobilization;
- Private sector development;
- Communication (road, rail, inland water transport, information and communication technology, and telecommunication), electricity, energy and power sector development;

- Governance (reform in civil services, judiciary, law and order, and strengthening of local government);
- Health and nutrition;
- Development of women and children and establishing their rights;
- Education;
- Rural development (including food security, disaster management, social safety nets, expansion of micro-credit and rural non-farm activities, employment, and development of growth centers);
- Agriculture (crops, fisheries, livestock, horticulture, and agro and biotechnology) development;
- Protection and development of the environment;
- Water resource management;
- Adivasi/ethnic minorities and physically, mentally, and socially disadvantaged people; and
- Housing.

The discussion was also divided into two sessions. The first session was common and dedicated to discussing various facets of poverty (causes, nature, and depth), as well as recommending strategies to achieve pro-poor economic growth. The second session was devoted to topic-based or sector-based discussion. The major steps in discussion covered in the second session were: (a) setting spectral targets to reduce poverty; (b) suggesting strategies to achieve those targets; (c) identifying actions or programs needed to implement those strategies; and (d) indicating appropriate design and implementation mechanisms to accompany those actions or programs so as to achieve optimum benefits for the poor.

During the group discussions there was a special emphasis on issues such as pro-poor growth, gender equity, sectoral good governance, the rural–urban nexus, and special problems of different socio-economic groups, sustainable development, and balanced regional development. After the group discussions, the groups presented their reports in the plenary session which was followed by open floor participation.

Regional consultations

Six regional consultations were held in six divisional headquarters of the country under the joint leadership of the National Poverty Focal Point (NPFP) and the office of the Divisional Commissioners. The consultations, like the national consultation, were said to have been representative as members of the civil society, specialists, academics, local government functionaries, journalists, professionals, poor people, ethnic minorities, etc. More or less, each consultation drew 200 participants and they were divided in 12 groups. Each group discussed a topic that was given to them. The meetings were split into three sessions: (i) the first session was general in nature focusing on the broad spectrum of poverty; (ii) the second session discussed detailed on the given topic, and finally (iii) floor participation where the participants enjoyed free discussion on any issue they wanted.

Before the regional consultations there was a meeting of the divisional commissioners with the NPFP and the chair of the National Steering Committee. While the meeting provided the commissioners guidelines of selection of participants for discussions, outline of regional level consultation meetings spelling out the structure, features, composition of discussion groups, and allocation of time for different sessions, general guidelines for effective participation and recording of output was developed by the NPFP and endorsed by the NSC. Members of the NSC, secretaries to the government, and other higher officials including the Minister for Finance and Planning were said to have participated in the consultation programs and bolstered the enthusiasm of the participants. NPFP officials participated in the regional level consultations and stayed throughout the discussion but did not take part in discussion. Moreover, every group had a moderator for smooth running of the discussion.

Face to face with the poor

It was said that the policy planners sat with small but uniform groups of the poor and the vulnerable people in dialogues to share as to what they were thinking about their situations. Ten such groups comprising garment workers, housemaids, potters, snake charmers, fishermen, cobblers, sweepers, tea garden workers, industrial workers, and adivashis/ethnic minorities were consulted. The PRSP claimed that the consultations added a new dimension to the participatory process brining the poor directly into the PRS consultation and preparation process.

Interfacing with development partners

It seemed that there were strong contacts with the international lenders or in the words of the government, development partners. There were two formal sittings with the Local Consultative Group (LCG)[9] and the LCG members were briefed about the preparation process. The LCG members also exchanged views with NPFP and NSC members and many from the NPFP took part in meetings organized by LCG sub-groups. The PRSP claimed that apart from formal sittings there were numerous informal discussions between the NPFP members and LCG members.

2: Bangladesh's policy ownership and independence in PRSP: a reality check of actors, process, and influence

Policy ownership refers to full engagement of national actors in the entire process of policy formulation and implementation. It necessarily implies that the need for development must occur in the mind of key national actors. In other words, it can be said that development goals have to be the felt need of the country. Though the government becomes the key stakeholder in leading the process, the role and contribution of people's organizations such as trade unions and other professional organizations, civil society organizations (CSOs), political parties, bureaucracies, and key political institutions particularly the parliament are essentially important. Indeed, the contribution and participation of various stakeholders in policy process qualify national ownership of a development strategy.

Bangladesh traditionally prepared a Five-Year Plan (FYP) for national development. But in 2000 the ruling government abandoned the traditional FYP and decided to prepare a Poverty Reduction Strategy Paper (PRSP) in response to the World Bank and IMF recommendation. Bangladesh's PRSP titled as *Unlocking the Potentials: National Strategy for Accelerated Poverty Reduction* (NSAPR) was the principal national planning document in place. Initially the full PRSP contained three-year development matrices, which expired in June 2007 however, the then interim government,[10] without providing any public note on the raison d'être, extended the life of the NASPR by one year through an executive order.

In the preceding section the architecture of the formulation of the PRSP was described in detail. Officially the PRSP argued that it was prepared with wide engagement of various actors and institutions amounting to the representation of the people at large. But invariably, in all countries undergoing a PRSP regime the notion of participation and ownership, cardinal elements of the World Bank and IMF prescribed process conditionality, was challenged and contested. Presumably Bangladesh is not an exception to global practices and realities. Moreover, there have been clear and strong criticisms about the ownership of Bangladesh PRSP as well. Indeed, the debate about the ownership constitutes the rationale of the research.

Thus, this section seeks to broadly analyze the depth of ownership of Bangladesh in the PRSP and in doing so the following issues have been taken into consideration: (i) genesis of the decision of making a PRSP for Bangladesh, (ii) the key actors and their scope and nature of contribution – parliamentary and political engagement, (iii) the dynamics of civil society engagement, (iv) responses of line ministries, and (v) external and technocratic influences – the LCG and the consultants. It also briefly focuses on the macroeconomic agenda contained in the PRSP to examine whether there has been any strategic shift from the SAP. Finally, the section attempts to provide an analysis as to why Bangladesh is so susceptible to the leverage of the lenders in general and the BWIs in particular.

The section while drawing on the insights gained through in-depth interviews of key actors at various levels, also uses secondary materials to corroborate the insights.

Bangladesh's PRSP: whose agenda is it?

Although the decision to prepare a PRSP was taken in the BDF 2000 meeting, the document succinctly de-linked it from any linkage with multilateral or bilateral assistance whatsoever. Only the Finance Minister gave a slight hint in his foreword message that developing countries now had to prepare a PRSP to access World Bank and IMF soft loans (GoB: 2005).[11] But like many others[12] Mahmud (2006) clearly spelled out that the preparation of the PRSP in Bangladesh was directly connected to the entry of the World Bank and IMF program assistance under a medium-term policy framework. He further argued that the timing of the finalization of I-PRSP was significant because immediately after the formulation of I-PRSP and its joint assessment by the World Bank and IMF, the government successfully applied for the IMF's program lending under the PRGF and the World Bank's Development Support Credit (DSC) under the PRSP umbrella. Both lending arrangements were linked to a medium-term policy framework involving disbursements of funds in a series of installments. Those who favored a medium-term development strategy argued that the enthusiasm for the use of a FYP suffered a huge decay in terms of relevance in a market-oriented liberalized policy environment with reduced role of public investment and institutional incapacity of the Planning Commission. The Fifth Five Year Plan, the last until then, was said to have represented an attempt to shift from quantitative investment allocations to strategic and policy planning. Even when the idea of FYPs was no longer fashionable in the wake of the rise of economic neoliberalism, expert opinion in the country was in favor of having a well-articulated medium-term development strategy. Thus, they argued that in the absence of the FYPs, a PRSP process could be a good chance of being seen as a continuation of a nationally owned planning process. In their opinion a PRSP was therefore a political demand (Mahmud: 2006).[13] Muhammad[14] agreed that the planning process suffered a serious decay but he attributed the decay to the acceptance of international organizations' hegemony by the national government. The influence contributed to the shifting of economic policies from the strategies used to be contained in the FYP. He argued that this eventual contradiction between the economic principles in practice and the principles in the FYP made the planning process gradually irrelevant. He further argued a PRSP was a retreat because what we actually needed was not the abandonment of the FYP but a further focus on poverty reduction with implementable strategies coming out of the shadow of neoliberalism. Akash[15] contested the demand for a new strategic document instead of an FYP. He argued the demand was for a special focus on poverty reduction and not for a new strategy because "the need for FYP was felt internally, formulated internally, approved internally and implemented internally providing local ownership and on the contrary PRSP emerged from outside". Hossain,[16] criticizing the matrix approach of a PRSP, viewed that the PRSP was like the NGO projects which also contained some matrices to please the donors but the matrix approach did not enable us to see a long-term vision of the country. The pertinent point that arose was that what led Bangladesh to move forward to a PRSP entailing three-year policy matrices, unlike the FYP, remained unaccounted for in the document. The document did not clarify why the previous FYPs failed and what improvement the PRSP would bring about. On the other hand, clearly it established the links of a Bangladesh PRSP with the multilateral aid access. The link was even reported in the minutes of National Steering Committee.

The dynamics of engagement of key actors

Upon analysis of the formulation process it appeared that the major key actors were the National Steering Committee, line ministries, civil society organizations, and parliament. But above all of these were the consultants attached to the NPFP and the thematic groups (TGs) in the line ministries. The lead consultant along with another consultant was actively engaged in the NPFP and the NSC.

While the national steering committee consisted purely of senior bureaucrats with the principal secretary to the Prime Minister as the head and Member (Secretary equivalent), General Economics Division (GED) in the Planning Commission as the member-secretary, the TGs comprised government officials and hired consultants. However, some TGs such as the thematic group on macroeconomic issues were reportedly to have been comprised of government functionaries only. In the architecture of the PRSP formulation no direct link for political leadership is evident. Beside the formal actors, there had been active and constant engagement of the multilateral and bi-lateral donors with the NSC and TGs through the LCG.

PRSP and parliamentary engagement

Parliament is the highest political institution that provides opportunity for the electorate to be represented through their elected representatives. It ensures a national engagement in issues that may permeate national life. The PRSP is necessarily a national agenda that clearly seeks to reduce the national poverty level. Moreover, poverty itself is a pervasive issue and demands different connotations in different circumstances. Thus, in order to attack poverty we need to engage parliament to ensure a broader national representation. The other critical side of parliamentary engagement is that it is the only organization that may ensure a broad-based national consensus and eventually would lead to ensuring national ownership. Given the importance of parliamentary engagement, the issue of parliamentary involvement in the PRSP received strong academic value and popular support.

> Bilateral donors and European Commission have expressed concern over the fact that "the role of parliaments in the preparation, approval and monitoring of country strategies has generally been limited and is a concern that has been expressed".
>
> (Rahman: 2005)

A PRSP, as a national development strategy was supposed to be politically determined. There are naturally many critical issues involved in a development strategy and they require political support to be realities. As far as the national development agenda is concerned the pertinent question that arises is whose business it would be to present before the nation the strategic vision? Would they be bureaucrats, consultants, or international lenders or donors? If we critically analyze the parliamentary engagement in Bangladesh we find that it was a mere orientation. After the preparation of the draft document of the PRSP, some selected MPs were invited to a workshop held under the support of the Bangladesh Institute of Parliamentary Studies (BIPS) – a UNDP sponsored project working to promote parliamentary efficacy in Bangladesh. The meeting was held in a 5-star hotel near the legislative building. Thus, by no means can it be said that it constituted parliamentary engagement. It was just sharing the draft PRSP with some invited MPs and of course, not all MPs. From 330 standing MPs, only 44 participated in the workshop held on two different days. The first day, 14 May 2005, was devoted to the inaugural session and the second day, 17 May 2005, provided an opportunity for floor participation.

The reason for organizing the workshop, as mentioned in the welcome speech, was that it was being forced upon them by the European Union and some bilateral donors, as the latter questioned the limited participation of national parliaments. Parliamentary involvement was seen as an opportunity (as if a charity)[17] for the MPs to reflect upon the draft PRSP that seriously undermined the prerogative role of national legislators to lead the national development agenda to be envisioned, visualized, and set by them through policy debates, contestations, and presenting policy alternatives. Moreover, the PRSP was seen as being formulated by technocrats.[18]

While the PRSP was claimed to be a national development agenda, the idea should be evolved in and prompted by the parliament, particularly since Bangladesh chose to abandon its traditional FYP. The parliament should have provided policy directions based on which subsequent participation of other stakeholders could be held. The reason behind the failure of dedicating a special session to discuss the PRSP in the floor of parliament was mentioned neither in the workshop nor in the PRSP document.

On the face of the discussion, it is very convincing that the participation was low, less critical and hurriedly managed to please donors to prove that it is nationally owned. The interesting point to note is that the workshop was organized with the support of an aid agency and both the (then) Prime Minister and the Finance Minister were absent in the discussion. The frustration of the MPs was clear when it became apparent that their contribution would not be taken into consideration. The workshop itself recorded some frustrations:

> Khondoker Delwar Hossain, then MP and Chief Whip of Bangladesh parliament[19] appreciated the valuable discussion made by his fellow

> parliamentarians and hoped that these would serve to enrich the ensuing final document. Being a veteran parliamentarian, he critically reviewed the role of the parliamentarians in policy intervention. He observed that unlike India, parliamentarians of Bangladesh have peripheral role in deciding policy options of the country. Referring to a case in point, the budget bill, he observed that parliamentarians of India make more meaningful contribution to the budget through the respective standing committees apart from debating the budget on the floor. Given the tradition in Bangladesh, he observed that there was almost no possibility of tabling the draft PRSP in the parliament as suggested by a few colleagues during their discussion. He voiced frustration whether the valuable suggestions given by parliamentarians during the discussion would merely be confined to paper.
>
> (Rahman: 2005, 19–20)

Members of the parliament (MPs) were skeptical about the intent and ownership of the PRSP in Bangladesh and thus they urged that the PRSP should give importance on the human aspect of poverty reduction and development. MPs voiced this concern during a consultation workshop on PRSP. The (then) Speaker of the parliament said that the PRSP should be people oriented. MPs were also apprehensive about the implementation of PRSP as they thought that the multilateral Bank would impose many conditions in the name of PRSP. An MP told that the formulation process of PRSP violated the basic principles of participation.

The Chair of the Parliamentary Standing Committee on Planning also voiced his frustration in the workshop that despite being the chairperson he had little briefing about the preparation of the Annual Development Plan (ADP). It should be noted that ADP is the blue print of development activities of the government of a given year (Rahman: 2005). Another MP commented that the recommendations made by the Parliamentary Standing Committee were neglected in the PRSP and thus demanded discussion on the PRSP on the floor of parliament (Rahman: 2005). The chair of the Parliamentary Standing Committee on Agriculture also lamented that the government did not pay attention to the recommendations made by the committee. He criticized that the draft failed to go into deeper analysis on agriculture particularly on subsidies (Rahman: 2005). However, he titled his presentation as 'PRSP by IMF' and it implied that MPs in Bangladesh were truly convinced that the exercise was necessary to comply with BWIs requirements.

Thorough analysis of the presentations and deliberations of the MPs with some minor exceptions suggests that the discussions were mainly on social sector issues. Critical analysis of previous development models induced by the IFIs that had a significantly negative impact on the country's development was absent. The lack of discussion on the macroeconomic issues was most evident.

> We told for a political decision on PRSP. We suggested for sharing it with MPs. Our Finance Minister told that it would not give any result talking to MPs. Practically he did not want their involvement. But MPs during various sharing discussion sessions with us strongly demanded parliamentary and political discussion on PRSP.
>
> (A civil society network leader revealed this during an interview)

The apprehension about the exclusion of recommendations made by parliamentarians eventually came true. As mentioned, there was not much discussion on critical issues. The Chief Whip of Bangladesh parliament (2001–06) indeed understood that these recommendations might be confined to paper. That is what did happen in reality. In the workshop there had been the following broad suggestions:

- A stronger analysis is needed on the consequences of trade liberalization and open economy.
- The PRSP draft document should be tabled in the parliament for discussion.
- A special parliamentary committee to be formed to review the PRSP.
- A national body based on broad-based consensus should be formed to supervise the monitoring of the PRSP.

In the final document none of the recommendations were included. The PRSP was not tabled in parliament for discussion and no parliamentary committee whatsoever was formed either to review or monitor the progress of the PRSP. The monitoring committee consisted of some academics representing civil society and some senior bureaucrats. The two core consultants earlier engaged in the PRSP formulation were also involved.[20]

To conclude, it appears that parliament was not actively involved in the process and nor did it provide any strategic policy guidelines as to the development of Bangladesh. The Parliamentary Standing Committee recommendations were not entertained and even the suggestions made in the workshop were not fully taken care of. Issues concerning the macroeconomic agenda were not reviewed even nominally and no presentation was made on them in the workshop with MPs.

Parliamentary non-engagement can be interpreted by both historical and practical reasons. Historically, parliament is ignored in policy formulation in Bangladesh. Even budget discussion is neither effective nor productive (Jahan and Amundsen: 2012). During the ecstatic days immediately after independence the involvement of parliament was even less than marginal. There were practical reasons in that the ruling coterie believed proactive parliamentary involvement might deter the entire process. It was almost obvious that the PRSP was essentially linked to the IMF's PRGF. Thus, the government did not want to risk the process by giving MPs chance to speak openly and criticize donors, particularly the WB-IMF. However, the important point to highlight is that there had been weak demand for parliamentary process. Political parties, civil society organizations, and other opinion builders definitely failed to generate momentum for greater parliamentary involvement. The other reason could be that the political stakeholders did not want to be critical about the World Bank and IMF policies and strategies. The competing political forces always want to enjoy the blessings of the international lending and aid agencies to secure regime legitimacy.

PRSP and the Civil Service

The engagement of civil servants in a country like Bangladesh in public policy formulation process is very important since the country lacks strong political institutions to represent public voices. In the preceding section it became fairly clear that parliament as the most representative and powerful political organization failed to ensure its engagement, let alone lead the process. Thus, bureaucrats with wider exposure to national reality and development demand may significantly contribute to national development strategy. Moreover, their professional mastery demands them to lead the process. The other significant point is that bureaucrats are the organs of the state that contribute to the implementation of the strategies.

However, the presence of senior bureaucrats in the NSC and the higher proportion of participation by the public officials within the line ministries in the TGs may take on the appearance of the entire process as being bureaucratically driven. Extended discussions with public officials, at various levels, revealed that the presence of public officials on the committees did not mean true engagement. They did not have a leadership role in most of the cases. There were one or two cases where they had to lead the process but not with an independent mind but to serve others' opinions[21] and they primarily served to provide legitimacy to the process.

> "A deputy secretary in a workshop organized by the World Bank said I had heard of it only when I was invited to the workshop and it was about two years later since the document had been prepared". Thus, this is the level of ownership of the government officials.
>
> (Revealed by a government official who was present in the workshop)

> We have not seen it. We do not know much about it. The document is very clumsy. We are not clear that it was developed for greater development. Truly we are not informed.
>
> (Views made by a deputy secretary)

In the beginning there was a proposal for constituting a high powered National Poverty Reduction Council (NPRC) with the Prime Minister as the chairman and the Finance Minister as the executive chairman. It proposed to include a number of ministers, senior civil servants, private sector and civil society representatives but in the end it did not come into fruition. Thus with the absence of the NPRC, the NSC virtually became the most significant body to spearhead the activities concerning the PRSP. A strategic document to deal with poverty, the number one problem of the country necessarily would expect some strategic and visionary thrust from the NSC though it may be contested if a NSC staffed by civil servants should at all be entitled to do so. A reading of the minutes of nine consecutive meetings of the high-powered NSC starting from the first, does not reveal any strategic guidelines or vision regarding the poverty reduction agenda. It appeared that they were mostly engaged in facilitating activities to be done by others. The obviously intrinsic deficiency of Bangladesh's PRSP was that it never received any visionary guideline from either the political policy makers or from the senior policy makers in the civil service.

The NSC was powerful in terms of getting things done[22] but not in terms of setting the vision. It did not even encourage the members to play a critical role. This was disclosed in interviews with the staff members of the Planning Commission who attended meetings as aides. A secretary who was a member of NSC also expressed his frustration that their presence was required just to validate the process.

> The steering committee was powerful but not participatory. Excepting 2/1 secretaries most participants did not speak out.
>
> (Viewed by a staff member of the Planning Commission who used to attend the meetings)

While it appeared that the NSC was bestowed with higher administrative authority, the scenario in terms of engagement in the line ministries may be more illustrative to understand the depth of ownership and participation. The TGs in the line ministries played the critical role of creating the background paper on the themes they were assigned. In terms of the terms of the reference (ToR) the TG should involve officials from line ministries, civil society, and consultants. To understand the magnitude of ownership and engagement, particularly that of the civil servants a special research focus was put on the Ministry of Women and Children Affairs and Ministry of Establishment (now, Ministry of Public Administration (MoPA)). Based on the experience, and insights gained through in-depth interviews with the career civil servants, the points of ownership are discussed in Annex 4.2.

The issues of the TGs occupied a huge importance in the meetings of the NSC and of course, it was primarily because of the involvement of the consultants. Reading between the lines of the minutes it appeared that the NSC wanted the consultants to be engaged in the TGs and in the national poverty focal point in the Planning Commission to prepare the PRSP. The government officials invariably exposed that there were truly no major discussions in the Ministries.

Box 4.3 Civil servants on PRSP

PRSP is not our own agenda. It's a prescription. We are donor dependent country and thus we had to accept both PRSP and MDG to comply with donors' requirement. These are products of globalization process.

An official commented in MWCA

Desk officers were not involved in the preparation rather the consultants involved in the TG did it. Thus, the implementation of PRSP has been automatically weak.

To me PRSP is just a book. I don't know what it contains. I don't have any interest even. I don't feel any sense of a new start due to PRSP for poverty reduction. The targets set in PRSP are ambitious; they are not set in the perspective of the capacity of the state. We wanted to have done all things. In other word we have set so many indicators and targets just to give the sense of getting so many things. To me most of them are junk.

Views of a midlevel civil servant

PRSP is imposed and does not draw spontaneous ownership. It has to be understandable and involve huge participation.

Views made by an official works in planning section in a ministry

Consultants prepared the TG report. In the line ministries no discussion or consultation was held on TG report and policy matrix. GED perhaps failed to make the line ministries properly understand about the entire process of ownership. Today, the line ministries say that they don't understand PRSP.

Commented a staff member of the GED, Planning Commission

It was not fully participatory but had some participatory elements. There has not been any evaluation of the implementation of the document. Development planning is poorly conceived in Bangladesh.

Commented a secretary and the member of NSC

PRSP was a conditionality from the WB – the IMF. Some people are doing business with it. This is bogus and is not our plan. Leadership in policy development is important. The political government did not desire the development of institutions that are crucial for policy autonomy.

A joint secretary commented

PRSP is the outcome of donors' idea. Of late donors are working on preparing documents. The need for extensive research was huge. But the WB-IMF doesn't give opportunity to carryout research. We are too not interested in research. Without local research a macro document like PRSP targeting to reduce poverty is neither feasible nor desirable.

A midlevel official working in ERD commented

The experience in the Ministry of Women and Children Affairs suggested that in some social issues such as gender the contribution of civil society was substantial but the leadership was with the consultants. Consultants in collaboration with CSOs primarily prepared the documents, set the matrices and targets, and the Ministry only played the role of getting them approved from the higher authority such as the Minister or the Secretary through the routine channel of bureaucracy. The resultant impact was that the civil servants could not see it as their own agenda that would have to be implemented by them. Various statements made by officials from mid-level to senior level during the interviews illustrated the overall lack of political and bureaucratic involvement.

> Here in Bangladesh civil service was willfully destroyed in the assumption that an efficient and strong civil service might create trouble to the political leadership. We were exposed to martial law for many years and they also took the opportunity. Everything has been done to make civil service ineffective.
>
> (A former cabinet secretary)

While it was evident that the involvement of the public officials was quite shaky, their perception concerning the PRSP was remarkable (Box 4.3). Every one interviewed believed, with certainty, that the PRSP was an imposition of the World Bank and the IMF. They were not convinced that a document prescribed by the multilateral donors might come to the help of poverty reduction. This resultant view might be one of the major contributory factors of their apathy to the process.

The predominance of the consultants both in the TGs and in the NPFP and the resultant leadership expose a special scenario of incapacity of public officials in leading public policy. The quantity of participation and engagement may be low for many reasons but what could justify the ignorance of public officials about the PRSP? It is important to note that the civil service, unfortunately, has always been a victim of populist politics of both elected and authoritative regimes. Successive governments in Bangladesh did not apply any kind of comprehensive plan to streamline the civil service in order to cope with a changing environment (CPD: n.d.). Today's failure may be attributed to that inaction of successive political regimes. Civil servants reported that indeed they were not ready to prepare a PRSP.

> The civil service suffered huge career compromises and thus failed to interact. Failure of the civil service paved ways for donors to form a

> nexus with CSOs. The CSOs failed to uphold national interest. Our civil service was not prepared to prepare a plan like PRSP. They were not ready to accept the PRSP instead of 6th FYP. The PRSP was developed within the time frame given by the IMF. There was not any program to orient the civil servants. We accepted it because the government was committed to doing so.
>
> (Comment of a civil servant)

More importantly, while the global scenario was that in every country both the World Bank and the IMF encountered serious resistance, in Bangladesh the civil servants tended to see the PRSP in isolation. Research did not find any civil servant who was aware of the evolution of the PRSP from the structural adjustment program. It would not be an exaggeration to say that while the global and local situation demanded civil servants to become critical about the international political economy, civil servants in Bangladesh remained as the obedient students of the World Bank and the IMF. Thus, the situation could not be better than this for a less enterprising and uncritical bureaucracy.

The lack of research-based policy development undermined the scope of engagement of the civil service. Line ministry hardly does maintain any relevant data and every time donors facilitate preparing the reports, documents, and mission statements to be presented either in national or international forums. Culturally bureaucracy has been dependent on the donors. Today, bureaucracy has lost its self-esteem and leadership role. Arbitrary decisions seriously affected the mainstream bureaucracy i.e. the administrative service. While the members of the administrative service provide policy leadership and implementation leadership both in the National Secretariat and field administrations, the bifurcation of roles in the ministry between planning and administration squeezed out the opportunity of the administrative service officials to lead development planning. It is important to bring the administrative service officials into research and policy leadership by eliminating the existing economic cadre of the civil service at the ministry level. Developing a strong administrative service could only be a better response to the criticalities of globalization and its complex influences.

PRSP and civil society

The research clearly indicates three dimensions concerning civil society participation in the PRSP. The first dimension was that most of the prominent civil society organizations remained either silent in the entire process or were busy during the time of the PRSP formulation with issues relating to governance and political reforms. The second dimension was that only a network and some other organizations were actively engaged in the PRSP process. However, their position was to lobby for inclusion of the demands of various groups of the people. They criticized the IFIs in some cases but did not totally reject the PRSP. The third stream was a group of individual economists who appeared highly critical about the entire package of PRSP.

> Whose civil society is it? They are donor driven civil society. I am also donor driven. It is Dhaka based. Where is their connection with people?
> (Comment of the head of a civil society network)

Before we discuss the engagement of the CSOs, let us take note of the existing scenario relating to civil society in Bangladesh. The common feature of civil society in Bangladesh is that they are mostly NGO backed and politically divided and dependent on foreign sources for funds, and most of funds come from the Northern countries. There is a strong view about Bangladesh civil society in that they are attendants of Western elites; they partly criticize and partly accept the policies espoused by the Western masters. The other strong view is that while civil society should be independent in their thinking, civil society in Bangladesh is NGO backed and consists of members of consultancy groups that are organically linked to the WB, IMF, ADB, or UNDP. Thus, in reality, it is almost near impossible for them to criticize the Western hegemony other than subscribing the policies of the West.[23]

The booming of civil society organizations in Bangladesh took place after the 1990s at a time when two major incidents took place concomitantly – in the international order, the collapse of socialism and in the national front, the fall of autocracy. The then political environment strongly supported the emergence of civil society organizations in the 1990s. However, soon most of the civil society organizations became beneficiaries of the funds of the Western governments and aid agencies and divided in line with the divide in national politics.[24] In reference to the PRSP, many critics argued that given the embedded character of civil society they could not raise questions as to the fundamental crisis of the World Bank and IMF led neoliberal paradigm. What they could do at best is suggest cosmetic changes. Thus, the inaction of the majority of civil society organizations may be attributed to the latter's dependency on international, bilateral, and multilateral donors. International funding agencies not only expected their local cronies to remain silent but also influence their research agenda and findings.[25] The statistics from the donors suggested that various civil society organizations received millions of dollars for activism and research on governance alone. Annex 4.1 presents a list of the local CSOs/NGOs which were supported by Western donors. In my view it is enough to draw critical insights into why civil society appeared so naïve in the process of PRSP formulation in Bangladesh. The funding perspective clearly unfolds a patron-client relationship between CSOs and their Western donor-partners. While all major donors backed the PRSP approach, the CSOs had little space to criticise it. Consequently, a significant portion of civil society (due to their dependency on Northern funding sources) remained silent; however, some CSO networks tried to seize the opportunity of engagement in PRSP process. These networks viewed that at least theoretically people were for the first time encouraged to talk on issues concerning a development agenda that would eventually affect them. *Campaign for Good Governance* [in Bengali *SUPRO* – Sushashoner Jonno Procharavijan], a network of local organizations, took two positions at the same time: they criticized the IFIs but also endeavored to engage in the PRSP process. In fact, among the CSOs only SUPRO played a pivotal role in raising awareness on the limitations and contesting issues of the PRSP. They organized workshops, dialogues, and a national convention throughout the I-PRSP and PRSP formulation process. They translated the PRSP document, originally written in English, into Bengali. They also translated the I-PRSP into Bengali. Recognizing the fact that development strategy of the poor countries more or less since 1960s has been dependent on the foreign actors, they appeared more critical about the implementation of the PRSP rather than formulation[26].

> PRSP has been as if a consultancy work. A consultancy work is obviously different from the work of the economists with passion and commitment and cannot project long-term development vision. A few decades ago our vernacular economists upon return from abroad receiving higher degrees used to challenge the Western development thoughts but now they do not talk on them anymore. Now they have equalized their consultancy rate. The country has fallen under a culture of imperialism. Now critical development thinking, such as land reform, has been substituted by issues like governance, accountability etc.
>
> (A civil society member commented)

People's Empowerment Trust (PET) with support from Action Aid organized dialogues with peasant groups, workers, environmentalists, teachers and students, ethnic minorities, and political leaders during the I-PRSP formulation period and came up with a number of policy recommendations. Major recommendations of PET included:[27] (a) the government should not submit to the pressure of the multilateral donors to prepare a PRSP for aid rather develop national development strategy involving people within national planning structure; (b) land reforms, tenurial reforms minimum wage for farm laborers as adopted by Abu Zafar Obaidullah Committee on Agrarian Reforms in 1984; (c) fair price of agriculture products and expansion of subsidies; stopping de-nationalization of profitable state owned enterprises (SOEs); (d) special protection to local industries; (e) enforcement of ILO Conventions including trade union rights in private sector industries and export processing zones (EPZs); (f) introduction of education loan and subsidies to poor students; (g) allocation of at least 8 per cent of the national income or 25 per cent of the main budget for meeting costs in the education sector as recommended by the UNESCO; (h) ensuring transparency of large NGOs and (i) one-third block-grant of the national development budget to local government institutions for facilitation of people-centric development planning.

The significant feature of the civil society activism was that a group of mainstream economists of the country not only severely criticized the process but also challenged the fundamentals of the PRSP.[28]

Despite participation of some networks and individual economists, civil society in Bangladesh failed to create greater societal engagement in the entire process and more importantly to create a demand for a national development agenda insulated from international influence.

> We don't count the poor, the beggars, and laborers as part of the civil society. We think that the urban elite only constitute the civil society. When issues concerning the WB-IMF-WTO emerge we see many international NGOs fund civil society activism in our country.
>
> (Commented a senior journalist)

The main point of failure, as stated by a civil society network leader, was that the entire process lacked coordination and moreover, those who could have led the process were involved in various capacities [as consultant to NPFP, background paper writer in the TG, etc.] in the making of the PRSP. While lack of coordination may be a great problem, the crucial point would be the inaction of the resourceful civil society organizations for their organic connection to Western hegemony. The members in the civil society who at times held workshops, seminars, and roundtables on issues, particularly on accountability in politics and governance,[29] did not play any significant role during the PRSP process and let the entire process go unchallenged. A major shift among the professional economists has also significantly contributed to the inaction. Many of those who were critical a few years ago about blanket liberalization and deregulation, today work for setting arguments for far greater integration of the national economy with the globalization process; this shift in the mindset has been possible because of the fact that they have been more or less the consultants of the donors.

The failure reveals the limitation of civil society activism in Bangladesh. Civil society activism is urban-based, or to be more realistic Dhaka-based, and mostly led by the elite in every sense of the term. Most of them are consultants living off fat remunerations or represent resourceful business houses and politically influential groups. The palpable and seemingly intentional failure now should lead the people who have a belief in the action and strength of the common people to start a new countervailing force to establish a true paradigm shift in development strategy.

Political dimension of participation and ownership in the PRSP process

Here two issues are addressed: the nature and dynamics of political activism and government's collective stance on PRSP. Bangladesh politics is characterized as being heavily confrontational. This confrontational nature left a black cloud over the political culture of Bangladesh. Since the restoration of democracy in 1991, the opposition continuously boycotted proceedings in the national parliament. Finally, the nature of confrontation rose to the extent that an emergency intervention backed by the military was imposed in January 2007 to avert the prescheduled national election, arguing that it might destabilize the entire political scene in the country.

In such a confrontational scenario one might be astonished to see the convergence of two major political parties in terms of economic strategy, who since independence ran the country at different times. The decision of the PRSP was taken a few months before a new government was installed in October 2001. This regime took an opposing view to the previous one. After installation the new regime overthrew many of the decisions of the immediate past government, which is customary in Bangladesh politics, but to remarkably the government did not say anything against the PRSP rather it started preparing an I-PRSP.

In the entire period of the PRSP formulation no major political party made any effort to destabilize the process, either in parliament or outside. The parliamentary parties did not try to raise the issue of the PRSP in parliament. This inaction signifies that the major political parties of Bangladesh accepted the market reality and the influence of the international lenders in the economy as a fait accompli.[30]

Look at the language of a senior leader of the then opposition:

> With a view to ending poverty for good in Bangladesh, the Awami League government also started the process of preparation of the PRSP in November 2000 under the dynamic leadership of our late finance minister Mr. SAMS Kibria … The first meeting on the PRSP, based on 'Comprehensive Development Framework' (CDF) and the 'Sector wide Approach Programme' (SWAP) was held on 16th November 2000 chaired by late Mr. Kibria … I, however must point out that, in the preparation process of PRSP, the present government violated the basic principle of 'participation', to be precise 'comprehensive participatory process' as claimed in the Executive Summary of the draft PRSP
>
> (Khan: 2005, 27)

From the above quote it emerges that the political party in question was not critical about what the PRSP contained rather they tried to criticize the government for not ensuring comprehensive participation. It means they accepted the PRSP for granted. They did not offer any policy challenge. It reflects the policy convergence between the donors and Bangladesh's major political parties.

Many critics argued that the convergence was intrinsic in the rent-seeking behavior of the political establishments irrespective of party colors. Development budgets in the peripheral economies are still largely dependent on the foreign loans and assistances, which are the major gateway to serve petty political and self-interests. In other words, the rent-seeking behaviors of the political parties make them unable to criticize the damaging policies of international organizations.[31]

Another important argument to illustrate the inaction of the political parties is that it is widely perceived that in most political parties in Bangladesh the culture of policy debates is totally absent. This, in fact, leads the parties to embrace the inability to argue with alternative policy paradigms in the face of international policy influence which is incarnated in a well-articulated way with sound technical and methodological propositions. During the interviews, senior leaders of the two major parties admitted that the culture of policy debate or dialogue would have made the situation far better.

Box 4.4 An insider's experience

He served in the government for about 35 years and was mostly engaged in development planning activities. Many a time he led initiatives. This time in the PRSP he was very instrumental as well. Looking back he shared many issues of frustration during the interview. He stated that development vision always comes from the political leadership rather it is their prerogative as they represent people. The bureaucrats and professionals set the strategies to realize the vision and however, the bureaucrats are also engaged to implement the strategies. But what happened actually in case of the PRSP they did not ask us anything about the PRSP but only when a team of the BWIs was coming. <u>In the entire process of three years the Finance Minister asked me only twice about the development of the document. Now you draw your conjecture as to the ownership of our political leadership in the PRSP. The team inside [government] was very weak</u>.

He further said we look at the dictations of the WB-IMF in implementation of our policies. The Finance Ministry was never ever committed to the implementation of a five-year plan. In conclusion, upon reflection of his long career and close engagement in the PRSP he commented with utter lament "In this country economic policy making has always been reactive and never ever been proactive".

Source: Interview with the author

While that was the common feature of the major political parties, let us take a stock of the government's position. It is important to see how the government as a collective political body itself was involved in the process to lead the nation with independent thinking. A close scrutiny of the process suggested that no formal political leadership was in place to guide and lead the process. There was no monitoring from the cabinet. A [former] minister revealed that there was no effective discussion in the cabinet, and they did not have involvement at the input level. He believed that the cabinet should have had a sub-committee to ensure upstream ownership. However, the entire issue was left to the Finance Minister. But how was he involved?

Three incidents may well illustrate the political leadership's ownership crisis over the PRSP agenda. The throwing of the PRSP document on the floor by a cabinet member (former Minister for Planning), in the presence of the WB Country Director, testifies to the lack of coordination in the government. Professor Rehman Sobhan, a dedicated political economist and analyst of the political economy of Bangladesh for about half a century commented on the entire drama, "The Minister's [Moyeen Khan] attitude reflected a serious lack of coordination within the government regarding PRSP. Terming the PRSP as a 'three-year development plan' he said that donors are actually not inclined to provide support in line with the document. 'That's why our finance minister has now rushed to Washington to solicit funds from the International Monetary Fund under PRGF', he added. Rehman Sobhan asked the donors' to 'tear up' their country assistance strategies if they really want to support the country. 'We have to get access to your documents for review as you have in ours'" (*The Daily New Age*, Dhaka: 6 August 2006). The detail of the episode is narrated in Bangladesh's different daily newspapers. The country's leading English daily's headline read '**Moyeen Khan** [the then planning minister] **flings PRSP book to floor, calls it a trash**'.[32] The incident of throwing the document itself reflects that it lacked even serious government ownership; otherwise it would have not been possible for a cabinet member to throw it down. Moreover, after the incident the minister was not criticized by the government for his action.

The other incident is the experience of a senior public servant who had the privilege to coordinate the entire issue of the PRSP preparation. His experience was narrated in Box 4.4. It is important to note the title of the presentation of a [then] Treasury Bench MP, who was the Chair of the Parliamentary Standing Committee on the Ministry of Agriculture, made in the PRSP sharing session with the MPs. From his narratives it appeared that having been convinced he deliberately entitled his presentation *PRSP by the IMF.* He appeared to have been conspicuously unhappy with the entire process (Rahman: 2005). In the same program the [then] Chief Whip of the Treasury Bench was clearly apprehensive about the implementation of recommendations made by the MPs. These major incidents unequivocally expose both the World Bank and IMF's influence and the lack of commitment and coordination in the government. Later on, we also witnessed that the business community collectively condemned the diktat of the IMF. Twelve business associations (all most all leading associations) in an unprecedented move issued a joint statement against donors, especially criticizing the IMF's policy influence. This statement appeared in all national dailies on 2 August 2007. This business move against the donors is an important example of donor influence over the development agenda.[33]

Engagement of donor's local consultative group (LCG)

A PRSP, as a national development document, should be insulated from the influence of the donors who have a bad track record for their policy guidelines in Bangladesh. Moreover, the concept of policy independence discourages any form of donor involvement in the process of policy construction (Ohno et al.: 2005; Johnson: 2005; Ishikawa: 2003). But in the case of the Bangladesh PRSP, a structural link of the donors through the LCG with the NPFP was actively maintained. The NPFP met with the LCG several times and tried to account for the entire process of the PRSP formulation. Similar to NPFP which created twelve thematic groups, the LCG, with representatives from various multilateral and bilateral donors, created sub-groups. The IMF and WB led the LCG's sub-groups on macroeconomic stability and pro-poor growth and financial sector reforms interacted with and influenced the government's thematic groups (LCG: 2004). The names of the LCG sub-groups that were linked to the government's mandate of macroeconomic stability and pro-poor growth were 'macroeconomic development' and 'technical assistance'. The term 'technical assistance' is important because it necessarily gives the impression of policy leverage by the donors. Christine Wallich, the then country director of the WB, as chair of the LCG, submitted comments on the draft PRSP on 7 April 2005 to the Principal Secretary to the Prime Minister, and the Chair of the NSC. This strong and active engagement flies in the face of the weak to non-existent engagement with civil society or parliament. There is no doubt the active engagement centered on the fact that the LCG were donor led and donor focused. The government was obligated to listen and obey.

Participation or compliance with IFIs policy leverage

> … [i]n Bangladesh no representative from the poor people specially trade unions were [ever] invited in pre-budget discussion or in preparing PRSP. Even IMF and World Bank Dhaka office did not discuss with trade unions, though I wrote letter to them. So it is evident both IFIs and government did not change their principle for which they are continually criticized. IFIs and rich people in the govt. are preparing paper to eradicate poverty, those who have no idea about poverty – the pains of poverty.
>
> (A trade union leader)

The one-size-fits-all approach was the major issue of contention during the SAP regime. The approach being primarily neoliberal in nature served the interest of the developed countries situated in the North at the cost of the developing and poor countries' development aspirations. PRSP is necessarily a retreat of IFIs in the face of the global movement against the hegemonic nature of the World Bank and IMF development strategies. It is thus imperative to scrutinize the participatory process regarding how the critical issues such as privatization, deregulation, etc. were taken into consideration while preparing a PRSP.

> PRSP was done to qualify PRGF. However, we tried to take the opportunity to make it also work as a planning document. But essentially the goal was PRGF. The macroeconomic targets were not systematically drawn and the targets were developed based on the IMF furnished data to show higher growth that our political leadership appreciated very much. The Finance Ministry being influenced by the IMF led the process in the core economic issues.
>
> (A close witness observed in the planning commission)

It is important to mention that since the 1980s Bangladesh has been exposed to the World Bank and IMF development policies and the impact of liberalization on the economy has always been a highly contested issue. The increase in growth failed to arrest the increase in the level of poverty and rather massive inequality has been a dominant feature as well as a daunting challenge for the economy. However, even if rigorous research on the previous strategies and their impact was imperative, the government deliberately avoided doing any research on the grounds that they did not have enough time. While the plea of time constraint is unsubstantiated, the intention of the government in keeping things as 'business as usual' cannot be denied.

> The recommendations of the consultations were neither made public nor reflected in the PRSP document.
>
> (A planning commission official)

However, the participatory process raised serious questions. The faults in participation eventually resulted in perpetuating the donors' leverage on the economy of Bangladesh. The flaws in participation were essentially linked to the perception about a PRSP. The officials interviewed categorically believed that the essential objective of a PRSP was to enable Bangladesh to obtain a PRGF loan and it was reflected in the composition of the thematic groups. The groups dealing with core economic issues did not involve participants outside the Finance Ministry. Another official in the Finance Ministry stated that in the thematic group they tried to avert difficulty in obtaining the PRGF. While that was the bottom line, economist Anu Muhammad[34] argued that when any country accepted the hegemony of the World Bank and IMF no opportunity remained open to go beyond the neoliberal paradigm of development. Funding conditionality of the IFIs is geared to a neoliberal development model and thus, eventually, the so-called pro-poor attitude, even though remaining in the PRSP, becomes rhetorical as historically IFIs policies hit the poorest class across the world hardest, including Bangladesh.

> We do not take decision that where we should spend money; others do it. It's an awful situation. We don't decide who would be the consultant; the

> donors decide. We have failed to develop our own development strategy. We always want to listen to them.
>
> (A civil society member)

The active involvement of the LCG and ultimate approval capacity of the World Bank and IMF board reflected that the PRSP had to be prepared under the influence of the IFIs. In response to the critique that participation was needed some economists argued that the World Bank and IMF were heavily exposed to widespread criticism and discredit during the SAP era for the failure of polices and based on the previous experience they did not want to take the onus of policy failure in the PRSP regime. Thus, they added participation as a condition to avert the responsibility but the same old policies had to be implemented.

Professor Anu Muhammad[35] further argued that it was important to note that Bangladesh's PRSP did not give any strategic recommendations to promote the manufacturing sector and industry[36] in the economy and if any economy failed to provide a plan for basic industry it automatically conceded vulnerability. While the government boasted of creating provisions for more allocation of funding to the agriculture sector, Anu Muhammad commented that given the pattern and nature of hybrid cropping and multinational involvement, the majority of the allocation would go to serve the multinationals. The same situation occurred within the power sector where a significant amount of the funding allocation would be used as a subsidy to foreign companies.

Though participation was one of the primary conditions of the PRSP, the number of consultations and involvement of people from various professions were very much limited. Only in the divisional cities were consultations involving the general public held. The major drawbacks of the divisional consultations were that they were government administration led and selective. The criteria for invitation were given from the NPFP as if it aimed to validate the pre-determined issues. Moreover, the entire consultation process suffered a huge lack of transparency. The consultation reports were neither made public nor was it reported that the recommendations were incorporated in the main document of the PRSP. The consultations seemingly were not geared to soliciting sector recommendations. Many of the civil society members questioned the efficacy of the consultations, as they did not incorporate professional organizations and organizations that represented the people.

The important question is that the critical issues such as privatization, deregulation, corporatization, etc. did not emerge in discussions, or consultations. Barkat (2006) aptly questioned the credibility of the consultations. The issue of land ownership is fundamental to the poor; thus, he suggested that it was not acceptable that the participants did not raise any questions of land ownership in the consultations. Poverty in Bangladesh is linked to structural injustices that are linked to the policies of international organizations. There was no discussion on the issue. While the PRSP was being prepared in

Bangladesh the largest jute mill, not only of Bangladesh but of Asia, was shut down but no questions were raised on the issue by any laborer. Economist M. M. Akash[37] argued that the majority of the population were the peasants and laborers but their participation in the process was marginal. Economist Prof. Tariq Saiful Islam was also highly critical of both the contents and approaches of the PRSP as means of poverty reduction.[38]

The PRGF conditions also negated the impact of consultations. Under PRGF arrangement the country had to comply with the Funds' specific reform agendas and the majority of them are linked to blanket privatization and liberalization (Bull, Jerve and Sigvaldsen, 2006; Saleh, 2011). An analysis of the IMF report (IMF: 2007) suggests that their thrust was still linked to SAP assumptions. In the report the IMF appreciated the actions of the government for carrying forward some previously stalled reform agendas: corporatization and privatization of public sector banks.

> The TG (Transitional Government[39]) has undertaken a number of previously stalled reforms, motivating the World Bank to proceed with a budget support operation (Development Support Credit IV) that was approved on May 29 … The TG moved swiftly on decisions related to some stalled reforms. It has approved corporatization of the remaining nationalized commercial banks (NCBs), one of the two PRGF structural performance criteria for March … The pace of reform implementation has also picked up in other areas. In addition to the reforms agreed for the sixth review, the TG approved the sale of the remaining minority shares of Rupali Bank; intervened to manage the failing Oriental Bank that had previously been given effective immunity … placed the new container terminal at Chittagong port under private management; raised electricity tariffs by 5 percent in March, and fuel prices by 16–21 percent in April, and established a committee to regularly review and recommend fuel price adjustments. More comprehensive energy sector reforms are being initiated in consultation with the World Bank and the AsDB (underlining the author).
>
> (IMF: 2007, 4–6)

Let us look at the [underlined] issues raised in the report of the IMF. If the components of the Washington Consensus are very much in place then what change did the consultations bring forth? Privatization, corporatization, divesting fund, and consultation with the multilateral bodies, everything of the neoliberal paradigm and policy leverage are there. Two noticeable things are in the report. First, it is evident that the PRGF has certain conditionality, which is beyond the knowledge of the people and outside discussion or consultation. Second, the energy sector reforms should be in consultation with the World Bank and the Asian Development Bank. In other words, the IMF report is a clear indication of the policy of ignoring the people and parliament. If government and the IFIs maintained clandestine policy negotiations then the PRSP exercise becomes superficial and an eyewash. The IMF report at least proves this assumption. Mahmud (2006, 24) while substantiating the obvious influence of the lenders argues:

> … [T]he PRSP policy agenda is likely to have been preempted to some extent by the policy framework agreed under the World Bank and the IMF programme lending. There is also a question of mindset of the government policymakers, namely, their perception about what is expected of the PRSP. After all, the PRSP had to be approved by the World Bank and the IMF's respective Boards. An illustrative example is provided by the PRSP policy matrix for the power sector. In line with the World Bank's general reform agenda, the policy matrix has avoided proposing the creation of any additional power generation capacity in the public sector. It is the World Bank, which has now reassessed its policy stance in this regard and has recently agreed to provide an IDA loan of $ 275 million to set up a power plant under government ownership. A power generation company will be set up for this purpose and the plant will be run initially under management contract given out through international bidding. The Bank has come up with this idea particularly in view of the country's severe power shortage and the government's apparent lack of capacity to attract independent power companies. Ironically, the Bank appears to be more proactive than the government policymakers in deviating from its own professed privatisation policies and finding an innovative state-market mix (underline mine).

It is very remarkable to note that Mahmud mentions the World Bank's general reform agenda includes reducing the power of the public sector to influence a policy or to have at least a voice in policy creation. It means the broader reform guidelines of the World Bank and the IMF influenced the framing of local policy matrices. The PRSP ownership became a mockery as eventually the PRSP had to be approved by the World Bank and the IMF board of directors. Before that it goes to the board a joint World Bank and the IMF committee would evaluate the strategies. Thus, every country PRSP has to come under joint scrutiny. It is common knowledge that if the World Bank and the IMF finally approves it then country ownership or participation just becomes this stylized mockery, because practically no country can bypass the strategies set by the World Bank and the IMF. Thus many argued that eventually ownership in a practical sense meant the commitment of the borrowing country to implement the strategies that the World Bank and the IMF approved. Therefore, development of authentically homegrown and nationally relevant strategies based on the local realities in terms of socio-economic, historic, and geographic peculiarities do not matter with this kind of World Bank and the IMF understanding of ownership. The same experience is evident across other continents and countries (Guttal and Mulaluan: 2003).

> An economics professor from Bangladesh said that the Bank and Fund had to be viewed in perspective. "We feel everyday their power and privilege. The office of the IMF is in the Central Bank and the IMF is present at the Central Bank meetings. Their privilege to set policies is not written in conditionality, but they make use of oral conditionality as part of their power and privilege."
>
> He had been examining World Bank and IMF documents for 3 decades in Bangladesh, before and after "structural adjustment programmes", and they remain consistent. "Only the words change," he said. "Now, privatization is called restructuring public institutions. 'Rationalisation of prices' is used instead of raising prices. The PRSP continues the same programme as structural adjustment."
>
> He added that the World Bank and the IMF had built a support base in the country, and institutions had been restructured in a way that there are beneficiaries among the elite who speak on behalf of the World Bank and the IMF.
>
> (Khor: 2006)

It is evident that the boasting of country ownership by the World Bank and the IMF is just rhetoric. Another incident further strengthens this finding. In 2006–07 FY budget speech the Finance Minister of Bangladesh hinted about some protection measures for the local business but the IMF were very critical of that move. The audacity of the criticisms by the IMF went to the extent that all the trade bodies of Bangladesh who are generally perceived to be not critical to the World Bank and the IMF in an unprecedented move for the first time issued a joint statement coming heavily down on the IMF and their policies.[40]

Another disappointing feature of misplaced loyalty demands attention. While the government failed to table the draft PRSP before the parliament for discussion, they made time to be accountable regarding the implementation of the PRSP to the donors in the development forum meeting. The meeting was virtually the PRS Implementation Forum Meeting. As discussed earlier, in the orientation meeting with MPs the Finance Minister was not present and neither was any important government functionary. But at the meeting with the donors not only the Finance Minister was present but also the Prime Minister. That meeting decided the implementation progress of the PRSP in Bangladesh. A critical analysis of the minutes of the NSC reveals that both the NSC and NPFP were primarily occupied with the PRS Implementation Forum meeting at that time. They put things together very hurriedly to present before the Bangladesh Development Forum (BDF) meeting and sometimes the slow pace caused significant frustration. A resolution[41] reads "failure to prepare the PRSP within the stipulated time will result in generating ominous consequences regarding accumulation of foreign assistance and national image". It is a bizarre that foreign aid via the PRSP was linked to 'national image'.

An accidental-coalition[42] and the practical ownership of PRSP in Bangladesh

The preceding section exposes both the inadequacy of scope and level of active engagement of major local stakeholders in the preparation of Bangladesh's PRSP. The inadequacy leads to the questions of how had it been possible to prepare the PRSP while all those expected actors appeared so naïve. In an interview the lead consultant boasted of creating an enabling environment. In his language, an 'accidental-coalition' smoothed the way. The coalition at that time comprised three individuals;[43] the Principal Secretary to the PM and the head of the NSC, the Finance Secretary, and the lead consultant. According to the lead consultant they enjoyed an excellent coordination of thought and process, which was instrumental in having the document prepared. While the three individuals belonged to professional groups, the absence of other actors such as political leadership seemed to present no problems in either terms of legitimacy or contribution. Since in the estimation of the government the issue of ownership would not be more than rhetoric in the PRSP, it deliberately decided to delegate the responsibility to this 'accidental coalition' – a team of technocrats for developing the PRSP quickly complying with the IFI conditionality to guarantee access to PRGF loans. Moreover, the local political environment was not very compelling for ensuring political participation in the PRSP. Thus, it appeared that the 'accidental-coalition' was central to the entire process. While we still hear many things about national ownership in a PRSP, in reality Bangladesh's experience proves that the meaning of national ownership was reduced to the interface of a group of individual professionals. The most unfortunate part is that the entire nation was either blind or indifferent to the blunder.

While many critics rightly argue that the PRSP is nothing but window dressing, it is important to note that the World Bank and the IMF for the first time gave an opportunity to prove national ownership in development agenda linked to World Bank and the IMF concessional loans. The failure of a loan receiving country such as Bangladesh in ensuring national ownership should arguably be attributed to national actors including the government and major political parties. Not only did Bangladesh miss out in the opportunity but also it failed to prove institutional potential to spearhead its own development policies and thinking.

Eventual disappearance of PRSP: was it a crisis of ownership or was PRSP inadequate or both?

Bangladesh returned to its traditional five-year plan framework in 2011 with adopting the sixth five-year plan (SFYP: 2011–15) by abandoning the PRSP model. The SFYP did not though account for any clear clarification as to why PRSP was scrapped. Looking critically at the Bangladesh Prime Minister's Message and the Preamble of the SFYP, it appeared that it was understood by the leadership that a PRSP model could not provide a longer-term trajectory to help the country beat poverty, and move towards a higher growth pathway. According to the words of the Prime Minister:

> [W]e must live up to our reputation; and as a nation with the history of supreme sacrifice of 3 million lives, we do have the potential and strength to achieve a status of middle-income country within a decade. Our government has, therefore, decided to revert to mid-term five-year plan process from the three year PRSPs
>
> (GoB: 2011)

The preamble of the SFYP spells out that it is anchored within a greater vision under a perspective plan (2010–21) to take the country to higher level of development i.e. middle-income status. From the tacit justification for reverting to SFYP, it appeared that the country needed a big push to the economy through an ambitious development plan which could not be possible by a PRSP model steered by donors. And this makes sense given that any development plan that lacks a country's ownership could not live up to the country's expectation. It implied that Bangladesh needed its own way of formulating a development plan within its own context of development potential and challenge. So, PRSP seemed to have been both; it lacked ownership; it was also inadequate.

Notes

1 Bangladesh Development Forum meeting is the annual meeting of lenders and donors, both bilateral and multilateral, where Bangladesh presents its commitment to donor induced reform agenda and reviews the progress of earlier reform initiatives. The meeting also decides the donors' commitment for loans to Bangladesh.

2 The section draws on GoB (2005), *Unlocking the Potential: National Strategy for Accelerated Poverty Reduction* (NSAPR). Indeed NSAPR is Bangladesh's PRSP.

3 *Joint Staff Advisory Note on the Bangladesh's Poverty Reduction Strategy Paper.* Approved by Steven Dunaway and Anthony Boote (IMF) and Praful C. Patel (IDA), December: 2005 Available at: www.imf.org/external/pubs/ft/scr/2006/cr0653.pdf; last accessed on 11 December 2017.

4 Vide memo number PD/Admn-2/17–34/2003/607 of the Planning Division, Ministry of Planning, GoB.

5 The decision to expand was taken in the second NSC meeting held on 13 November 2003. The 22 members were Principal Secretary to the PM, Secretaries of the Finance Division, Economic Relations Division, Ministry of Environment and Forest, Ministry of Agriculture, Ministry of Education, Ministry of Health and Family Welfare, Local Government Division, Disaster Management Division, Ministry of Women and Children Affairs, Ministry of Social Welfare, Power Division, Planning Division, Ministry of Fisheries and Livestock, Ministry of Commerce, Ministry of Science and ICT, Ministry of Land, Ministry of Water Resources, Rural Development and Cooperatives Division, Programming Division, and General Economics Division.

6 They were Dr. Hussain Zillur Rahman, Executive Chairman, Power and Participation Research Center (PPRC) and Dr. Kaniz Siddiqui, Economics Department, North-South University.

7 The choice was Dr. S.R. Osmani but ultimately he did not join the group. Dr. Quazi Mesbahuddin Ahmed revealed this information during an interview with the author.

8 Although the government frequently uses the term 'development partner', many academics and policy analysts prefer to call them as bilateral and multilateral lenders. There are others who want to remain in between the two positions and they call them diplomatic missions [in case of bilateral relations] and multilateral organizations.

9 The LCG is a joint platform of the DAC donors' representatives and the Economic Relations Division (ERD), representing the Government. LCG provides opportunity for development dialogues and discussions between donors and the government. LCG has several sectoral groups for partnership at sector level.

10 In the wake of extreme confrontation on the political front, on 11 January 2007, a military backed caretaker government took over power in the country. This interim government later was forced to hold a general election in 2008 to return power to an elected political regime. This interim government is popularly known as 1/11 government echoing the 9/11 of the US.

11 The necessity of PRSP in accessing World Bank and the IMF loan was recognized in the first meeting of the National Steering Committee, National Poverty Focal Point, held on 6 October 2003. The minutes of the meeting are unofficial.

12 The lead consultant himself also recognized during the interview that PRSP was a response to BWIs conditionality but he defended that it does not mean that ownership of the formulation of the strategies cannot be achieved.

13 The lead consultant echoed the same view during an interview.

14 Interview with Prof. Anu Muhammad.

15 Interview with Prof. M.M. Akash.

16 Interview with Zakir Hossain of Nagorik Uddyog – a civil society network.

17 The Secretary, Bangladesh National Parliament Secretariat advised the MPs to seize the fullest use of the opportunity provided by the workshop in his presidential address in the workshop opening session.

18 The Speaker of Bangladesh National Parliament credited the scholar [read consultant] for formulating the PRSP in the same workshop.

19 Between 2001 and 2006.

20 It drew criticisms as one of the leading economists of the country commented during the interview with the author that it was not ethically sound to have the same persons posted to monitor what they have produced earlier.

21 For example, the thematic group on macroeconomics. Finance Division single handily organized the activities [under aggressive and direct influence of the IMF]. Maybe that was the reason to exclude all other actors.

22 The NSC did many things compromising the existing rules in the plea that they have to complete the PRSP within the stipulated time. The recruitment of consultants may be a good example. They did not bother with official procedures. However, while they remained so keyed up to complete the document within a timeframe that was presumably not given by the political authority is a valid question. However, the total analysis would prove that all those were for PRGF loans.

23 These views emerged during interviews with members of the civil society.

24 During the interviews all members of civil society admitted these common features of Bangladesh civil society.

25 Professional economists and senior researchers of the Bangladesh Institute of Development Studies (BIDS), the government owned think-tank made these comments at a press conference on 28 November 2007. They highlighted several downsides of foreign funding for research. Source: *The Daily New Age*, Dhaka 29 November 2007.

26 This was revealed during interviews with senior executives of SUPRO.
27 Source: Draft Summary of the dialogues on "BANGLADESH: A National Strategy for Economic Growth and Poverty Reduction". The report was made available through personal communication with Prof. M.M. Akash, the then chair of PET Trust.
28 For example: Islam (2004), Ahmad et al. (2004), Barkat (2004), Ahmad (2004, 2004a), Akash (2002, 2002a), Muhammad (n.d.), Muhammad (2007), Sobhan (2002a, 2002b).
29 Holding seminars and workshops on politics drew heated cynicism from a group of independent minds since these activities are purported to have promoted a depoliticisation process in Bangladesh in order to serve the interest of the Western hegemony. Even the sources of their huge fund also cast doubts. See for an analysis Mazhar (2007).
30 All major economists confirmed the convergence during the interviews. The lead consultant in response to a question that whether he would apprehend any chance of discontinuity after the regime change confidently replied that he did not think so.
31 A detailed feature of rent seeking behaviour may be obtained from Barkat (2002).
32 For details; http://archive.thedailystar.net/2006/08/06/d60806012217.htm; last accessed on 12 December 2017.
33 For details; http://archive.thedailystar.net/2007/08/02/d7080201085.htm; last accessed on 12 December 2017.
34 Ref: Interview.
35 Commented during face-to-face interview
36 A core member in the NSC admitted the lack. He added other missing areas, which include labor issues and public administration.
37 Source: Interview.
38 Prof. Islam, a famous economist and also a professor of Economics, University of Rajshahi, opined the view several times with the researcher.
39 They termed the military backed caretaker government as a Transitional Government (TG). This government took over the power on 11 January 2007 in the wake of severe political confrontation in Bangladesh. The TG ruled the country for about two years. The donors and external actors were also supportive to the unelected regime.
40 *The Daily Star*http://archive.thedailystar.net/2007/08/03/d70803020225.htm.
41 Fifth National Steering Committee (NSC) meeting.
42 The term was used by Hossain Zillur Rahman, the lead consultant to the NPFP during an interview with the author. It was accidental because it was not planned but eventually during the formulation process they were able to establish this coalition to finish the task in an accelerated way. Since the Principal Secretary to the PM was a part of the coalition, it was easier for them to ensure government's internal political buy-in.
43 Respectively they were: Dr. Kamal Siddiqui, the then principal secretary to the PM, Mr. Zakir Ahmed Khan, the then Finance Secretary, and Dr. Hossain Zillur Rahman, professional economist and researcher.

Annex 4.1

Table 4.A1 Local Consultative Group [LCG] support to CSOs/NGOs in Bangladesh on Governance Research[1]

Organization	*Project Time/ Status*	*Amount*
PRIP Trust	2002–2006	$ 345,000
	2004–07	$10.16m
Transparency International [Donor Consortium]	2003–07	$ 7.2m £4.320m
Transparency International, B	2003–	$8,95,000
	Ongoing	$ 50,000
	Ongoing	£4.5m
	2000–03	$3,00,000
Centre for Policy Dialogue [CPD]	2003–09	$3,12,500
	2004	$1.3m
	2004–09	$4.6m
Bangladesh National Women Lawyers Association [BNWLA]	2000–03	$2.7m
	2003–06	$5,00,000
	2000–02	$2,17,000
Nijera Kori	2001–08	$8.5m £5.325m
Heirich-Bowell-Foundation/PRIA	2001–06	$5,00,000
World Bank/ PROSHIKA	2001–02	$2,00,000
Mass Line Media Center and others	2000–05	$3m
Bangladesh Center for Development Communication and Journalism [BCDCJ]	2000–02	$1,87,500
	2003–05	$1,87,500
Academy for Educational Development [AED]	Ongoing	$1,53,040
	2001–06	$7.4m
	2001–06	$5.3m
Bangladesh Bar Council	2003–04	$18,166
Bangladesh Legal Aid Services Trust [BLAST]	2003–08	$4,00,000
Madaripur Legal Aid Association [MLAA]	2001–04	$3,00,000
Madaripur Legal Aid Association [MLAA]	Ended 2002	$32,000
Bangladesh Society for Enforcement of Human Rights [BSEHR]	Ongoing	$5,20,000
Coastal Development Center [CODEC]	Ongoing	$3,36,575
Acid Survivors' Foundation	2001–04	$4,46,364
	2004–09	$0.9m
	2001–04	$1,72,615
BRCT		$3,83,333
Manusher Jonno Foundation/ CARE International	2002–07	$26.4m £16.52
Heirich Boll Foundation/ Bangladesh Nari Progoti Sangha [BNPS]	2002–04	$1.3m

Organization	*Project Time/ Status*	*Amount*
BNPS	2000–03	$4,85,000
	2002–03	$4,85,000
Ain-O-Shalish Kendra [ASK]	2000–03	$4,08,000
	2003–06	$5,00,000
	2000–03	$1,76,630
Nari Uddoyag Kendra	2004–07	$4,18,000
Democracy Watch	Ongoing	$3,33,333
	1999–2002	$3,96,400
Khan Foundation	2002–03	$2,00,000
SAMATA	2001–03	$1.7m
	2001–08	$10.3m £6.457m
Rupantar, Khulna	2000–07	$2,35,000
	2002–06	$5,60,163
Naripokhho	2004–06	$2,46,000
Manobik Sahajjo Sangstha [MSS]	2000–02	$3,53,429
	2000–03	$1,98,000
Association of Development Agencies in Bangladesh [ADAB]	2000–03	$1m
Election Monitoring Working Group [EMWG]	2001	$1,00,000
Rights Jessore	Ongoing	$57,000
Phulki	2000–05	$3,20,600
Centre for Women and Children Studies [CWCS]	2000–03	$2,38,453
Association for Community Development [ACD]	2002–03	$4,70,000
Karmojibi Nari	2000–03	$1,47,000
North South University	2001–03	$1,40,000
	2003-04	$1,98,640
Rangpur Dinajpur Social Service [RDSS]	2002-05	$6,83,421

Source: http://www.lcgbangladesh.org/inventory/13_inventory.pdf (Last accessed 10 July 2007).

Note: 1 This is only the tip of the iceberg. There are other sources of funding to work on various issues. Many of the organizations mentioned here draw funds from those sources too. Moreover, many civil society members in their individual capacity are engaged in consultancy taking funds from both bilateral and multilateral sources. Moreover, the data presented here account for a situation of almost 10–15 years back. Now, the donation from Northern donors to the local CSOs has presumably increased. Most European donors and USAID prefer to work through local CSOs and NGOs in order to strengthen them.

Annex: 4.2

The inside story of the civil service's engagement in PRSP: the saga of the ministry of establishment (now ministry of public administration) and the ministry of women and children affairs

In order to closely monitor the process we have selected two government ministries: the [then] ministry of establishment [now ministry of public administration] and the ministry of women and children affairs. The selection was based on various reasons. The ministry of the establishment is the lead ministry in managing career civil servants who supposedly play critical role in policy formulation and implementation. Moreover, the Southeast Asian experience suggests that an enterprising bureaucracy is key to national development and poverty reduction. On the other hand, promoting good governance was one of the major supporting strategies of Bangladesh's PRSP and thus identifying issues and implementing policies in order to promote bureaucratic efficiency and accountability arguably should be at the heart of governance interventions.

Gender issue has earned a huge currency in the development and policy literature of Bangladesh and it has crosscutting linkages. The ministry of women and children affairs deals with gender-related policies in government as the lead ministry. The ministry has good rapport with many civil society organizations and networks that promote gender-related issues. The major aim in selecting the women affairs ministry thus was to study the behavior of the civil society organizations vis-à-vis the ability of public officials to contribute to policy formulation.

The methodology included: scanning internal documents of the ministries and long interviews with key informants of the ministries working at various levels. The researcher, who once worked in the women affairs ministry as senior assistant secretary, enjoyed wonderful access to the documents and had effective discussions with the key informants.

Having scanned the documents available in MWCA it appeared that the Joint Secretary (Development and Planning) officially led the activities. However, there were two separate technical committees on gender and children. The committees seemed to have representative involving participation of members of Dhaka based women activists, female academics, members of INGOs, Western embassies, and donors including some government officials. No document recording the activism of the parliamentary standing committee was found out. The responsibility of preparing the document on gender and children issues was given to consultants. The estimated budget suggests that they were given handsome remuneration managed from various embassies to prepare the draft write-ups. The class character of those involved in suggests that elite women activists and rights activists took part in the process in MWCA. During interviews with the key informants in the MWCA it was revealed that hired consultants managed everything ministry officials were not even consulted over the separately written draft reports on gender and children. To utter surprise it was found that though there were tall talks in the PRSP matrix concerning gender and children issues, there was no special program after the introduction of PRSP was taken. The officials suggested that it was just business as usual.

The experience in the ministry of establishment was more disappointing. It took several days to identify who the focal person from the ministry in PRSP process was. In the end it was identified that the joint secretary career planning and training (CPT) represented the ministry. Later he was promoted and transferred to another ministry. However, I had a long discussion with him. In the CPT wing I had also discussion with other officials including the [then] incumbent Joint Secretary. It was reported that the ministry had no effective participation in the entire process particularly on governance process. The lead consultant confirmed that he managed the writing of the paper on governance and admitted that scant attention was given to the issue. Despite attempts the desk officer failed to find any file or document concerning the ministry's involvement in the PRSP process. Similar to the MWCA experience, PRSP did not deliver any special program for public officials in order to enhance efficiency and professionalism.

In the MWCA despite several attempts no document concerning the involvement of the parliamentary standing committee was found. However, the parliamentary standing committee on the ministry of establishment held its meeting on 5 April 2005 and came up with a number of recommendations and observations after critical discussions. While the major observation is that the committee argued that though the ministry of establishment had a critical role in human development and promoting good governance, it was not given the lead role.

The recommendations *inter alia* included: establishment of a permanent commission for public administration reforms such as the Department of Administrative Reforms and Public Grievances in India, the Malaysian Administrative Modernization and Planning Unit (MAMPU), the Headquarters for Administrative Reforms in Japan; rationalization of the number of divisions and ministries to promote administrative efficiency and best use of human resources; establishing three separate Public Service Commissions based on the recommendations of Public Administration Reforms Commission (PARC), 2000; provisioning training for officers engaged in development administration at field level at home and abroad; the gradual abolition of quota system in public service; engaging the ministry of establishment in the good governance matrix as the lead ministry; and developing a permanent promotion system based on efficiency and meritocracy.

A critical look at the PRSP suggests that not a single recommendation was entertained finally. What a weird parliamentary engagement!

While in the MWCA the involvement of a foreign fund supported civil society members and donor agencies were proactive and spontaneous, no such involvement from civil society members in civil service issues under the governance folder was recorded. The vital question was how could poverty be tackled while an effective and forward-looking public administration was totally bypassed.

Finally, both the ministries revealed that consultants played key role in the PRSP process in Bangladesh. These hired consultants served the role of contractors in developing the document. The failure of bureaucracy is really huge and the nation must pay attention to it.

References

Ahmad, Qazi Kholiquzzaman. "Bangladesh: An Alternative Paradigm" in *South Asian Journal*, Issue: 4 [April–June] 2004.

Ahmad, Qazi Kholiquzzaman. "Poverty Reduction Strategy Paper: Repackaging Old Medicine" in *Bangladesh Economic Association Journal 2004* [in Bengali]: 2004a.

Ahmed, Quazi Mesbahuddin. *From I-PRSP to PRSP: Steps and Processes*, Presentation made the Meeting of the National Steering Committee (NSC) with the Local Consultative Group (LCG) in Bangladesh, held on February 26, 2004.

Akash, M.M. "Poverty Reduction Strategy Paper: What, Why & for Whom", Action Aid Bangladesh: Dhaka: 2002.

Akash, M.M. "Whither PRSP (Poverty Reduction Strategy Paper)?", Action Aid Bangladesh: Dhaka: 2002a.

Barkat, Abul. "Bangladeshe Baideshik Riin o Shahajjoyo Kotokhani Prpyojon: Goto Tin Dashakaer Aviyaggatar Political Economy" [How Much Foreign Aid Does Bangladesh Really Need? The Political Economy of Last Three Decade's Experience] in *Bangladesh Economic Association Journal 2002* [in Bengali]: 2002.

Barkat, Abul. "Bangladeshe Dariddro Ussched o Raash: Udbeger Bishoy" [Poverty Elimination and Reduction in Bangladesh: Issues of Concern] in *Bangladesh Economic Association Journal 2004* [in Bengali]: 2004.

Barkat, Abul. "Ekjon Adariddrrer Dariddrro Chinta: Bangladeshshe Dariddrrer Rajnoitik-Arthoniti" [in Bengali] (Poverty Thinking of a Non-poor: The Political Economy of Poverty in Bangladesh), Welcome Address presented in the Regional Seminar titled Poverty Reduction: Poverty Reduction Strategy Paper and Reality and Regional Cooperation: Politics vs. Economics, jointly organized by Bangladesh Economic Association and the University of Rajshahi: 2006.

Bull, Benedict, Morten Jerve, Alf and Sigvaldsen, Erlend. "The World Bank's and the IMF's use of Conditionality to Encourage Privatization and Liberalization: Current Issues and Practices", Report prepared for the Norwegian Ministry of Foreign Affairs as a background for the Oslo Conditionality Conference; SUM Report No. 13: 2006 [Available at: https://www.duo.uio.no/bitstream/handle/10852/32692/Bull.pdf; last accessed on 12 December 2017].

Centre for Policy Dialogue [CPD] "Reforming Public Administration for Improved Performance and Accountability", *National Policy Dialogue Report*: Dhaka: n.d.

Deb, U.K., Raihan, A. and Ahmed, M.S. "The Poverty Reduction Strategy for Bangladesh: A Review of the Finalisation Process and Interim Measures", in *Revisiting Foreign Aid: A Review of Bangladesh's Development 2003*. University Press Limited and the Centre for Policy Dialogue: Dhaka: 2004.

Government of Bangladesh (GoB). Bangladesh: A National Strategy for Economic Growth, Poverty Reduction and Social Development, *Economic Relations Division* [*ERD*], Dhaka: 2002.

Government of Bangladesh (GoB). *Unlocking the Potential: National Strategy for Accelerated Poverty Reduction*, General Economics Division, Planning Commission, Dhaka: 2005.

Government of Bangladesh (GoB). *Sixth Five-Year Plan 2011–2015: Accelerating Growth and Reducing Poverty*, General Economics Division, Planning Commission: 2011.

Guttal, Shalmali and Mulaluan, Jenima Joy Chavez. "Poverty Reduction Strategy Papers: A Poor Package for Poverty Reduction" in *Anti Poverty or Anti Poor? The Millennium Development Goals and the Eradication of Extreme Poverty and Hunger*, Focus on the Global South, Bangkok: 2003.

IMF. *Bangladesh: Joint Staff Advisory Note on the Poverty Reduction Strategy Paper*, Approved by Steven Dunaway and Anthony Boote (IMF) and Praful C. Patel (IDA), IMF, Washington DC: 2006.

IMF. *IMF Country Report No. 07/234* [BANGLADESH: Staff Report for the 2007 Article IV Consultation], IMF, Washington DC, 2007.

International Development Association (IDA) and International Monetary Fund (IMF). "Bangladesh: Joint Staff Assessment of the Interim Poverty Reduction Strategy Paper", Approved by: Meiko Nishimizu and Gobind T. Nankani (IDA), Steven Dunaway and Shigeo Kashiwagi (IMF): 2003.

Ishikawa, Shigeru. "Ex Ante Determinants of Regime Transition: China, Vietnam, and Russia Compared": 2003 [Available at: http://www.grips.ac.jp/forum/pdf02/Ishikawa_ex_ante.pdf; last accessed on 10 December 2017].

Islam, Muinul. "Poverty Creation or Poverty Reduction Under PRSP: A Case for Reviewing and Rethinking the Role of the State in Bangladesh" in *Bangladesh Journal of Political Economy*, Vol. 21, No. 2: 2004.

Jahan, Rounaq and Amundsen, Inge. "The Parliament of Bangladesh: Representation and Accountability". CPD-CMI Working Paper 2: 2012.

Johnson, Omotunde E.G. "Country Ownership of Reform Programmes and the Implications for Conditionality", UNCTAD, G-24 Discussion Paper Series, No. 35: 2005.

Khan, Muhammad Faruk. "Poverty Reduction Strategy Paper – A Parliamentarian's Perspective" in Rahman, H. Zillur (ed.), *Parliamentarians and the PRSP Process: Bangladesh Experience, Bangladesh Institute of Parliamentary Studies*, Dhaka: 2005.

Khor, Martin. "Oslo Conference Finds World Bank, IMF Still Pushing Conditions", *SUNS*# 6152: 2006.

LCG. *Inventory of Government and Donor Thematic Groups*: 2004 [Available at: http://lcgbangladesh.org/Education/reports/PRSP%20thematic%20groups%20rev%20Sept%2004.pdf; last accessed 12 December 2017].

Mahmud, Wahiduddin. *Monitoring Donor Support to Poverty Reduction Strategy in Bangladesh: Rethinking the Rules of Engagement*, ERG Occasional Research Paper, Economic Research Group, Dhaka in association with Commonwealth Secretariat, London: 2006.

Mazher, Farhad. *Khamoter Biker o Ganashaktir Utthan* [in Bengali] [The Perversity of Power and Emergence of People's Power], Diganta Media Corporation, Dhaka: 2007.

Muhammad, Anu. "Development Strategy and Problems of Democratisation in a Peripheral Country: The Bangladesh Experience", in *Radical Notes*: 2007.

Muhammad, Anu. "From Mills to Malls: Globalization and Economic Transformation in a Peripheral Economy: Bangladesh Experience in Share The World's Resources": (n.d).

Ohno, Izumi et al. *True Ownership and Policy Autonomy: Managing Donors and Owning Policies*, National Graduate Institute for Policy Studies and GRIPS Development Forum: 2005.

Rahman, Hossain Zillur (ed.). *Parliamentarians and the PRSP Process: Bangladesh Experience*, Bangladesh Institute of Parliamentary Studies (BIPS), Dhaka: 2005.

Saleh, A.Z.M. (ed.) "IMF's Loan and its Implications on Bangladesh Economy" in *Bangladesh Economic Update*, Vol. 2, No. 2, Unnayan Onneshan – the Innovators: 2011.

Sobhan, Rehman. "Policy Independence and Political Accountability", Centre for Policy Dialogue, Dhaka: 2002a.

Sobhan, Rehman. "The Political Economy of the State and Market in Bangladesh", Centre for Policy Dialogue, Dhaka: 2002b.

The New Age. 15 May 2005: Dhaka.

The Daily New Age. 6 August 2006: Dhaka.

5 Independence in development agenda and lessons from the PRSP regime

Quest for a new model for Bangladesh

Building on the findings regarding Bangladesh's national ownership in the PRSP that served as the development model for Bangladesh during 2003–2010, this chapter discusses policy implications for Bangladesh's true ownership in adopting a national development agenda. The analysis of this book primarily captures the nature and scope of engagement of principal stakeholders in the formulation of PRSP; it also examines the extent of independence of engagement of stakeholders. Bangladesh, ever since its independence has been deeply influenced by the World Bank and the IMF and also other donors in terms of development policy choice; this influence was further strengthened in the 1980s with Bangladesh's engagement with the SAP. The analysis of the historical interface between development partners and the government of Bangladesh in development policy formulation underscores that this relationship is very strong and symbiotic. Therefore, this analysis makes an important contribution to existing knowledge regarding the political economy of development agenda setting in developing countries. Though this case study is largely devoted to Bangladesh's own context, yet it may also serve as a good reference point for many aid recipient countries struggling to demonstrate leadership and ownership in their development journey.

The first section of this chapter recaps the major findings regarding policy ownership in Bangladesh's PRSP; and the final section presents a model for Bangladesh's policy independence within the context of Bangladesh's changing development financing regime. This book argues that Bangladesh's steady progress in social and economic development warrants Bangladesh's to redefine its own pathway to ensure its autonomy in development policy making. Foreign aid will have still a role to play in Bangladesh's development; however, the country must strategize to undercut the policy influence of aid and international donors.

Recap of key findings

Scrutinizing the evolution of the PRSP process, it appears that the PRSP did not automatically emerge as the result of local demand to deal comprehensively with poverty reduction in Bangladesh. It was rather an imposition from the World Bank and the IMF in order to enable Bangladesh to access the IMF's PRGF loan. Thus, arguably Bangladesh's chance to be independent in the PRSP formulation was very slim. By capturing the formulation process, it is manifestly clear that the major stakeholders have played an insignificant role to contribute to build the theoretical underpinning of the PRSP. There was instruction from the Planning Commission as to who should be invited to the discussion meeting and it affected the autonomous environment of discussion in the meetings. All major stakeholders seemed skeptical about the contribution of participation to the PRSP formulation. On the face of it, essentially quality, credibility and effectiveness of participation in the formulation process could be contested. In essence, it seemed that the participation process was to comply with the World Bank and the IMF instructions concerning stakeholder consultation.

Review of participation of an individual group of stakeholders provides many lessons and interesting findings. The engagement of public servants in the process was highly nominal in various line ministries as the bureaucracy seemed ambivalent about the strategic and procedural dimension of PRSP. The comments of the interviewed public servants testify that civil servants failed to understand the political economy of development cooperation. Public servants, in reality, appeared to have leased out their responsibility of preparing the PRSP or for that matter country's development agenda to consultants. The bureaucratic failure is an outcome of the historical apathetic attitude of the country towards developing an efficient and enterprising public service in Bangladesh.

National parliament also encountered the same experience. Parliament did not play as such any directional role; nor did it hold any formal discussion on the draft PRSP in the parliament house though parliament was expected to be a major stakeholder. However, UNDP organized a consultation meeting with some MPs as part of informing the MPs. This indicates the level of stewardship of the parliament in development policy in Bangladesh. Nevertheless, it was later on identified through cross-checking the final PRSP document that their (MPs) recommendations on the draft were not seriously considered. Though PRSP marked a shift in development planning as with PRSP Bangladesh opted for a three-year planning process instead of the traditional five-year planning, the reasons for this shift were not discussed in the meeting involving parliamentarians. To one's utter surprise the closure of the largest jute mill,[1] Adamji Jute Mill, considered then as the largest jute mill in South Asia, was not even questioned or challenged in the discussion although it was common sense that MPs as political leaders would discuss this at least to demonstrate their pro-laborer commitment.

It was evident from analysis that political leadership took a decidedly compromised role in PRSP. They did not want to be expressly unfriendly to the World Bank and the IMF policies and so they did not demand a thorough discussion on the PRSP in parliament. Nor did they discuss it formally in their party forum. All major political parties maintained that strategy. This seemed a strange policy convergence between major political parties as Bangladesh is much known to the international community for its confrontational political culture. The convergence among major political parties was most unlikely though, but it happened because the major political parties seemed to have already endorsed much of the neo-liberal political and economic ideologies.

This study finds that the mainstream civil society organizations (CSOs), particularly those who were active in governance and political agendas were invariably donor dependent for financial resources. Many of the CSOs are active in areas that are appreciated by Northern donors but they preferred not to question the PRSP. Indeed, they did not make their voices heard. They did not actively engage them in PRSP formulation process. Many academics term this acquiescent attitude as civil society's embeddedness with Western donors. This novel finding provides new insight into the agenda and strategy of civil society in the developing world.

Though the civil servants, political leadership, the parliament, and CSOs were naïve in the PRSP formulation process; on the contrary donors and consultants played an important role. Donors, gathering under the umbrella of the Local Consultative Group (LCG), maintained constant rapport with key government agencies particularly the Finance Division; Ministry of Finance. Officials in both Planning Commission and Finance Ministry revealed that the macroeconomic thematic group did not involve any members either from the civil society or other groups and moreover, they used IMF supplied data to make the economic development projection credible. Government's commitment to donors again was reflected with the fact that the government held a meeting with donors in regard to the PRSP implementation instead of holding such a meeting with national actors such as political parties, national parliaments, and other key stakeholders. And the Minister for Finance was present in the meeting, though he skipped the meeting held with the parliamentarians.

Consultants were actively involved in the preparation of the PRSP. They also enjoyed freedom and autonomy in their work. In the Thematic Group (TG) and in the National Steering Committee (NSC) consultants played the main role in setting the agenda since there was clear lack of strategic leadership and direction from both political and bureaucratic leadership. NSC was in essence a titular committee.

One of the lessons learned from PRSP formulation is that the role of local research is significantly important to counteract the pressures of donors. Unfortunately, research, both at government level and in political parties, was missing and as a resulting impact both bureaucrats and political leadership felt less competent while they negotiated with their counterparts from international organizations. During the interviews many argued that without research the full potential of the nation could not be achieved. Neither any political party, nor the parliament, nor the Finance Ministry undertook any form of research to crosscheck the PRSP agenda from a national perspective.

However, this lack of due diligence is not only reserved for the PRSP process. In Bangladesh hardly any public policy is supported by rigorous research. In most cases policies are developed by donor engaged consultants and PRSP was no exception.

Though failure of neo-liberal policies and lack of ownership during the SAP regime apparently led the World Bank and the IMF to adopt PRSP as an approach to poverty reduction in poor countries, the current research observes that there has not been any major change in strategies and approaches of the World Bank and the IMF since the neo-liberal paradigm. The research findings on the PRSP experience in Bangladesh and the available literature on the PRSP experience in other countries (particularly EURODAD: 2007 and WDM: 2005) strongly hold the view that there has been virtually no change in the World Bank and IMF development strategies and approaches. These institutions are still pursuing the same neo-liberal policies with a clear lack of national ownership.

The broader understanding of the current research is that national ownership of development policy or strategy demands a strong will and commitment of national leaders to build a self-reliant economy. Development strategies and policies should assume eventual 'graduation' (or an 'exit plan') from aid and be supported by a concrete vision and realistic measures for growth promotion and domestic resource mobilization. Policies should move beyond mere slogan and be truly imbued with equitability and growth sustainability.

My professional experience of working in several line ministries and UNDP for close to two decades convinced me to reiterate that no major development strategy or reform measure was undertaken without the assistance and influence of donors. It in fact reflects a subservient attitude for the functionaries of the government. Given this dependency, one has valid reason to doubt if Bangladesh has understood the spirit and essence of policy ownership. A senior civil servant, who was at the leadership role in PRSP formulation process, during discussion with me commented that the political leadership is totally indifferent to the necessity of policy ownership. This observation is further supported by the analysis of Professor Nurul Islam, who has very successfully combined both national and global experience of policy making and who was Bangladesh's first deputy chairman of the Planning Commission just after the independence of Bangladesh and who has been overseeing Bangladesh's economic development for over four decades living in the United States. To quote him:

> [T]he role of the government has been usually one of reacting to the policy prescriptions of donors in the light of their political feasibility or costs/benefits, rather than one of proactively formulating its own views or programs, independently analyzed throughout for policy dialogue with donors. To the extent that this is true, there is not much felt need on the part of the government policymakers for independent research or

> analysis. However, when there is a 'hue and cry' among the local experts/professionals against the particular policy advice/prescriptions of the donors, the government seems to be responsive to the opinions of the independent experts, especially in areas where it is politically convenient to disagree with the donors
>
> (Islam: 2010, 2)

Quest for a new model of ownership in development agenda

Bangladesh's steady economic progress calls for a new pathway to establish ownership in the area of national development strategy. The changing scenario of the country's development financing also indicates that Bangladesh can no longer be fully dependent on aid and donor policy prescriptions. Bangladesh's development trajectory should be built around its own needs, priorities, and opportunities. Against this understanding and building on findings of the PRSP regime, this book argues that the country should take some proactive measures to strengthen its institutional ability, political culture, and people's true engagement for better policy making being independent of any external influence. Bangladesh needs to create a culture that would allow different stakeholders to engage in the development planning process of the country. As the private sector is taking a leadership role in development, their constructive contribution would help the country develop a more business friendly growth pathway addressing the key challenges to business environment. CSOs, professional bodies should also be encouraged to interact with government systems during development of any policy strategy. However, it is encouraging to mention that an environment of collaboration has already started but this needs to be deepened to ensure effective results of such engagement. On the political front, Bangladesh's political parties should live up to the expectations of the country; and in doing so the parties need to revisit their role and agenda. Research, policy debate, or dialogue is to some extent a missing element in our political culture and governance and thus, in effect, the political leadership suffers from capacity constraint. In today's world academic enlightenment of political leadership is crucial for effective policy leadership.

The role of bureaucracy is enormous in economic development. The contribution of an enterprising bureaucracy in the developmental states of Southeast Asia is aptly recorded in the economic development literature. While political leadership is changed with an election, public servants continue with duties of office till retirement. This feature enables public servants to gain more skill and expertise on public policy issues and thus, their input and contribution has much importance. The analysis of the findings illustrates that Bangladesh stands with a non-innovative, uncreative and an uncritical bureaucracy. While there are some historical reasons for that, the nation now must develop a highly professional, innovative and extremely motivated bureaucracy. Human resource planning within the bureaucracy must undergo huge reorientation. The prevalent structure of bureaucracy may not be helpful to attain that goal. Thus, an overhauling of the current structure should be started to fit the purpose. Civil service has to be designed in a way that it pulls the best of the talented minds of the nation. Moreover, the present apathetic culture towards policy research needs to be dismantled. The junior level and mid-level public servants, particularly, should deliberately be linked to research environments. They must be interested in taking the research results into the policy formulation process. Historically, little importance was given to research results while policies were made. But, the research insulation made Bangladesh's bureaucracy and political leadership less informed and critical about political economy of development cooperation. Bangladesh should opt for a research/evidence-based progressive and result oriented bureaucracy that could withstand the hegemony of international organizations.

Towards a strategic leadership model for autonomous development agenda: can Bangladesh draw lessons from other countries?

Echoing former French President Charles de Gaulle, ownership in development agenda is too important a matter to be left to the government alone. Collaboration among key stakeholders is an imperative now. Ownership does not necessarily mean that a particular policy agenda is owned by the country but truly it should mean that the agenda is developed through true engagement within the context of national development priorities and is meant to be implemented. The key challenge that the ownership crisis can pose is that it contributes to low sustenance and incoherence of policy resulting in poor implementation and results. It is important to understand that all countries are unique in a sense that one country's example and experience could not be fully photocopied. This uniqueness calls for greater and deeper analysis and understanding of ownership agenda. Any individual country must look at its agenda from its own point of view. Therefore, a more systematic administrative and policy approach is being undertaken in other countries of the world to build an effective policy regime in development. A new regime aspires to depict certain features, building institutional capability, strengthening partnership and engaging professional research. Korea has continued to be a good example of such a model. The government partnered deeply with the Korea Development Institute (KDI) that enabled the government to scale up its institutional ability, utilize research findings, and knowledge and partner with both the research and private sector. This seems a good approach where engagement of major stakeholders could be achieved and at the same time research knowledge could be utilized. The failures of flagship reforms models, both SAP and PRSP, of donors again proved that there is no 'quick fix' in development. Thus, Shimomura and Ohno (2005) stressed the need for trial and error in ensuring true ownership. By trial and error, it means finding the best approach and strategy for the country through repeated test and experiments.

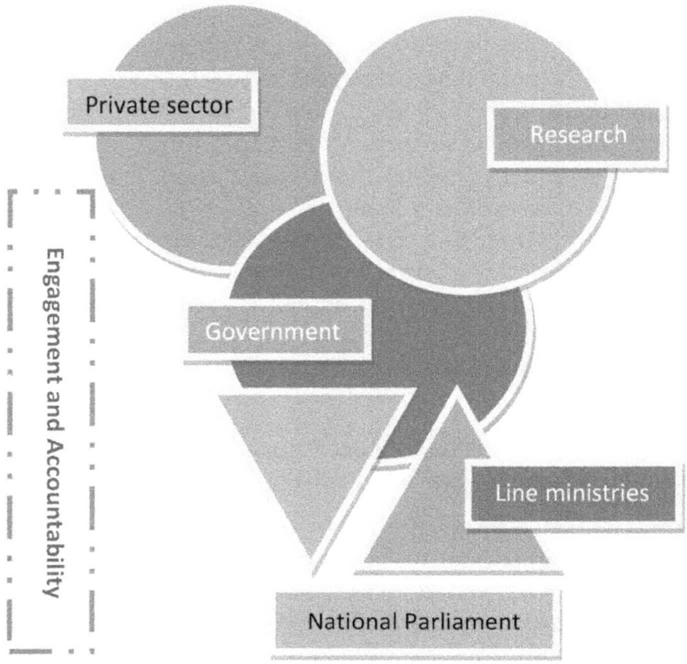

Figure 5.1 A triangular model for development agenda setting

Nonetheless, development aid will continue to play some role in economic development of the emerging economies including Bangladesh, a triangular partnership of local actors will be a key factor to achieve effective policy regime for development for Bangladesh in general and to utilize development aid effectively aligning with government's development priorities in particular (Figure 5.1). This triangular partnership indicates deeper collaboration between government, private sector, and research. At this point of its development, government cannot unilaterally work for development policy ignoring private sector's engagement and without utilizing research inputs. However, this engagement itself will also require a strategic framework so that effectiveness of engagement could be ensured. Moreover, building a new research institution for development policy analysis or consolidating the already prevalent one(s) would be highly important. Having realized the importance of research, Korea built KDI and allowed it to grow autonomously. The interface between government ministries and research would strengthen the agenda setting environment in terms of ensuring the scientific and professional approach to development agenda. This will further ensure efficient and strategic use of resources. This new model also needs to embrace its eventual accountability to the national parliament. So, major development strategies should be mandated to require strategic guidance and critical deliberations from the parliament. On the other hand, all ministries and agencies should ensure stronger collaboration across the government to ensure a whole-of-government work culture. Any loose relationship in this chain will affect the objective of the greater partnership. Weak leadership from government ministries will likely result in weaker collaboration with private sector and research.

While the Korea-KDI model may be considered a success story of the past, India's new model serves as an example of the present time. The Modi government, having come to power, dismantled the traditional planning commission established in 1950, and instituted the National Institution for Transforming India (NITI), also called NITI Aayog[2] in 2015 with robust development aspirations. NITI Aayog serves as the 'Think Tank' for government of India by providing both directional and policy inputs. It blends two major roles through its two different hubs, Team India Hub (TIH) and the Knowledge and Innovation Hub (KIH). The TIH presents the leadership role, while KIH the strategic and technical role. The prime minister of India heads the NITI Aayog, while some ministers and development professionals are members of the NITI Aayog. Senior level government officials provide management support to it. It implies that systematic approach to strategic leadership is important to manage and undertake development from an autonomous point of view. As Bangladesh aspires to be a middle-income country by 2021, it is time for Bangladesh to look at the good practices around the world and build its own model for effective development planning. Experiences of Korea and India could be a good starting point for Bangladesh.

Notes

1 It was then done as part of government's privatization policy. This decision was seriously contested.
2 http://niti.gov.in/.

References

EURODAD. "Untying the knots: How the World Bank is failing to deliver real change on conditionality": 2007 [Available at: http://www.eurodad.org/uploadedfiles/whats_new/reports/untying%20the%20knots%20-%20how%20the%20wb%20is%20failing%20to%20deliver%20real%20change%20on%20conditionality.pdf; last accessed on 12 December 2017].

Islam, Nurul. *Role of Experts in Policy Advice: Lessons of Experience*, Bangladesh Institute of Development Studies (BIDS), Dhaka: 2010.

Shimomura, Yasutami and Ohno, Izumi. "Introduction and Overview" in Ohno, Izumi et al. *True Ownership and Policy Autonomy: Managing Donors and Owning Policies*, National Graduate Institute for Policy Studies and GRIPS Development Forum: 2005.

World Development Movement (WDM). *One size for all: A study of IMF and World Bank Poverty Reduction Strategies*, London: 2005.

Index

Note: Page numbers in **boldface** indicate tables; those in *italics* indicate figures.

www.ingramcontent.com/pod-product-compliance
Ingram Content Group UK Ltd.
Pitfield, Milton Keynes, MK11 3LW, UK
UKHW011013180926
475701UK00004B/729
* 9 7 8 0 3 6 7 5 8 9 4 1 7 *